DATE DUE			
OCT 1 1984			
JAN 2 '86			
FEB 17 '86			
FEB 2 1 1986			

Friends and Neighbors

GROUP LIFE IN AMERICA'S
FIRST PLURAL SOCIETY

Friends and Neighbors

GROUP LIFE IN AMERICA'S FIRST PLURAL SOCIETY

EDITED BY

MICHAEL ZUCKERMAN

TEMPLE UNIVERSITY PRESS

Philadelphia 82

Temple University Press
© 1982 by Temple University. All rights reserved
Published 1982
Printed in the United States of America

Library of Congress Cataloging in Publication Data
Main entry under title:

Friends and neighbors.

  Includes index.
  Contents: This Tory labyrinth/by Wayne
Bodle—"Fullness in their posterity"/by
Barry Levy—Diversity and its significance in
an eighteenth-century Pennsylvania community/
by Laura L. Becker—[etc.]
  1. Middle Atlantic States—Social
conditions—Addresses, essays, lectures.
2. Middle Atlantic States—History—Colonial
period, ca. 1600–1775—Addresses, essays,
lectures. 3. Pluralism (Social sciences)—
Addresses, essays, lectures. 4. Cultural
relativisim—Addresses, essays, lectures.
I. Zuckerman, Michael, 1939–
HN43.F74   306'.0973   82-3254
ISBN 0-87722-253-3   AACR2

Publication of this book was partially supported by
The Philadelphia Center for Early American Studies.

Contents

Friends and Neighbors

GROUP LIFE IN AMERICA'S
FIRST PLURAL SOCIETY

CHAPTER 1

Introduction:
Puritans, Cavaliers,
and the Motley Middle

MICHAEL ZUCKERMAN

American historians have always had an oddly obtuse
relation to American history.

When the essential life of the land was local, they attended obses-
sively to the national scene. Now, when localities have never mattered less, they rush to recover local history. When the republic was
largely unentangled in foreign alliances and intrigues, they pursued
diplomatic history avidly. Now, when the nation's every domestic
policy depends on international conditions and contingencies, they
relegate such study to the remote reaches of their discipline. When
their countrymen cared to read and shared something of a common
religio-literary culture, they dismissed native thought derisively.
Now, when scarcely one adult in a dozen reads a single book in a
year, they lavish admiring attention on the history of American
ideas. When the unmistakable business of the country was business, they addressed themselves singlemindedly to political history. Now, when business is unimaginable apart from the politics of
regulation, taxation, and subsidy, they turn to social history.

At every juncture, they have averted their gaze from the glare of
power. Again and again, they have gone looking where they would
cause no deep disturbance even on finding anything unsettling. If
they have rarely until recently paid any regard to the less savory
losers in their history, they have hardly accorded any serious scrutiny to the real winners, either. Insofar as they have plumbed the

3

decisively victorious elements of their past, they have done so at a very discreet distance.

It may be, of course, that there is nothing remarkable in their reticence. Historians need not be any more aware than other people of the profoundest commitments of their culture. Prevailing powers and premises resist undue illumination. They leave the limelight to others, who are ordinarily too preoccupied with the vindication of their own unavailing visions to examine very closely the forces that confine them to the stage and keep them from any prominent part in producing the show. But it may be, too, that the disinclination of historians to challenge the dominant authorities and attachments of their society explains some of the peculiar imbalances in their work.

In the writing of American colonial history, no tradition has been more elaborately or assertively set forth than the regional tradition of New England. And yet, in the actual unfolding of American destiny, no colonial region has been less relevant.

For all their ambitions to found a city upon a hill, the puritan colonists departed from the ascendant line of Anglo-American de-velopment almost from the first. By persisting in intolerance as the rest of the English empire came to new accommodations to religious diversity, they consigned themselves to inconsequence in the wider world of Western Protestantism. By failing to garner gold or grow staples, they confirmed their insignificance in the estimation of metropolitan mercantilists.

New Englanders of the first generation understood all that. New Englanders of the next generations understood it too, though more darkly and self-deceivingly. Cotton Mather caught their anguish in his adamant insistence that the venture of his ancestors "must live" in his *Magnalia* because it might not "live any where else." And New Englanders ever after consoled themselves for their regional isola-tion and unimportance with an overcompensatory inflation in liter-ature of claims they could never sustain in life. By the beginning of the nineteenth century, while many of the real masters of New England were contemplating secession from an America in which their aspirations were repeatedly rebuffed, and their interests as well as their pretensions repeatedly ignored, a generation of New England historians and litterateurs were busily fashioning a fusion of the young nation with their own slighted section. Following a habit of the regional mind as ancient and audacious as the *Magnalia*, they pronounced the American Revolution itself a mere fulfillment of New England principles, and America but New England writ large. Their equations have been advanced as ardently and arrogantly in every generation since.

Through its first two centuries and more, the South needed no such consolations. As long as it provided political leadership for the entire nation and as long as it maintained agricultural prepotency in a country that depended on agriculture, it had no need of the sort of histories that proliferated in New England. But as slavery came to seem a peculiar institution in an age of egalitarianism, southerners embarked on a more energetic investigation of American history. And after their secession failed, they came to a more exquisite solicitude still for the past, and a more poignantly sophisticated consciousness of history than New Englanders ever managed or, for that matter, required.

Of all the colonial regions of America, the Middle Atlantic alone never needed a distinctive history. While Southerners and New Englanders maintained the power of their peculiar principles, the politicians and businessmen of Pennsylvania and New York made off with the massy substance of power itself. While southern and northern provincials struggled to align their sectional idiosyncrasies with national developments, men of the middle states were without incentives to such local consciousness. They simply held hegemony. Their principles and practices were increasingly inseparable from those of the emerging and expanding nation.

From the first, the people of Pennsylvania, New Jersey, and New York acted under conditions of cultural pluralism that only came to characterize the rest of the country in the nineteenth century. More, the middle colonists accepted those conditions where their contemporaries resisted and even, in New England, anathematized them. The settlers of the Quaker colonies and the Duke's province instituted at their founding a religious liberty whose achievement occasioned strife in Virginia over a century later and in Massachusetts and Connecticut for fifty years after that. The politicians of the Middle Atlantic provinces operated in partisan environments unparalleled in America and advanced ideas of legitimate group interest undreamed around the Chesapeake and Massachusetts Bays. The merchants, farmers, and mechanics of the middle colonies labored in economic arenas and upon economic ethics of legitimate self-interest long before their peers in other places.

Indeed, almost all the lineaments of American liberalism were normative in the valleys of the Delaware and the Hudson before they were even broached along the James or the Charles. The

5

Middle Atlantic did not need a special history because its ways were so substantially the ways of the westering nation. "American" history was adequate to the region's requirements because "American" history was so nearly the history of the Middle Atlantic configuration writ large.

Only now, as the petrochemical complex of the Southwest outstrips the wealth and influence of Wall Street and as issues of giant organization and individual hedonism displace the classic questions of nineteenth-century liberalism, does the Middle Atlantic become visible in its own right. Only now, as its accustomed dominance decays, does it become for the first time a subject of intense historical study.

Of course, there was always some sporadic study, and even some significant study, of the middle colonies. Carl Becker's *History of Political Parties in the Province of New York*, and Charles Lincoln's contemporaneous and complementary account of conflict in pre-Revolutionary Pennsylvania, set the perspective of the only notable impingement of colonial historiography on general American historical writing that we have ever had, namely, the Progressive interpretation of the Revolutionary movement.

But such study was never sustained. Even at its flood, it failed to reach shores regularly washed by waves of southern sentimentalism and New England filiopietism. At its ebb, it barely left a rippled trace.

As the Progressive tide subsided, genteel scholars grew wary once more of the theme of social conflict. Division uninformed by any exalted issue sullied their story. Discord unredeemed by any honorable end defiled the gracious design of their saga. And incessant struggle for pelf and position undid their efforts to inspire a loftier notion of the nation.

The social grace of the planters of provincial Virginia and the religious zeal of the saints of seventeenth-century Massachusetts allowed the scholars alternatives to the American obsession with acquiring and accumulating. But the milling pluralism and feebly principled pursuit of profit of Pennsylvania, New Jersey, and New York afforded no refuge from the commercial culture from which the scholars were fleeing in the first place.

Indeed, even if the middle colonists had covered their covetousness with a patina of elevated ethics, their history would still have been less accessible than the histories of New England and the

Chesapeake. Puritanism and the plantation provided central strands around which narratives and analyses of those regions could be spun. The proprietary provinces between them could not be comprehended so conveniently. Their very pluralism precluded their being caught in catch phrases or seen in simple sequences. And just because they offered no single thread on which to string their history, they were consigned to obscure precincts of the past.

Puritanism in particular made New England accessible to historians. For the course of puritanism suggested an evolution intellectuals are conditioned to see and prepared to appreciate: the decline of religion, the decay of the traditional community, and the emergence of market relations and individualistic orientations. Tönnies called it the transition from *gemeinschaft* to *gesellschaft*. Others, from Maine and Marx through Durkheim and Weber to Redfield and Warren, propounded other labels in other languages but asserted essentially the same development. It is our preeminent—almost our only—account of western modernization. Inevitably it makes New England the preeminent—sometimes almost the only—focus of our formative years.

Of all the colonial regions, only New England began with a measure of medieval community from which departures could be calculated. New York and East Jersey commenced as commercial polyglots, and West Jersey and Pennsylvania became similar settlements soon enough. None of the middle colonies ever attained a steady state, and, except for Pennsylvania, none of them ever even achieved a vision of such a state. Diversity dogged them all from their founding. Flux afflicted their earliest existence. And population changes born of the highest rates of immigration and natural increase in English America extended their initial instability.

Unremitting alteration also occluded the other way in which scholars might have admitted the mid-Atlantic settlements to their darling drama of modernization. For insofar as historians do not impose their own models of change on the past, they incline to recapitulate the perceptions of the process articulated by participants. And exactly insofar as the Middle Colonists encountered an environment of recurrent dislocation, they were unlikely to express themselves in the idiom of Jeremiah or allege regrets for good old days and ways. As social psychologists have suggested, an unstable milieu induces a preparedness for novelty, a habit of habit change. Men and women who expected a certain fickleness in affairs, and adapted relatively readily to it, were little given to lamentations for lost *gemeinschaft*. They had never known a time of tranquility, so they never grieved its going. They had always ridden the whirligig, so they reconciled themselves to its revolutions. The very acceptance of inconstancy that let them play the principal part in our lived history left others who busied themselves bewailing the eclipse of community a larger role in our academic annals.

By the dawn of our own scholarly day, then, historians were already disposed to attend unduly to New England and the South. For reasons technical to their own discipline as well as motives incident to their own ideology, they were already prone to discount the Middle Atlantic area. And therefore they were primed to provide what the ruling temper of the era after World War II would have required in any case.

As intellectuals scurried for foxholes in the flush of the Cold War, early American historians found themselves fairly close to cover. Having always concentrated on the puritan and cavalier colonies, they had no trouble emphasizing the religious uniformity, ethnic homogeneity, and political placidity that seemed essential to true Americanism at the time. Having for years confined their chronicles to the regions east of the Hudson and south of the Delaware Bay, they hardly had to strain to give their accounts of the country's origins the gloss of idealism and the sheen of solidarity that seemed imperative in the anti-Communist crusade.

But if the iron insistence on orthodoxy of Cold War culture took historians ever more urgently to New England and the South, the searing conflicts of the late 1960s led them anew, and as importunately, to the Middle Colonies. If the will to see America congenial and consensual directed them to settlements where planters and preachers prevailed, an emerging apprehension of American unsettledness impelled them to territories where none held such hegemony.

As it did, some of the best early American historical scholarship of the 1970s came to focus on the middle provinces. The finest explorations of the imperial context were those of James Henretta, Stanley Katz, and Robert Ritchie—all of them set in New York. The most elegant and engaging of the synthetic histories of a single colony was Michael Kammen's depiction of provincial New York. The most evocative historical geography was James Lemon's study of southeastern Pennsylvania. The richest interpretation of acculturation in the new land was Stephanie Wolf's reading of assimilation in a German town outside Philadelphia. The most comprehensive account of the life of a colonial family was Randolph Klein's record of the Shippens of Pennsylvania. The fullest rendition of the material and mental worlds of the poor and laboring people of an early American settlement was the work of John Alexander, James Hutson, Jesse Lemisch, Gary Nash, Charles Olton, and William Williams on Philadelphia.

Beyond even such excellences were the recent treatments of conflict in the middle colonies. Separately, they were unsurpassed. Together, they were unrivaled in their sophistication, their sweep, their suggestiveness, and, indeed, their power to precipitate conflicts all their own. Patricia Bonomi's magisterial mosaic of factiousness in New York may have stood above such scholarly brawls, but other researches of significance only engendered them. Wolf's examination of Germantown, our most convincing account of ethnic accommodation, appeared at exactly the same time as Thomas Archdeacon's canvass of the first half-century of English dominion in New York City, our most compelling exposition of ethnic animosity and exploitation. Gary Nash's investigations of the social structure of Philadelphia, our most resourceful revelations of class cleavage, jostled in the journals with Sung Bok Kim's reconstruction of landlord-tenant relations on the New York manors, our most ingenious and intricate denial of class antagonism. Edward Countryman's studies of the dissolution of effective authority in revolutionary New York, our most powerful delineation of social conflict, came out contemporaneously with Alan Tully's survey of mid-eighteenth-century Pennsylvania politics, our most subtle inquiry into the muffling of such conflict.

These works posed problems, set agendas, and developed dialogues where nothing but isolated voices and extended stretches of silence had been before. They forged a discourse that has become at once the liveliest and the most provocative in the current colonial literature. And more than that, they lifted that literature itself to a new level. They made it integral to the exploration of subsequent American social processes.

As long as early American history confined itself primarily to New England and the South, it consigned itself to findings whose significance was primarily moral. It could convey the virtues and graces of worlds we had lost, but it could make no other connection to the plural society we had become. It could afford no other illumination of evolving structures or even of effective attitudes in the nineteenth and twentieth centuries.

The new colonial history that confronts the middle colonies confronts, as if for the first time, that modern American people. It permits the formative era to appear formative because its preoccupations are continuous with those of the later republic rather than disjunctive by definition. And those preoccupations, in turn, impart an unprecedented energy to the search for an adequate conception of our colonial past.

In the midst of such surging interest, moreover, the disposition to dwell on more marginal yet manageable regions diminishes. For those more marginal regions are no longer so manageable. The same expansion of scholarship that has quickened the study of the mid-Atlantic area has shattered the coherence that conditioned the appeal of its northern and southern neighbors, and especially of New England, by revealing unsuspected irregularities there. Such diversities may be paltry by comparison to the robust multiplicities of the middle colonies, but they are sufficient to dissipate the long-standing presumption of an essentially homogeneous region possessed of an essentially unified mind.

Indeed, the discovery of diversity that animates the investigation of the Middle Provinces utterly disconcerts the study of New England. Over the past thirty or forty years, that study has depended on the paradigm propounded by Perry Miller, and over the past decade it has become ever more evident that the paradigm can not sustain such weight. On its own terms, the postulation of a unitary regional consciousness stands increasingly exposed as an idealization of certain strands of thought among many prevalent in the area at the time. On terms beyond itself, the insistence on the primacy of mind appears increasingly plainly as a measure of Miller more than of early New England. Dissertations by the dozen, and articles and books by the score, elaborate a new social history of the eastern settlements that dispenses entirely with old reliances on notions of a New England mind. Miller's synthesis no longer binds the scholarship even of early New England. And of course it never did illuminate configurations elsewhere or afterward, despite his ambition to lay bare the beginnings of American culture.

Nonetheless, no other synthesis has arisen in its place. The town studies that seemed to herald a new history of the northern provinces have merely multiplied, without adding up to anything in their own right. If anything, their multiplication has divided New England immoderately and perhaps irreparably. It has demonstrated that Dedham and Andover do not even typify the other towns of Massachusetts, let alone the communities of the rest of the region or those of any other precinct of English America.

Just as we can no longer credit the inference from a few ministers in and around Boston to an entire population across New England, so we can no longer proceed serenely from a town or two by the Bay to the full range of settlements east of the Hudson. The unveiling of local variation has ended all that. And the discovery of a vaster variation has made unmistakably evident that New England itself is no model of America. Its intellectual evolution does not provide a purer laboratory specimen of the national mind, as Miller supposed. Its communal modes do not exhibit more plainly the pattern of the national fabric of politics and society, as some of the new social historians have suggested.

The wonder is only that we ever thought otherwise. The fallacy of the natural laboratory, purer than the rest of the republic, was exposed at least a generation ago in community studies, in the collapse of the quest for the aboriginal American small town. As sociologists learned to their chagrin, the untouched Anglo-Saxon town they had sought so long was an ignis fatuus. Its very purity precluded insight into social processes in the messier mass of American places that were ethnically mottled. Its insularity impeded understanding of ordinary American communities and their entanglements in wider worlds.

An old joke tells of a drunkard looking for a lost key, late at night, under a lamppost. A passerby stops to help. The sot and the samaritan search together for a while, unavailingly, until the samaritan asks the sot if he is sure they are looking in the right place. The man answers amiably that, as a matter of fact, they are not. The key is down the block where he dropped it, but the light is better by the lamppost.

For far too long we have been looking for keys to American culture under New England lampposts. The unmistakable import of the local studies of the last decade is that the light is not even any better there.

Today it seems increasingly clear that the configuration of American civilization first found its essential contours in the mid- and South-Atlantic regions, and especially in the province of Pennsylvania. In political, economic, social, and even religious life, Pennsylvania provided the pattern for the nation more than Massachusetts ever did.

In politics, the pluralistic modes of the middle colonies spread irresistibly in national affairs. The very creation of the new nation caused men of many backgrounds to come together as they never had before outside the Middle Atlantic area; and just as the demographic diversity of the Hudson and Delaware River settlements precipitated partisanship and an ethic of legitimate opposition in the region, so the establishment of new arenas and institutions spurred a similar development in the country at large. We are only beginning to appreciate the importance of ethno-religious rivalries in a context of multicultural fragmentation. But we can already see that such a pattern of politics could never have originated in New England, where more than nine-tenths of the white population was English and almost nine-tenths of the tiny company that was not was Scottish, Scotch-Irish, or Irish. We can conjecture that the normative national pattern could hardly have had its sources solidly in the South, where markedly more cosmopolitanism obtained than in New England but where English hegemony still prevailed in every province, generally by about a two-to-one ratio of Englishmen to all other Europeans together. We can infer, therefore, that the pattern emerged from a mid-Atlantic matrix, where heterogeneity inhibited such hegemony. In New York and New Jersey, the English were barely a majority of the white inhabitants. In Pennsylvania, they were little more than a third of the free settlers. Amid such multiplicities, a politics of ethnic antagonism and alliance appeared in Pennsylvania, New Jersey, and New York before it emerged in the South or was even imagined in New England.

In economic action and attitude, Americans of later ages also followed in paths prepared by the middle colonists. While agriculture languished in Massachusetts, the farmers of the Lancaster plain made Pennsylvania the granary of the Atlantic economy and a pattern for the planters of the Chesapeake. While business stagnated in Boston, Philadelphia became the principal entrepôt and New York the second city of America. And while puritan precepts encumbered enterprise in New England and slavery subtly infected every ambition in the South, premises of possessive individualism unclogged middle colonial commerce. Entrepreneurs, speculators, promoters, and profiteers found their fairest fields in New York and Pennsylvania.

In social mores, in matters of manners ranging from the family to patterns of settlement, Americans also disdained the norms of New England and appropriated the modes of the middle colonies. As men and women made their way across the continent, for example, most of them planted themselves on the land on isolated farmsteads and in crossroads communities that derived directly from the Delaware Valley. Most of the rest made their way to cities which explicitly modeled themselves on Philadelphia or, later, New York. Geographers and folklorists have shown that the cultural inheritance of New England was confined to a thin band of settlement in the northern tier of the new nation, whereas the influence of the mid-Atlantic provinces was much "more pervasive," extending over "an enormous area from the Upland South to the Old Northwest and beyond the Mississippi." Historians have traced similar influences in the same vast arc, which Rowland Berthoff once called "Greater Pennsylvania." And if that "Greater Pennsylvania" was primarily a product of frontier elements in the province, other contours of the emergent national culture were set by elements closer to the confluence of the Schuylkill and the Delaware. As the American family assumed its modern form, for example, it emerged along lines already normative among Quakers for generations. Pennsylvania Friends were the first to attain a fair facility at the sort of family limitation that was so desperately desired and ultimately so largely achieved among the aspiring classes of the nineteenth century. Friends were the first to affirm in principle the kind of companionate marriage founded on the kind of parity between husbands and wives and parental indulgence of children that has struck foreign visitors as peculiarly American ever since the age of Andrew Jackson. And Friends were the very first group in all the Western world to maintain the modern sentimental family, predicated on privacy, intimacy, and a loving surveillance of children.

Even in religion, the Middle Atlantic exhibited more fully than any other colonial region the shape of things to come. New England and the South presented fragments, at best, of the nineteenth-century synthesis. The middle colonies presented the synthesis itself. Their diversity promoted a rule of religious pluralism in the republic that has persisted to this day.

The puritan provinces of New England never did embrace principles of pluralism and only grudgingly made a place for a few of its institutions. In Massachusetts, as late as the 1770s, almost three-quarters of the churches were still within the Congregational fold, and almost three-quarters of the towns offered their inhabitants no choice of cult or communion. In the South, to the time of the Revolution, a much more extensive nonconformity lodged alongside a continued clinging to canons of Anglican establishment. The middle colonies alone maintained a truly modern multiplicity in life and—apart from a limited local establishment in New York—in law. In New Jersey, not a single denomination enlisted as much as 25 percent of the population. In Pennsylvania, Quaker meetings constituted but 10 percent of all ecclesiastical societies. And while even the limited range of election that other colonies allowed came late, the wider variety that Pennsylvania permitted was as old as its original proprietor's first Frame of Government.

On the whole, however, early American historians have paid perfunctory attention to these questions of ecclesiastical pluralism. Habituated to seeking the significance of colonial religion primarily in New England puritanism, they have confined themselves to telling, in ever more intricate and ingenious detail, an essentially parochial tale. For neither the institutional milieu that conditioned subsequent American church life nor the specific institutions that constituted its most vital elements derived in any influential way from colonial Congregationalism. Toleration owed almost nothing to the intransigent orthodoxy of Massachusetts. Voluntaryism made its way more haltingly in the puritan provinces than anywhere else from Maine to Georgia. Separation of church and state came to Connecticut and Massachusetts a full century and a half after it was settled principle in Pennsylvania and New Jersey. And virtually every particular church of eventual consequence to the country found its followers outside New England in its formative years. The great democratic denominations of American Protestantism, the Baptists and the Methodists, grew most mercurially in the back country and most laggingly in puritan precincts. The next most numerous group, the Lutherans, commenced their march across the continent from Pennsylvania. The next, the Presbyterians, set off from their Scottish and Scotch-Irish seats in the middle and southern colonies far more than from their consociations in the Connecticut Valley. The Episcopalians remained more nearly in the East, became the preferred confession of America's elite, and owed their origins to southern planters and Philadelphia gentlemen. The Catholics overspread the country in the nineteenth century, became the true church of America's masses, and traced their founding faithful to Maryland and Pennsylvania.

14

Scholars who assume the ultimacy of puritanism in the national experience cannot penetrate any of these denominational dramas because New England had so small a part in them. They cannot grasp the grander drama of America's advancing acceptance of the inviolability of conscientious conviction because Congregationalists had so anticlimactic a role in it. They can only commend themselves to an ethereal muse of the "mind," and in her austere theater declaim their melancholy theme.

The significance of the middle colonies was widely recognized in the era of the Revolution. Geography may have helped make the Middle Atlantic the meeting ground when Americans gathered to declare their independence and devise their constitutions. Geography may even have influenced the establishment of the national capital in a succession of sites in New York, New Jersey, and Pennsylvania. But more than mere geography made the area between Hudson's river and Mason and Dixon's line the most American of all the seaboard regions. Its mixed multitudes of strangers enhanced its attractiveness to the restless men and women whose mobility made possible a people. Its divergent creeds and customs eased its assimilation and, indeed, mediation of the extremities of others. And its demographic diversity and institutional complexity enriched its inspiration of the great sketch of the nascent nation that appeared at the culmination of the colonial era.

St. Jean de Crèvecoeur's *Letters from an American Farmer* proclaimed the Americans new men in the New World. Brought into being by a "strange mixture of blood, which you will find in no other country," they had coalesced into a "new race of men," motivated by "new principles . . . and . . . new opinions." Refusing religious establishment, they multiplied churches. Scorning hierarchy, they boasted a social order in which every man enjoyed the bounty of his own labors on the land.

If Crèvecoeur's celebration of the distinctive democratic character of the colonists was an idealization, it was an idealization that disclosed as much as it concealed. Even as it obscured the slavery of the South and the establishment of the East, it revealed a society to itself. And the society was essentially its middle regions writ large. Crèvecoeur had spent almost all his American career in those parts, and they provided him his perspective as well as his particulars. The diversity and disestablishment he hailed as generically American were primarily properties of New York, New Jersey, and Pennsylvania. The yeomen he set so appealingly against the dispossessed masses of the Old World held their "fertile farms in these middle provinces." The backcountrymen who presented "America in its proper light" begged the Lord's blessing on William Penn. In much the way that another Frenchman, fifty years later, would attempt to apprehend America by modeling its ideal-typical tendencies, Crèvecoeur tried to understand processes more profound than the manifestations that met a surveyor and sometime soldier of fortune in his inveterate travels. To do so, he projected an American prospect from a middle-colonial point of view.

Yet his projection served more to open the issue of the national character than to settle it. He saw that the nature of the new society was to be sought primarily in the mid-Atlantic provinces. He even grasped something of the significance of their diversity for the expansion of ambition, the evolution of religious indifference, the amplification of technology, and the modification of manners in the land. Nonetheless, his most celebrated thrust was not a conclusion but a query: "What, then, is the American, this new man?" And his question has outlasted his answers. The very diversity he emphasized eluded him in the end. His perception that the middle colonies posed the problem did not, of itself, confer a solution.

No one else has done much better than the vagrant Frenchman in the two centuries since. Many have seen as he did that the Middle Atlantic settlements were the cradle of American culture. None have successfully specified how. Many have sensed as he did that their religious and ethnic multiformity must have been ingredient in their importance. None have determined how disparate peoples did actually live together. None have discovered the consequences of their intermixture for provincial society as a whole, for its component communities, for their constituent ethnoreligious elements, or for individuals. It is an irony that has not gone unnoticed that, despite our recognition of the salience of cultural pluralism in the middle colonies, we have never had a theoretical frame for ethnoreligious research there. As a recent review of the historiography of the region reminded us, "to recognize ethnicity is not to understand it."

The pieces in this collection do not provide that comprehensive theoretical understanding. They do bear Crèvecoeur's question in mind, and their findings do bear upon it, but they do not finally allow a decisive answer to it. Indeed, they do not even resolve any noticeable number of the less cosmic controversies that have come to characterize middle-colonial history. On the contrary, they often deepen those disputes, giving them new dimensions and unprecedented indicators. The old issues are old just because they *are* issues, and very vexed ones at that.

Even where the essays do offer answers, they are as often inconsistent, one with another, as mutually supportive. It would be tedious to tally the discrepancies here, let alone to attempt to unsnarl the tangle of confirmations and contradictions, but it would not be inappropriate to explain something of their origins.

This is an anthology assembled after the fact. Though its entries were all written expressly for this collection, they were not composed in concert. Though its authors all did their doctoral studies at the University of Pennsylvania, they have not even consummated their research under common supervision, let alone come to common conclusions. They have made their own way to the middle colonies and kept to their own separate ways once there. They have begun from different disciplines, and they have ended with different dissertation directors. If they have never been at cross-purposes, they have never shared a single purpose in common, either.

Indeed, they have never even shared sources or methods. Unlike the contributors to a recent collection on early Maryland, they are not held together by an attachment to a particular archive such as the Maryland Hall of Records. Unlike the authors of a somewhat older volume on nineteenth-century cities, they are not bound by an enthusiasm for a specific device such as the extraction of mobility series from manuscript census returns. They pursue problems and people, by the means at hand that seem suitable. They do not depend on any routine that any other scholar can appropriate and apply mechanically to any other community. Their every essay draws on different sorts of data, or different facets of the same sorts of data. More than that, their every essay comes at different questions from different theoretical perspectives. Valerie Gladfelter begins from group dynamics and an extensive clinical experience. Deborah Gough starts from the sociology of religion. Others set forth from foci on acculturation, family, women, and war. Variously they avail themselves of wills and deeds, diaries, tax lists, meeting records, proprietary estate books, and soldiers' letters. And collectively they attain a complexity commensurate with their subject matter and exhibit an array of interests as plural as the societies they study.

17

If their collaboration holds together, it does so because they do share an awareness of the magnitude of the cultural recovery they are attempting. They have been talking to one another for years. They have participated in the creation of a community of scholars, and they have known the exhilaration that attends it. They have been able to believe that their separate investigations would resonate beyond themselves, to the reconfiguration of an entire society.

They have aimed, then, at nothing less than the life of the middle-colonial past as men and women of that pioneering plural society actually experienced it. They mean to move beneath the political and theological interests of the articulate few to the personal and associational experience of the inexpressive many. They seek the grounds of group relations and the sources of intimate identity.

In a couple of cases they are able to do so directly from personal documents. More characteristically, they have neither such overtly eloquent materials nor any inordinate concern for the elites who usually produce them. In the absence of explicit testimony, they penetrate the personal order by indirection and ingenuity. Susan Forbes teases friendship patterns out of witness lists on wills. Laura Becker discovers clues to informal mingling across ethnoreligious lines in the ledgers of tradesmen and tavernkeepers. Barry Levy elicits family priorities from dreary legal dispositions of property. Valerie Gladfelter discerns shifts in the eternal battle of the sexes in the disciplinary records of a Quaker meeting. By such attention to apparently impersonal data, these essays reconstruct the sensibilities of very real people. From dry leaves that drift down to us across centuries—from court records, mortgages, marriage certificates, and the like—they fan a flame of life in something of the fullness of its passions and purposes. If their accomplishment is an illusion, it is a grand one. It if is managed by means of inferences, the inferences are surely no shakier than those that go from literate and expressive elites to the society at large.

If anything, it is a defect of this collection that it lacks other contributions even more audacious in inference. The pieces here address difficult issues, make solid sense of recalcitrant evidence, and suggest solutions to significant problems. They give us a vivid view of the motives and mores of a colonial society in a measure of its intricate immediacy. But like so much of the "new social history," they still reflect the holdings of the repositories from which they derive as much as the wholeness of the life they are meant to illuminate. They are, in the aggregate, too attentive to the Quakers and too heedless of the unchurched. They are too fond of the family and too indifferent to the dissolute. They are too tied to the towns and too aloof from the crossroads communities of the countryside. They are too concerned with stable structures and too unmindful of transiency. They are too voluble about the respectable and too silent about the sordid. They make too little place for speculators and peculators, backwoods brawlers and backroads haulers, sluts and scullery maids. In short, they are only auguries of the reconstruction of middle-colonial life, not the reconstruction itself. For the rest, as Theodore Roethke once assured us, we will learn by going where we have to go.

Even in these auguries, though, there is much to mull. Together, the essays suggest serious defects in central theoretical orthodoxies of contemporary social science. Separately, they imply surprising significances in the multiplicities of the middle colonies.

Their animadversions on current theories of modernization are especially striking because they arise out of an area that was in many ways the most modern corner of the most modern country in the Western world. If the emergence and establishment of modern society occurred at all in the eighteenth century, it should have occurred in Pennsylvania. Yet these students of the communities of the commonwealth do not report its occurrence in any straightforward fashion. On the contrary, the evolution they observe dissolves the dichotomies and denies the directionality on which the very concept of modernization depends.

Virtually every version of the orthodox dogma posits a contrast between an initial "traditional" state and a subsequent "modern" one. Virtually none of these accounts of middle-colonial communities sustain such a simple progression. The counterpositions that come so easily in abstraction are harder to come by in concrete historical contexts.

Sometimes the effort to apply such oppositions leads ineluctably to paradox. In Wayne Bodle's consideration of the countryside around Valley Forge, for example, the privatism of the farmers, which could be seen as a symptom of modernity, conditioned the incapacity of the American army to wage guerilla war and thereby assured that American independence would be preserved by military means almost wholly traditional.

More often the predication of polarity leads to deeper and more substantive difficulties. At a distance, dualistic accounts seem illuminating. Up close, antitheses fuse in middle terms that cannot be clearly allied with either extremity. Intimate familiarity yields mediations between the elegant antagonisms of the grand theorists.

These mediations emerge most forcefully in the sphere of the family. Family must occupy a problematic place in any dichotomous treatment of traditional corporatism and modern individualism, and its position proves equivocal indeed in these essays. Nancy Tomes finds it impossible to "unravel the two affiliations" of religion and family because they were "so effectively intertwined." Where theories of modernization require a rivalrous relation between public and private attachments, Tomes reveals a variety of ways in which "kinship became a model for the group solidarity the Quakers wished to foster." Forbes also finds the family a "mediator," inextricably entangled in atomistic and collective enterprises alike. And Levy discovers that and more.

Just as Tomes uses visiting as a vehicle to come at social relations that would be inaccessible otherwise, Levy utilizes landholding to pierce the privacy of the home. When he does, he finds that historians as well as high theorists can concoct controversies out of ideological abstractions. For landholding has been at the center of a squabble about the course of modernization that has captivated colonial historians in recent years. James Lemon has shown that settlers of southeastern Pennsylvania held land as a commodity, for speculation, status, and exchange, and he has called their enmeshment in market relations evidence of their essential modernity. James Henretta has countered that farmers of the northern colonies customarily acquired land for their own productive purposes, and he has declared their usage proof of their persisting traditionalism. But where both Lemon and Henretta accept the appropriateness of the terms of modernization theory and argue only over the timing of the passage from one pole to the other, Levy embarrasses the theoretical assumptions they share and vitiates the very terms of the theoretical issue they join. By intense examination of land transactions, he reveals the Quaker family as an intermediate element in a situation too complex to be caught in contrapuntal categories. Quaker fathers did not acquire land for use, but they did not accumulate it for speculation and exchange, either. They secured it for their families. And their families maintained neither a market orientation nor a traditional one in any simple sense. They were more solicitous of extended lineage than any other families in English America and, at the same time, more sensitive to the narrow nuclear unit than any other families in the Atlantic world. They submitted to the meddling of the meeting and, simultaneously, pioneered in privatism. They cannot be ensconced comfortably among the agents of tradition or modernity, yet they cannot be set aside, either, because their primacy in the economic development of the Delaware Valley is undeniable.

Close examination of the immediacies of familiar affairs upsets the directionality of modernization as much as it disconcerts the dichotomies of the concept. For modernization demands a simple linear development. Its exegetes may differ in their verbal descriptions of that evolution—from use values to exchange values, tribal brotherhood to universal otherhood, and many more—but they do not differ in their dogmatic insistence on its headlong irreversibility. And yet, as Tomes suggests, actual historical experience was kinkier than high theory allows. The social and economic changes of the eighteenth century did not destroy or even enfeeble older attitudes toward kin and community among her Quaker diarists. On the contrary, those traditional loyalties "intensified rather than deteriorated."

Others also observe this paradox of the exaggeration of tradition in a modernizing milieu. Their observations signify their skepticism about modernization theory and, more, their faith in finding something better by attending to the consequences for collective life and individual ambition of pluralism. Indeed, it is exactly at this juncture that their critique of received theory merges into their efforts to elaborate alternatives. On their accounts, the course of middle-colonial modernization never did run smooth, and the reasons for its irregularity were inseparable from the heterogeneity of the region.

Pluralism promoted paradoxes all its own. As a form, it was quintessentially modern, but its formal modernity did not dictate a corresponding substantive modernity. Rather, its very permissiveness protected communities and cultures such as those of the Scots of East Jersey, which were able to maintain under pluralistic auspices the utterly nonmodern habits they brought with them from the northeastern Lowlands. As Ned Landsman shows, the Scottish settlers of East Jersey actually fortified their old ways in the New World. They perpetuated customary communal networks. They remained withdrawn from politics and submissive to authority. They preferred tenantry to the isolated farmsteads to which they were entitled. And where they had met a fair measure of religious pluralism in Scotland, they drew together in redoubled devotion to

Presbyterianism in East Jersey. The very heterogeneity of their new environment impelled them to a clannishness they had never known before, a Scottish solidarity that made them more monolithic and thereby less modern than they had been even in the old country.

Forbes finds a similar pattern in New Garden, where advancing diversity led Friends to look more to the meeting and less to their own separate sensibilities and interests for guidance. As the strangers came, the Quakers became increasingly dependent on collective controls. And Tomes too discerns an enlargement of Quaker insularity at a time of burgeoning social schism. In the midst of the most modern metropolis in America, affluent women of the meeting retired to the security of sectarian retreat.

All of these discoveries suggest questions about community and diversity alike. The capacity of the Scots to sustain a separate life among the English and the ability of the Quakers to remain within their own meetings amid multiplying masses make it unclear whether middle-colonial geopolitical units can be considered communities at all. And insofar as they cannot, it ceases to be self-evident that the men and women of the mid-Atlantic actually experienced the heterogeneity that the census counts suggest. Perhaps, as planners promoting racial integration have noticed in our own time, physical proximity did not dictate effective interaction.

Intriguing as these issues are, there are others even more perplexing, for sometimes propinquity did promote mingling. Quaker ladies of Philadelphia may have kept to themselves, but, according to Gough, their Anglican neighbors did not. New Garden Friends may have made their meeting their only allegiance, but, according to Gladfelter, Burlington Quakers met their non-Quaker acquaintances more amiably. Such differences suggest difficulties that resist simple resolutions. They invite empirical investigation of the prevalence of the two patterns and especially of the conditions under which one or the other occurred.

Some years ago, Sydney James suggested that the Quakers of provincial Pennsylvania might best be understood as a people among peoples. In that evocative phrase he meant to emphasize their steadily advancing acceptance of voluntary associational ways which would become normative for other Americans in succeeding centuries. But even in his own work the phrase admitted of two distinct interpretations, and in subsequent studies the imprecision has persisted. Some Friends, such as those of New Garden, embraced a more strenuously sectarian strategy, isolating themselves from the increasingly mixed multitudes around them. Others, such as those of Burlington, adopted a more latitudinarian attitude, accommodating themselves to rising heterogeneity by relaxing their own distinctive discipline. New Gardeners were one sort of people among peoples, Burlingtonians another. At this juncture we do not even have a solid sense of which sort was more common in the colonial era, let alone enough information to specify the conditions under which one or the other was likelier.

We have known that we do not know such things about the Quakers for quite some time. We are beginning to notice that we do not know them about other middle colonists either. In East Jersey, a Scottish people set itself off almost entirely from the rest of the region's peoples, while Scottish Quakers and Anglicans gave up their Old World affiliations for a Presbyterianism that deepened Scottish solidarity and separatism. In Reading, German and English peoples also placed a higher priority on ethnic than religious attachments, but not to the point of dissolving all religious differences within their respective national camps. And in Germantown, ethnic allegiances faded faster than denominational bonds in the face of the assimilative ambitions of the inhabitants.

In a plural society, every group is ultimately a people among peoples, one way or another. And because that is so, every group's identity must be problematic. Others faced their own ambiguities of aloofness and accommodation, and still others addressed still other dilemmas. It is not clear whether ethnicity defined people more than denomination did, or vice versa. It is utterly obscure under what conditions immigrants adhered to their ethnic communities or abandoned them and in what circumstances settlers stayed within their religious traditions or strayed from them.

It is clear only that these are crucial questions for the character of group life in America and that they—and others equally crucial on the sources of solidarity and the conditions of conflict in the midst of multicultural fragmentation—can be considered more closely in the mid-Atlantic region than anywhere else. The very diversity of the area demands the requisite attention to variation. Tribalism may have emerged among the Quakers of New Garden, but a far different familism appeared close by among the Friends of the Welsh Tract. Sects may have solidified in revolutionary Philadelphia, but privatism prevailed in the revolutionary countryside a few miles up the Schuylkill. So students of the middle colonies do not leap, like New England historians, from small parochial samples to the colonial universe. They do not pretend to have captured the meaning of early America in their local snares. But they do, together, suggest that such meaning may be found more amply and adequately in the middle colonies than anywhere else. For there we can confront most conscientiously the deep diversities of the country. There we can sift through disparate patterns with data rich enough at once to incorporate the full range of variables and to account for it. There the very complexity that sets such formidable difficulties sets, simultaneously, the conditions under which they can be dealt with.

The version of American history that is essentially New England local history writ large is, in the final analysis, a version of a genteel Anglo-Saxon racism. Just as such, it was immensely comforting to the Anglophilic elites of the nineteenth and twentieth centuries. By means of the metaphor of region, it provided them a model of cultural process in this country in which an appropriate social hierarchy prevailed and everything important moved in orderly imposition from the most virtuous people at the top to the benighted beneath them. On this model a united and enlightened New England dispensed to the other precincts of the nation; and as it did, region became an emblem of suitable social process more largely, in which a united elite would bring its bounty to the deferential orders below. This image was enormously reassuring to the embattled elites themselves—they were the ones who both produced and consumed it—but it had a grievous flaw. Its plangent premise of orderly imposition from on high and grateful acceptance from down under did not seriously touch the turbulent reality of America.

The middle-colonial model that is struggling to be born offers a different image of American development. It provides none of the reassurance that the New England model does, since its insistence on intraregional fragmentation and its implication of interregional indifference and isolation suggest some disturbing aspects of our national life. If we take the rendering of region as, again, a metaphor for social process more generally, then reorienting ourselves to the centrality of the middle colonies would oblige us to recognize conflicts at the very core of our culture and to reconcile ourselves to a discordant if not incoherent America. But the compensation would be a degree of realism and a chance to penetrate actual American social processes as the New England model does not and can not.

In effect, the exaggerated emphasis on New England gives us to ourselves as a single people. The insistence on the primacy of the middle-colonial pattern calls us to a reconfiguration of ourselves as a plural people, and calls us as well to the intricate untangling and ultimate acceptance of those multiplicities.

In effect, it brings us back to social history, and brings me back, a bit embarrassingly, to where I began. For in bidding us to take up such social history, rather than political history, and in urging it on a local rather than a national scale besides, I am right back to the evasions I began by lamenting.

And yet I hope—and even believe—I am being neither evasive nor irrelevant. Much of power and policy—more than we are yet comfortable in admitting—depends today on how we live in a world of diversity. At home and abroad, issues decisive not merely for politics but also for the very fate of man hinge on how we get on with others from whom we differ. In many ways, this is the one momentous issue by which modern man will be judged. And this is exactly the issue on which the experience of the middle colonies affords us our deepest, most durable, and most disturbing evidence. If we would know ourselves and our capacities for living with diversity, self-knowledge begins there. If we would utilize such knowledge for the enhancement of our lives, the record of our earliest efforts is richest there.

CHAPTER 2

The Birth of the "Modern Family" in Early America: Quaker and Anglican Families in the Delaware Valley, Pennsylvania, 1681–1750

BARRY LEVY

The career of the modern family in America began early in the Delaware Valley, at least by the late seventeenth century. From their first settlement, Quaker farmers and artisans lived in families featuring the basic elements that historians and sociologists have used to define the "modern" family: purified household environments, voluntary love marriages, financially independent conjugal households, and tender child rearing.[1] Quaker families also adapted well to the premodern Pennsylvania setting. Many historians insist, however, that the modern American family began in New England in the late eighteenth and early nineteenth centuries in response to significant economic, political, and social changes coinciding with early industrialization. Such interpretations rely on modernization theory and the centrality of New England to explain the transformation of the "traditional" American family into its modern, domestic form.[2] Social events in colonial Pennsylvania clearly challenge such interpretations.

Preparation for this article was assisted by grants from the Charles Rieley Armington Research Program on Values in Children, Case Western Reserve University, and by a summer grant from the National Endowment for the Humanities. Professor Michael Zuckerman's editorial assistance was particularly valuable.

26

The Birth of the "Modern Family"

There will be disagreements about whether the Delaware Valley Quaker families were totally modern or slightly less than modern (typologies are always inexact). The basic emotions, commitments, and forms were there, however. And what is essential is that a group using modern strategies—love and voluntarism instead of shame and coercion—was successful in a premodern American setting. In fact, the seventeenth-century Quaker family system mastered the Delaware Valley far better than did traditional English and Welsh families. In 1715 some 204 Quaker households, 60 Anglican households, and 43 Baptist or unchurched households lived in the fertile Chester and Welsh Tract countryside near Philadelphia.[3] These families lived differently according to their religious affiliation, and they were not equally adapted to life in colonial Pennsylvania. In the early Delaware Valley—hardly a "modern" place—the radical Quaker families thrived between 1681 and 1740. The middling Anglican families, although equipped with seemingly appropriate traditional habits, floundered economically, lost much of their previous religious identity, and gave less to the valley's social and economic development.

The Quakers' triumph was the first of many passages from public to domestic orderings in American life. Pennsylvania's thin social structure and miles of uncut farmland suited the Quakers' radical, privatistic strategy. The Anglicans struggled manfully to erect a public social order, but the Delaware Valley Quakers conquered this empty and wealthy environment by concentrating people's attention on the intricacies, feelings, and responsibilities of modern, noncoercive, domestic control. They seemed to have an effective antidote to the silence of early America: a devotion to silence itself. They introduced impressively a social form that in the nineteenth century would spread to other lonely American countrysides and cities.

The seventy-five Welsh Quaker and seventy-eight Cheshire Quaker families who settled between 1681 and 1690 along the Schuylkill and Delaware rivers near Philadelphia fashioned their family system from radical religious ideas and experiences and from the opportunities offered by Pennsylvania itself.[4] During an awakening in the northwest of England in the late 1650s, they had become religious radicals—Quakers. Experiencing a new revelation, they believed that the "light" or "grace" was born into every person (along with original sin), that it could be experienced in

27

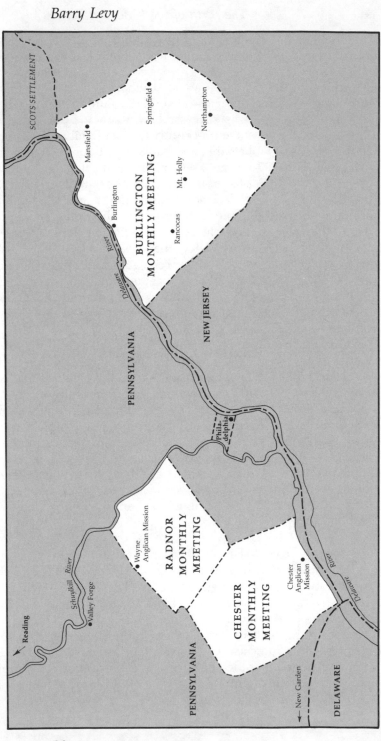

silent worship meetings, that it could be uttered when a "minister" spoke spontaneously from "Truth," and that it could be spread from one person to the next as one hot coal ignites another (a favorite metaphor).[5] Quakers therefore rejected the authority of learned ministers, traditional ceremonies, and even the final authority of Scriptural text. Their consequent emphasis on introspection, noncoercion, and love greatly influenced their thinking and feelings about family life. During the 1660s and 1670s these settlers had lived as a beleaguered and despised community in the Cheshire hills and Welsh mountains. In the 1680s and 1690s they came to Pennsylvania, as their records show, in order to realize frustrated communal and religious goals, to be organized most tellingly in their radical, involving families.[6]

Their new familial thinking helped impel them to emigrate. Being, typically, uneducated men and women, accustomed to an aural culture, their beliefs were simple and personal, based on direct religious experience, knowledge of Scriptures, and sharp judgments of people. They thought human relations sacred. Like many other seventeenth-century people, they often joined personality, religious faith, and social relations into one concept, "conversation."[7] What kind of "conversation" a person had, how "conversation" was developed, and how one person related to another through "conversation" were the vital issues of their communities and families. Quakers believed that people who owned the "Light" wholly or partly destroyed pride and sin and lived by the word of God or "Truth." Such people, they believed, had infectiously honest speech, gestures, and conduct, "holy conversation," which answered the "Light" in others. The settlers described themselves accordingly as having peculiarly selfless, tender, and "savory" "conversations." Thirty-six adjectives or adjectival phrases described the "conversation" of adults in sixty-two removal certificates from Wales to the Welsh Tract between 1681 and 1690. The adjectives most often used were "honest" (thirty-three), "blameless" (fourteen), "loving" (thirteen), and "tender" (nine).[8] They wanted simply to enjoy and to glorify God by maintaining families and communities in which "holy conversation" would be constantly shared and developed.

However, they also believed that people who suppressed the "Light" by worshiping their own prideful selves or other wordly idols brought confusion and conflict to human society and tended to corrupt others. They thought it necessary therefore to protect themselves and particularly their children from such worldly "carnal talkers." The settlers required their children, whose fragility they sensitively appreciated, to live within networks of holy human influence. The sixty-two removal certificates frequently described the settlers' children as being "loving," "modest," and "affectionate," while being also "poor," "innocent," and "weak."[9] Such recognition of children's loving dependence and fragility revealed a perception of children far removed from the traditional conception of children as resilient "little adults." Such fragile children were particularly vulnerable to "carnal talkers" and particularly in need of parental concern. Thus, one Welsh Meeting in 1690 praised the widower Griffith John, who had three "poor" children, because "all his endeavor hath been to bring up his children in the fear of the Lord according to the order of Truth."[10] Another couple were praised because they "by no means would be withheld of bringing their small weakly family along with them, to the very end, to have them brought up in the pure dread and fear of their God which they greatly feared would be wanting in their absence."[11]

Acquiring an environment for protective child rearing largely justified emigration. Keeping children in networks of "holy conversation" in Great Britain was usually too costly. Middling children were expected to provide much of the labor England required, at the least expense, and most children left home for service or apprenticeships at age ten.[12] Most Cheshire and Welsh Quaker emigrants were also middling or poor families from among the most economically colonized and poorest areas of Great Britain, where houses were small, land ownership rare, and farms small and pastoral.[13] And though Quaker children required an independent and secure economic future, even the paltry economic power Quaker families had individually and collectively accumulated was drained away by severe persecution from 1660 to 1688, when heavy fines fell upon Quaker patrons.[14] William Penn, the Quaker proprietor of Pennsylvania, thus wisely promoted his colony in terms of the relief it promised from such insufficiencies of estate. He told Pennsylvanians to form townships of 5,000 acres, with each farmer having lavish, contiguous holdings of 100 to 500 acres. He advertised that cheap land would permit a "more convenient bringing up of youth" and would end English parents' addiction "to put their children into Gentlemen's service or send them to towns to learn trades."[15] And the colonists shared his concern. When Thomas Ellis, a leader in the Welsh Tract, was challenged by George Fox in 1684 about the spiritual courage of migrating Quaker families, Ellis answered, "I wish that those that have estates of their own and to leave fullness in their posterity may not be offended at the Lord's opening a door of mercy to thousands in England especially in Wales who have not estates either for themselves or children."[16] It was a request that George Fox and other Quaker critics of Pennsylvania migration, who shared Ellis's childrearing ideas, could only answer charitably.

During the 1670s monthly meetings in Cheshire and Wales had worked diligently to place many poor parents' children in service with other Quakers. This had been the only option available. But abundant Pennsylvania real estate inspired Friends to think of rearing virtually all children at home with parents.[17] William Penn's settlement projections and the settlers' own practice answered this purpose. The Welsh Tract and Chester settlers chose a settlement pattern that supported community without restricting families' freedom to expand economically and geographically. Their plans also intelligently conformed to the traditions of Wales, Cheshire, and other highland areas, where dispersed farmsteads were the rule from the late Middle Ages. Quaker Pennsylvanians lived on contiguous farmsteads with their meeting houses placed near the center of each sprawling township. These highland Quaker practices, to be sure, appeared individualistic from the perspective of the lowland Massachusetts settlers' famed nucleated villages. But Thomas Ellis of Haverford honestly boasted in 1685 that the spatial organization of Quaker settlement ideally accommodated the settlers' familial and communal goals:

> About fifteen families of us have taken our land together and there are to be eight more that have not yet come, who took (to begin) 30 acres apiece with which we build upon and do improve, and the other land we have to range for our cattle; we have our burying place where we intend out Meeting houses, as near as we can to the center, our men's and women's Meetings and other Monthly Meetings in both week days unto which four townships at least belongs. And precious do we find other opportunities that are given as free will offerings unto the Lord in evening sometime which not intended but Friends coming simply to one another and sitting together the Lord appears, to his name be the Glory.[18]

Local Quaker planing was keenly communal. But highland tolerance of distance also allowed Friends to encourage families to be economically self-sufficient, to buy land for children with little worry about expanding outside the spatial limits of the community.

The men's and women's monthly meetings to which Thomas Ellis referred maintained "helpful" and "loving" care but also gave considerable freedom to individual families to manage their own affairs. Monthly meetings were composed of Friends in good standing from all the local worship meetings under their jurisdiction. The purpose of monthly meetings was, as George Fox said, "that all order their conversation aright, that they may see the salvation of God, they may all see and know, possess and partake of, the government of Christ, of the increase of which there is no end." Their aim was to construct an ideal speech community where the word of God would be constantly and infectiously exchanged in human relations, particularly those within households.[19] Thus newcomers were not recognized as community members unless they presented a removal certificate, an informed discussion of their spiritual personality, vouching for the high quality of their "conversations." When Friends got married in Chester and the Welsh Tract, they had their "clearness and conversation" inspected, and when disowned, they were denounced for "scandalous," "disorderly," "indecent," or "worldly" "conversation."[20]

But highlighting the central importance within this scheme of unsupervised, spontaneous familial relations, most of the business that came before the Welsh Tract and Chester men's meetings directly concerned the question of family formation. For example, in Chester, the men's and women's meetings sat together until 1705. Between 1681 and 1705, 43 percent of the business concerned marriages. The next largest category, discipline, accounted for 14 percent of the business,[21] and marriage infractions composed the majority of the discipline cases.[22]

Marriage was vital to the Quaker settlers because it involved the reproduction of intimate familial environments of "holy conversation" and therefore the rearing of the Quaker faithful. It was a time-consuming and delicate business, designed to combine a maximum of personal freedom with a dose of community control. Emerging landholders who emphasized parental character in child rearing particularly desired some control in marriage. But these settlers also regarded love and marriage as spiritual matters to be dictated by the "Light," which itself was too fragile and sacred to be bullied.[23] The Welsh Tract and Chester Quakers' marriage procedures were therefore unusually complex, voluntaristic, and generous. Entirely reversing relatively progressive Puritan marriage procedures, in which children were allowed a veto over marriages arranged by their parents, Quaker parents retained only a veto over marriages arranged by their children.[24] And even that veto was shaky. In cases when a couple sincerely fell in love, yet faced parental objections, they could ask the monthly meeting to persuade their parents to surrender, or even to give them sanction to marry in spite of parental opinion.[25] Accordingly, this veto depended upon the somewhat illogical expectation that young men and women permitted free courtship would refrain from discussing marriage until they had obtained the consent of all parents involved. For example, in 1713 the Chester women demanded that Hannah Vernon "acknowledge the sin of speaking with [Caleb Harrison] about marriage before she had consulted her parents" for approval of the couple's plans to marry. Hannah did so, with seemingly little embarrassment, and was wed.[26]

Thus, the final advantage in these procedures usually fell to the independent judgments of youth. Youth alone announced their marriage intentions to the local monthly meetings, and youth alone said their vows before God and witnesses. Such rituals and the doctrine of the "Light" provoked youthful assertion in matters of love. To help things along, young Welsh Tract women lobbied for their choices, filling the meeting house with supportive peers when they announced their intentions to marry. Such love politicking became so daunting that the Radnor Women's Monthly Meeting complained in 1725 that "this Meeting does not think it convenient that many young women accompanies any Friends when they go to propose their intentions of marriage to the Men's Meeting, and it is desired for the future that none go but are allowed by the Meeting."[27] And though a young woman freely selected her spouse from the first to the final stages of courtship, if at the last minute her inner testimony demurred, she simply changed her mind, no matter the inconvenience to the monthly meetings, the banished groom, or the expectant parents. In 1705, after approving the marriage of John Martin and Jane Hent, the Chester Men's Meeting was surprised that the marriage had not taken place. They reported that "the abovesaid marriage not being accomplished, two women Friends—Alice Simcock and Rebecca Faucit—spoke to Jane Hent to know the reason thereof, and her answer was that she could not love him well enough to be her husband. . . . she also said that she was sorry that she had to proceed so far with him."[28] This mild regret was the only apology the meeting would receive. And this was only one of a number of similar cases.[29] Radnor and Chester youth, particularly women, took marital love seriously and usually got their way.

Their assertiveness was also fostered by a deeper permissiveness. Traditional sanctions such as economic penalties and shaming were used lightly and sparingly. Meetings did ask couples to submit themselves before marriage to month-long inspections of their "conversations" by committees of the women's and men's monthly meetings in order to reassure the community about the fitness of youth in parenting and maintaining a proper household. But few couples were denied the privilege of marrying in meeting once they had announced their intentions. Youth with problems were warned off before the formal process began or had long been subject to the meeting's care. The meetings did seek to halt marriages between Quakers and non-Quakers and between youth who sought to marry without parental consent to assure peace and proper environments for children. But if such youth persisted, the meetings merely demanded that they come to meeting and condemn their waywardness. Only if they refused to "clear the Truth" were they disowned, and though many youth had to acknowledge their sins, few were actually disowned before 1740.[30]

Condemnations and disownments were posted publicly and doubtless caused shame and embarrassment. Nevertheless, the Quakers' use of shaming was remarkably mild compared to the methods traditionally used in English communities—a repertoire that included dunking, placing in stocks, cropping ears, branding with letters, dressing people in white gowns, hanging in effigy, and tarring and feathering.[31] By their own account, the meetings acted tenderly in "love" and "concern" to give "care" to Friends. Personal "honor," though a tolerated psychological fact, was less emphasized than the "honor of Truth." The approved sign of contrition was not red-faced humiliation or even embarrassment, but renewed love and deep sorrow for love's past absence. In 1720 Radnor women Friends were happy to report that a too permissive mother, Sarah W., "seemed tender and loving and said she was sorry that she gave way to anything that was a dishonour to Truth or gave trouble to Friends."[32] This was the properly dignified stance of contrition. The meetings recognized that excessive shame could break affectionate ties between wayward "tender plants" and the community. A delinquent Friend was often asked, as in the case of an illegitimately pregnant young Radnor woman in 1734, to "fight the shame" and "to come and settle somewhere among Friends where she might be under their care and instruction, hoping thereby she might be reconciled and reclaimed to Friends again."[33] Indeed, it was often the meeting that was traditionally humiliated. For example, Springfield meeting in 1715 complained about one obnoxious young man, John W., "for being one of the chief actors in dressing a man pretending him to be a dead man or corpse at Daniel Calverts and bringing of him into the house to affright the people." Nor was the meeting delighted to hear that "he being by some of them there reproved for it and was asked how he would answer it to the Monthly Meeting, his reply was it was but giving in a paper and they might get a box and call it W's box."[34] The Meeting did not make a box, and neither did it disown or scare John W.

Nor did Quakers use property heavy handedly to ensure compliance. Probate and meeting records reveal that young men and women who married out of the meeting were rarely disinherited. Radnor and Chester parents only delayed portioning wayward youth until their wills.[35] In this they followed the policy formally announced at the Cheshire Quarterly Meeting in England in 1689, "that if any Friends' child marry one thats no Friend, the parents of such child shall not communicate by way of portion unto such without the advise and consent of the quarterly meeting or whom they shall depute excepting at their decease, at which time the said parents are at liberty to do as they shall see meet."[36] In this, too, they punished "bad" Quaker children—that is, Quaker children who married non-Quakers, not Quaker children who married Quakers outside the meeting—much as parents in puritan Massachusetts favored good children who, no matter how obedient, received land usually when their fathers died.[37] On the other hand, thanks to generosity, wealth, and perhaps religious motives, Radnor and Chester Quaker parents gave land easily to good children. Among 139 second-generation sons in Chester and the Welsh Tract who married in the early eighteenth century, 71 percent received land— often by deed—before, at, or within two years of marriage.[38] Most nuclear families in Radnor and Chester were thereby economically autonomous at their conception, and in only one case did these Quakers' deeds contain a contractual clause, so common in seventeenth- and eighteenth-century New England, giving parents continuous and binding claim to the land or its products.[39] This is not to say that there were no communal controls over children, only that those controls developed chiefly from ties of intimate dependency and love.

The major method of knotting such ties was tender and careful child rearing. Even the local Anglican minister in 1714 observed that the "fatal weed of Quakerism" was "cultivated with the utmost skill and tenderness."[40] These Quakers' earnestness in child rearing cannot be overestimated. The Radnor and Chester Meetings helped support families with loans, charity, and child rearing advice. Traveling ministers reinforced the advice of the meeting. And that advice virtually never mentioned physical correction. Instead, it emphasized the impact of parental examples on children, the need to keep children from corrupting influences, and the need to recognize and encourage signs of the "Light" within the child.[41] After 1690 Quaker couples in Radnor and Chester could also expect meeting elders to visit them four times a year. The elders inspected the household's furnishings, sensed its spiritual atmosphere, questioned the parents, prayed with the family, and issued a report to the monthly meeting. Such reports helped scotch child rearing problems before they became uncontrollable. Thus, after one visitor's report, the Radnor Women's Meeting in 1720 dispatched Katherine Jones and Sarah Evans to go to R. P.'s to "advise R. P.'s daughters concerning their misbehaviors."[42]

And Radnor and Chester men often allowed tender child rearing to direct their lives. John Bevan of Treverigg, Glamorganshire, wrote that he emigrated to Merion, Pennsylvania, only because he was convinced by his wife that his four children were likely to be corrupted in Wales. "Some time before the year 1683," he wrote, "I heard that our esteemed Friend William Penn had a patent from King Charles the Second for the Province in America called Pennsylvania and my wife had a great inclination to go thither and thought it might be a good place to train up children amongst a sober people and to prevent the corruption of them here by the loose behavior of youths and the bad example of too many of riper years." Bevan loved Wales almost as much as his children and religion, "but as I was sensible her aim was an upright one, on account of our children, I was willing to weigh the matter in a true balance." In 1683, in his prime, Bevan went to Pennsylvania. In 1704, an old man, he returned to Wales, where he later wrote, "We stayed there [Pennsylvania] many years, and had four of our children married with our consent, and they had several children, and the aim intended by my wife was in good measure answered."[43] In 1741, Edward Foulke, a farmer in Gwynedd, Pennsylvania, wrote an exhortation to his adult children, advising them to rear their children carefully. He did not mention sermonizing or physical restraint but only exemplary parental behavior. He confessed he had occasionally been lax during their childhoods in being himself a perfect model. "It had been better for me, if I had been more careful," he wrote, "in sitting with my family at meals with a sober countenance, because children . . . have their eyes and observations on those who have command and government over them. . . . This," he added (referring implicitly to a generation of advice), "has great influence on the life and manners of youth."[44] But no matter how much Quaker men sacrificed or worried about child rearing, the major burden, as these examples also suggest, fell upon women.

Believing in women's centrality to child rearing, Quaker men gave them unusual authority in the Welsh Tract and in Chester. Uniquely in early America, Quaker women exercised some formal authority within their communities in the women's monthly meetings. The existence of those meetings sprang partly from a belief in the spiritual equality of Quaker men and women, but more profoundly from an appreciation of the importance of mothering to the Quakers' social strategies. Social equality was generally not practiced. Quaker women as individuals were not expected to be independent of familial responsibility or patriarchal power. Bequests to daughters rarely included land. And as Marylynn Salmon has shown, although Quaker men had control of the government in Pennsylvania from 1681 through the 1750s, Pennsylvania government held to the common law rule of *feme covert* whereby women lost all their property at marriage, and Pennsylvania courts interpreted this rule as strictly as English courts.[45] As individuals, women often had far less social status than men in Chester and in the Welsh Tract. Indeed, only eighteen of the thirty-one married women mentioned in the Welsh Tract removal certificates between 1681 and 1690 were even called by name. Typical was the Pennlyn Meeting's discussion of "Cadwallader Morgan and family," which spent forty words describing Cadwallader Morgan and said of his unnamed wife that she was "like-minded."[46] When married women received some comment, they were described chiefly as good mothers who had a positive influence on their children and occasionally on the community. The Garthgnvr Meeting said in the removal certificate of Ellis Pugh that "as for his wife Sina, we own her in her place as a good, careful, industrious woman; in things relating to her poor small children and family, wise discreet, and circumspect in her dealings and doings."[47] The persuasive Barbara

Bevan was described as "a nursing mother to some weak and poor among us."[48]

More than through the sometimes honored doctrine of spiritual equality, Quaker women gained some communal authority through motherhood. Inasmuch as Quakers' ideas about child rearing emphasized human relations and children's observations of parental behavior, Quakers had to save a place within their monthly meeting structure for maintaining holy female character and guiding the social reproduction of mothering. Thus the inclusion of women into the meeting structure and their separation into their own meetings developed partly from recognition of female spiritual equality but chiefly from a traditional understanding of women's natural talents (in the household) and an untraditional insight into the essential nature of early child rearing and domestic organization in maintaining and reproducing the religiously faithful. Accordingly, the women's meetings were not to be equal to or an imitation of the men's meetings; they were to have their own sphere, "distinct (as we may say in some aspects) yet in perfect unity with our brethren," as "the Women Friends in London" expressed it in 1674. They noted that "chiefly our work is, to help the helpless in all cases"—a fine description of the maternal role—and that "our provision is set apart for the supply of the household of faith and family of God."[49]

The distribution of tasks and authority between the men's and women's monthly meetings reflected, acknowledged, and asserted women's roles as mothers. While the Chester and Radnor Men's Meetings established worship meetings, collected and allocated money, judged the validity of old and new testimonies, and monopolized the power to disown men and women, the women's meetings dispensed small amounts of charity, visited families, disciplined women Quakers, and inspected the characters of young women who intended to marry. Demonstrating kindness, love, and charity, they were to define, enforce, and reproduce the standards of Quaker womanhood and motherhood. Women's meetings had to be separate. Frank discussions about the dark mysteries of female bodies, sexuality, and character frightened and embarrassed Quaker men, including George Fox, who nevertheless understood their necessity for reproducing good mothers. Defending in 1675 his controversial decision to establish separate women's meetings, Fox wrote, "There is some dark spirits that would have no women's Meetings, but as men should meet with them, which women cannot for civility sake and modesty sake speak amongst men of women's matters, neither can modest men desire it, and none but ranters will desire to look into women's matters."[50]

Despite early resistance in Chester, the Radnor and Chester mothers, meeting in closet, gained control over vital aspects of their communities. Given their role in marriage inspections, they were able to limit the males of the meeting to choices among women whose characters they approved. And their authority often extended beyond marriage and the meeting house. As a mother, Barbara Bevan could persuade her reluctant husband to travel across the Atlantic solely for the sake of their children. In 1725 the Radnor men had to listen carefully to "Gainor Robert's paper, directed to the Preparative and Monthly Meeting, expressing a concern that was on her mind that where any who committed anything that is a reproach to Truth that Friends should endeavor to bring them to a sense of their evil and be willing to bear the shame that we may be a good example to the succeeding generation."[51] A short time later, the Radnor men, their worry about the next generation refreshed, disciplined a prestigious male Radnor elder for marrying a cousin.[52]

Viewed from the inside, these families lived quietly, keeping faith with the "Light" and "holy conversation" by trying to maintain peace and love and by rearing their "tender plants" into a new generation of faithful Quakers. But muting their own vocabulary for a moment and viewing them along a sociological scale of family types, they must be judged as being basically modern. Quaker marriages were formed voluntarily on love; conjugal households were economically autonomous early in their careers; men and especially women were devoted to childrearing; and the scheme of childrearing was noncoercive and based on ideas of intimate spiritual communication in a nurturing environment. In his book *At Odds: Women and the Family in America from the Revolution to the Present*, Carl Degler established four criteria for the "emerging modern family," which he argued arose in the late eighteenth century: 1) "the marriage which initiated the modern family was based upon affection and mutual respect between partners, both at the time of family formation and in the course of its life"; 2) "the primary role of the wife was the care of children and the maintenance of the home"; 3) "the attention, energy, resources of parents in the emerging modern family were increasingly centered upon rearing their offspring"; 4) "the modern family on an average is significantly smaller in size than the family of the 18th and previous centuries."[53] The Radnor and Chester Quakers conformed easily to the first three of these criteria. They did not fit the fourth, though Robert Wells has shown that the Quakers of Pennsylvania were, as far as is known, the first group in America, beginning in the middle of the eighteenth century, to practice family limitation self-consciously.[54] The monthly meetings may also have been more intrusive and directive than modern social workers, school authorities, psychiatrists, neighbors, peer groups, and marriage couselors. (Their methods were similarly "caring.") But whether fully modern or just three-quarters modern or three-fifths modern, the Radnor and Chester Quaker families were clearly more modern than traditional, and therefore an ugly sight to local, traditional families and to Anglican authorities.

Suddenly surrounded by tender, loving Quaker families, Anglican neighbors naturally feared for the personal freedom and honor and public festiveness characteristic of English society. Before 1720, Anglicans, particularly those living in Chester County, reported frequently and shrilly on Quaker social radicalism and its dangerous, obnoxious influence. "In the year 1695, I came hither from Jamaica," wrote an Anglican layman, James Suder. "I not having my health there transported myself and estate here in hopes to find the same wholesome laws here as in other of the Majesty's plantations, and a quiet, moderate people; but found quite the contrary." He found loving Quakers virtually everywhere. He concluded, "We that are his majesty's subjects (which they are not nor never will be), we had better live in Turkey; there is good morality amongst them; there is none here."[55] Reverend George Ross battled the Quakers. Assigned to Chester mission in 1711, he struggled to defend the Anglican Church and English morality against the sway of the "mischievous brood of Quakers here."[56] "In no country of that Province," he wrote, "does the haughty tribe of that persuasion appear more rampant than where I reside, there being by modest computation 20 Quakers, besides other dissenters, to one true Churchman."[57] Inspired and then exhausted by the task, he preached in one town after another in order to contain the spread of the "seeds of apostasy" and "that fatal weed of Quakerism," which, he admitted, was "cultivated with the utmost skill and tenderness."[58] The Quaker's radical social design provoked militant Anglican missionaries to sacrificial dedication. Although sorely tempted in 1719 by an offer that "the worthy Governor of Maryland made me of a parish, worth in these good times in that province, not less than two hundred and fifty pounds per annum," Reverend John Humphry, Ross's successor, continued to live in the sleepy town of Chester on a salary of only £50 a year. "I could not prevail upon myself to leave this miserable people to the spirit which actuates the Quakers," he confessed.[59]

The Quakers' presence also revived the Anglican laity's enthusiasm for the Church in Chester County. Quaker zealots forced tradition-minded farmers and artisans to board the Mother Church or drown in the emerging Quaker social order. In 1704 "The Vestry of Chester, Alias Uplands, in Pennsylvania" petitioned the Society for the Propagation of the Gospel in Foreign Parts (SPG) for a schoolmaster "to instruct our children and youth" so they would not be "corrupted with the base principles they must need suck from Quaker masters and mistresses."[60] In 1706 the vestry praised their Reverend Nichols for his "industry and pious care to reduce the people here from Quakerism's errors and heresys to embrace true Christian principles," and in the same year the vestrymen proclaimed, "we are in love to this Church."[61] When their minister was sent elsewhere in 1709, they begged the SPG "to supply us with another missionary otherwise this poor church, seated in the very center of the Quakers, will quickly decay and become the object of derision to that people."[62] They hoped simply to preserve the dignity of their traditional way of life.

Although living among the Quakers in Chester and the Welsh Tract, the sixty middling Anglican families wanted to live in the Delaware Valley in proven English style. They belonged to, or joined, a religion that allowed parents to release children at relatively early ages to develop outside the household. Thus, although the SPG did send to Pennsylvania books like Bailey's *Practice of Piety*, which included discussions of household government and family devotions, the SPG chiefly stressed ministers, catechism, and communion—public people and events, not intimate environments.[63] Public socialization of children was usual and appropriate to the social realities of late seventeenth-century England. Farms throughout England were typically only forty acres or less; they could hardly be divided usefully among sons, and most farmers were tenants.[64] Parents thus often put their children out to labor between the ages of eight and fifteen in order that they might learn a trade or at least obtain subsistence from wealthier men and women. Mainly reflecting such child exchanges, Gregory King's contemporary assessment of the English population in the late seventeenth-century shows that upper class households were usually three times the size of middling ones.[65] These proportions were similar to those in a census of households in Montgomeryshire, Wales, between 1684 and 1687 taken by the parish clergy and Bishop of St. Asaph.[66] The practice of passing children up the social order served many social uses, including the reinforcement of hierarchy. By entrusting their children to men of wealth and position (and perhaps to the public rituals of baptism, catechism, and communion), middling English parents also limited their personal responsibilities and perhaps feelings toward their own children. Of course, Quakers like William Penn unsympathetically described the system: "They do with their children as with their souls, put them out at livery for so much a year."[67]

Nonetheless, traditional farmers and artisans hoped the Church would help them maintain such an open, public order in the valley. By 1707 they established two missions and built two churches in Chester and the Welsh Tract, St. David's at Radnor and St. Paul's at Chester. Satellite congregations developed in the backcountry at Concord, Marlborough, and Chichester.[68] The SPG poured over 4,000 pounds into the two missions before 1750; early congregations were large and "well affected"; pastoral care was constant and solid (ten of the twelve ministers in the two missions between 1701 and 1750 had spotless records).[69] The churches also had a core of talented laymen who served on their vestries. Jonas Sandelands, a small merchant in Chester, donated the ground for St. Paul's and was buried beneath the chancel; Jeremy Collet, a farmer, ran one of the first mills in Chester County; and Jasper Yeates purchased mills at Naaman Creek and served as burgess of Chester, Pennsylvania assemblyman, and provincial councillor. In ability and experience, they matched Quaker leaders like Andrew Job, John Sharples, and Hugh Roberts.[70]

In the 1690s, the Welsh Tract and Chester Quakers and Anglicans also shared almost equally in the valley's resources. Anglicans and Quakers carried on similar occupations; approximately 78 percent of the Quakers and 81 percent of the Anglicans were farmers. The rest were blacksmiths, innkeepers, cordwainers, and small shopkeepers and merchants.[71] A quarter of the Anglicans arrived in Pennsylvania before 1690 and over two-thirds before 1700. A number of them, such as John Test, Walter Martin, and Jonas Sandelands, had been in Pennsylvania before 1683, the beginning of the large Quaker immigration.[72] In the 1690s, the Quakers and the Anglicans also matched each other in wealth and land. An incomplete list of land-owners in Chester County, prepared in the early 1690s under the direction of Governor Blackwell, shows ten Anglican families with an average holding of 475 acres and sixteen Quaker families with an average holding of 450 acres.[73] A sampling from a partial tax list of 1693 shows eleven Anglican families with an average assessment of £0-5-8 and thirty-six Quaker families with an average assessment of £0-3-9.[74] These assessments, based on evaluations of land and live-stock, show that Quakers and Anglicans had similar capital hold-ings in the 1690s. But this roughly equal distribution of power and wealth among religious groups would not last long. Their family systems were far too different in form and purpose to support identical social and economic development.

Conventional historical wisdom holds that the Quakers' family system would flounder in a premodern setting, where the family's primary responsibility was the production of wealth, not the provi-sion of expert socialization of children and emotional support. Quaker emphasis on motherhood, on this logic, would overburden women with too many jobs; Quaker willingness to bankroll chil-dren's marriages would squander available resources; and Quaker emphasis on noncoercive schemes of child rearing would produce a feeble and unruly labor force. Nevertheless, analysis of seventy-two Welsh Tract and Chester Quaker families—their wills, inventories, tax assessments, deeds, and related court records—shows that mid-dling Quakers sought to, and generally did, protect their children from the "world" and did maintain nurturing familial love and peace by effectively accumulating wealth. To John Woolman's later worry, Quaker parents bought vast amounts of land, built large and comfortable houses, and distributed their wealth carefully and shrewdly to their children. A similar study of fifty-five Welsh Tract and Chester Anglican families shows that middling Anglican par-ents, unburdened by concern for delicate nurturance and protecting environments, were actually less economically aggressive and able.[75] They accumulated less land, built smaller houses, and distrib-uted their wealth carelessly and unwisely, occasionally in efforts to establish gentlemanly lines in Chester County. Modern strategies had their use in an unusual premodern setting such as Pennsylvania.

The Quakers clearly used the valley's chief economic resource, land, with more skill than did the Anglican families. For the protection of future generations and as a balm for family relations, Quaker settlers seized William Penn's generous terms for land. They bought an average of over 300 acres per family before 1690 and then continued to buy more land after prices began to rise. Quaker farmers purchased over 300 acres apiece, on average, after 1700, and 45 percent of all their land purchases occurred after 1690.[76] Typical Quaker immigrant fathers in the Welsh Tract and Chester collected over 700 acres by the time of their death; more than 70 percent accumulated over 400 acres. Such accumulations represented, in all probability, the highest average acreage per family of any religious group in early America.[77]

Quaker land use was consistent with Quaker religious goals. Friends did not plant much of their land. Analysis of crop and livestock listings in their inventories shows that the average Quaker family used about eighty acres of land for farming and grazing. The remaining 620 acres lay fallow and often uncut, awaiting children's marriages. Land purchasing was clearly child-centered, correlating closely with the number of sons in a family. The three Welsh Tract and Chester families with one son bought no land after 1690; nine men with two sons bought an average of 120 acres; twelve families with three sons bought an average of 260 acres; and twenty men with four sons or more bought an average of 410 acres after 1690.[78] Such purchases supported the voluntarism, gentle attitudes, generosity, and environmentalism that marked Quaker familial ideals.

The Welsh Tract and Chester Quaker families also distributed this land to their sons with care, generosity, and general profit. They gave over two-thirds of their sons over 200 acres of land. Thirty-three of thirty-eight Quaker families with more than one son practiced partible inheritance. Sixteen of thirty-nine Quaker fathers gave sons land by deed compared to only five of the twenty Anglicans. As these statistics suggest, in most cases Quaker fathers gave or sold land to their sons when their sons wished to marry. Indeed, in selling, they simultaneously supported new Quaker households and acquired additional money to portion daughters and buy land for the love interest of other sons. Many sons also fashioned productive farms from land their fathers lent them in order to earn their economic independence for marrying their piously beloved. For example, Ralph Lewis, who emigrated to Pennsylvania in 1683 as a servant to John Bevan, accumulated over 700 acres and sold or gave this land to his sons, not in order of their births, but when they wanted to marry. When Lewis could not afford to give a son land (usually when a son wanted to marry at an early age), he was willing to make a deal which profited the son, the whole family, and the Delaware Valley. Beginning in 1705, Lewis gave a 300-acre tract in Edgemount to his third-born son, Evan, who married that year. Next, in 1707, Lewis sold a house and land in Haverford to his second-born son, Abraham, who also married the year he received the land. Finally, in 1709, Lewis sold a house and large farm to his fourth son, Samuel, for the heavy sum of £300. After three years of hard work on the land, Samuel paid his father, received the deed, and married Phebe Taylor.[79] Such flexible and productive familial strategies were common. Love, land grants, and planting could be simultaneously and profitably exercised in the Delaware Valley.

The Anglican farmers and artisans had a less involving relationship to land. Although they bought more land than they might have in England and Wales, Anglican parents saw no need to bankroll every son's love story or to insure them all dignified and protected situations. Scattered returns have shown that the Quakers' and Anglicans' desire for land appeared similar in the early 1690s. However, by the end of this settling generation, the Quakers accumulated almost three times the land per family that the local Anglicans did. Accurate assessment of total land holdings could be documented for twenty-one of fifty-two Anglican families analyzed. The others left Chester County or were tenants (see Table 2-1).

Differences in capital holdings did not determine much of this difference between Anglicans and Quakers. Anglicans and Quakers had similar wealth in the 1690s. More important, Anglican farmers and artisans who had as many sons and twice the cash and goods as an equivalent set of Quaker neighbors bought far less land. In other words, Anglican farmers and artisans who easily could have afforded land for their children did not buy it (see Table 2-2). To take an extreme example, the Wade family, converts to the Church, sold most of their valuable real estate in Chester borough, though they had three sons.[80] Some Anglican families who arrived after 1690 may

45

Table 2-1. Land Given to Children by Chester and Welsh Tract
Anglican and Quaker Parents, 1681–1735

Acres of Land	Quakers (Chester, Welsh Tract)		Anglicans (Chester, Welsh Tract)	
	N	Percent	N	Percent
600+	27	52	1	5
500–599	8	15	1	5
400–499	3	6	0	0
300–399	1	2	4	19
200–299	8	15	5	24
100–199	5	10	7	33
0–99	0	0	3	14
Total	52	100	21	100

SOURCES: Chester County Wills and Inventories, Chester County Deeds, Chester County Court House, West Chester, Pa.; Philadelphia County Wills and Inventories, Philadelphia County Deeds, City Hall and City Hall Annex, Philadelphia, Pa.

have been discouraged by rising land prices, but these rising costs hardly slowed the Quakers, who bought land avidly after 1690.

Although they held less land per family than the Quakers, the Anglicans also used their smaller holdings less efficiently. Following traditional and lineal methods, they held their land until death or distributed it in dynastic fashion. Reflecting an indifference to providing comfortable places for all their children, only slightly more than half the Anglicans settlers wrote wills. Of fifty-three Anglican families studied, twenty either did not leave a will or left the area, fifteen clearly died intestate, and only eighteen left wills. Of seventy-one Quaker families studied, eleven either did not leave a will or left the area, eleven clearly died intestate, and forty-nine left a will. Five of the eleven Quakers who died intestate were old men who had already settled all their children; only two of the fifteen Anglicans who died intestate were similarly situated. Nor were the Anglican intestate fathers poverty-stricken: they averaged £165 in personal estate and 192 acres.[81]

The Anglican men who did leave wills tended to invest in the family line rather than in individual children. Thus even the most energetic and purposeful Anglican fathers chose just the wrong policies for a colony rich in soil but lacking cheap labor, desperate tenants, or a bonanza crop. Thomas Dawson, cordwainer and farmer of West Cain, tried unsuccessfully to establish a gentlemenly line in Chester County by heaping all his land upon one son. He had

Table 2-2. Comparison of Landholding among Welsh Tract and Chester Quakers with Personal Estates of £100–199 and Welsh Tract and Chester Anglicans with Personal Estates of £200–299

	Quakers		
	Estate in £s	No. of Children Sons	Acres
James Pugh	111	5	3	600
William Jenkins	158	4	1	700
Owen Evan	104	8	4	538
Robert David	123	6	4	600
Joseph Baker	150	3	2	1,230
Peter Taylor	152	6	4	500
Humphry Ellis	104	9	4	250
Total	902	41	22	4,418
Mean	129	5.9	3.1	631

	Anglicans		
	Estate in £s	No. of Children Sons	Acres
Thomas Smith	201	8	3	600
George Culin	245	8	5	351
Andrew Rawson	215	1	1	106
Peter Eliot	281	3	2	200
William Martin	273	6	3	170
Thomas Powell	235	2	0	189
Total	1,450	28	14	1,616
Mean	242	4.7	2.3	269

SOURCES: Chester County Wills and Inventories, Chester County Deeds, Chester County Court House, West Chester, Pa.; Philadelphia County Wills and Inventories, Philadelphia County Deeds, Philadelphia City Hall and City Hall Annex, Philadelphia, Pa.

three sons and three daughters, and by the early 1740s he had accumulated over 500 acres and held £219 in bonds. In 1741 Thomas Dawson deeded all his 551 acres, *post mortem*, to his eldest son Abraham, "for the advancement," he wrote, "of the heirs male of the body of the said Abraham Dawson lawfully begotten or to be begotten."[82] Dawson clearly did not want his estate dissipated among all his sons. In fact, fearing that his estate might fall into the hands of another line, he used his second son as a substitute heir. "If Abraham have no male heirs living," he wrote, "it shall go to my son Isaac's male heirs, and if there be no male heirs living, it shall go to my son Abraham's heirs or children or at pleasure to do as he thinks fitting."[83] Abraham, Dawson's privileged son, died in 1760, a moderately wealthy wheat farmer with a tenant on part of his vast land and two slaves helping him work the rest. Most of his land was not being used, however. Abraham left no male heirs and gave his land to his cousin and his brothers and the tenant's parcel to the poor of West Caln. Abraham also gave ten pounds to the local Anglican church.[84] Despite such grand gestures, he never rose to be a real gentleman. It was impossible to make a great fortune by concentrating land, English-style, in Pennsylvania.

Dawson's thinking was nevertheless common among Anglicans who left wills. Most Anglican fathers, who held 259 acres on average, favored one or two sons. Considering the will-leaving churchmen who had more than one son, two divided their land equally, eight gave it all to one son, and four determined that the land be sold and the cash be divided among all their children. Less than a third of the sons mentioned in these Anglicans' wills received land. Even counting gifts of cash from the sale of land as division of the estate, only six of fourteen of the will-leaving Anglican fathers with more than one son practiced partible inheritance.[85]

Policies of impartibility made good sense in England and Wales, but they made rather less sense in the Delaware Valley. There, to a degree that traditionalist farmers could not conceive, the tender, egalitarian relations of the child-centered family provided an unexpectedly fine way of organizing work and land in a near-wilderness. There, the Quakers' superior economic rationality emerged as a byproduct of their radical familial ideals.[86]

And in this setting, the Quakers' family system filled time more productively than did the traditional family. The Anglican settlers, like some later tourists, found the Delaware Valley furnished drearily with land, trees, and Quakers. For their amusement, sociability, and sanity, they supported, without the usual patronage of a gentry, expensive public sport and games. The Quaker meetings frequently and disapprovingly mentioned such events, doubtlessly organized by their more festive Anglican neighbors. In 1730, for example, the Gwynedd meeting spoke of "being sorrowfully affected with the prevalence of undue liberties such as shooting matches, singing, and dancing, and the like disorders."[87] Some Quakers got caught sipping excessively and riotously in Anglican taverns.[88] Though a number of Quaker youth and adults succumbed to these temptations occasionally, most found the approved alternative generally satisfying. They were to dissolve boredom and find company by making the trivia, responsibilities, and relations of private life fascinating, profound, and sacred.

Most visibly and mundanely, the Quaker settlers' unusual interest in the environments of their children's spiritual growth was reflected in concern for the setting and equipment of the home: ample chairs, tables, feather beds, and large, comfortable stone houses. Building few impressive public buildings, the Quakers used the Delaware Valley's resources to make family households warm, convivial, dignified scenes of the drama of life and spiritual growth. The publicly oriented Anglicans' houses reflected scant domestic involvement.

The first generation's probate inventories show clearly that among families of similar wealth, the Quakers spent proportionately more money on furniture, particularly bedding, than did the Anglicans. And a more detailed look at expenditures on bedding, when collated with the number of children in each household, shows that Quakers had entirely different standards of domestic living than did the neighboring churchmen (see Table 2-3).

By almost any standard, middling Anglican living arrangements were crowded while Quaker living arrangements were pleasant. The churchman Peter Eliot, for example, had a large personal estate

Table 2-3. Children and Bedding: Expenditures among Welsh Tract and Chester Quakers and Anglicans with Personal Estates £100–199, 1681–1735

Quakers	No. of Children	£'s Bedding
William Jenkins (1712)	3	17
Richard Woodward (1706)	8	24
Owen Evan (1723)	7	16
Joseph Baker (1735)	3	11
Peter Taylor (1720)	5	12
Humphry Ellis (1712)	7	12
Total	33	92
£'s bedding per child		2.78

Anglicans	No. of Children	£'s Bedding
Evan Evans (1731)	5	6
Morgan Hughes (1727)	4	2
John Test (1718)*	3	16
John Evans (1739)	3	4
Total	15	28
£'s bedding per child		1.86

Sources: Chester County Wills and Inventories, Chester County Court House, West Chester, Pa.; Philadelphia County Wills and Inventories, Philadelphia City Hall and City Hall Annex, Philadelphia, Pa.
*John Test was an innkeeper.

of £281. His household consisted of three children, his wife, and three servants, a total of eight people. His house had five rooms and only three beds. In the Eliot household there were almost two people to a bed, even if the servants went bedless.[89] The Quaker Morris Llwellyn had a smaller personal estate of £235 and also a household of nine people—himself, his wife and four children, and three servants. He owned a house with six rooms, and he owned twice as many beds—six to Eliot's three.[90] This meant only one person in a bed, if the servants slept on straw mattresses on the floor. Most significantly, all of the surviving houses from this period in Chester County—the Brinton House, the Pusey House, the Pratt House, the Sharples House, and the Collins House—were built between 1681 and 1730 by Quakers.[91] Almost all are large, built with stone, and suitable for modern families (Philadelphia suburbanites still occupy a number of these houses). Not one Anglican left such a domestic artifact. The middling Anglicans did leave their handsome country churches, particularly St. David's and St. Paul's, monuments to their attempt to erect a public world. But in the Delaware Valley it was easier to decorate your own home.

The Quakers also kept mentally occupied and alert managing the money needed to buy enormous quantities of land and large houses for themselves and their children. Although some Quakers did go broke, most Quaker farmers and artisans were able money managers who gracefully handled the financial burdens of their expensive family system. Perhaps lured by horse races, shooting matches, cockfights, and taverns, and certainly unconcerned about providing every son with a 200-acre farm, the Anglicans showed less interest and talent.

Quaker men were expected to internalize the values of thrift and financial shrewdness that Benjamin Franklin, knowing many Quakers, would later make famous. Men who failed received cautionary community attention. Fathers were expected to consult the monthly meetings for advice and aid at the first sign of dangerous indebtedness. When the Radnor Monthly Meeting discovered that Rowland P. was falling behind in his payments to various local Friends, for example, they called him to meeting "to speak with him and advise him to satisfy his creditors."[92] In such cases the meeting appointed a committee of successful men to help him balance his books. In similar fashion, slow or retarded youth were also cared for. The Chester Men's Monthly Meeting in 1723 recorded the following about an orphan, Rachel N.:

> It being made appear that Rachel N. being now of age and not capable of managing her portion left her by her deceased father, Thomas N., therefore Thomas Martin, a Friend of Goshen Meeting, to take care of her and manage her portion by putting it out at interest and not to let her have any of the principle without the consent of the Meeting.[93]

In order to protect children, the meetings also inspected the finances of marriage agreements, particularly second marriages.

The Chester Court of Common Pleas records and the Chester and Radnor Monthly Meeting minutes show how well or poorly individual families did in staying out of serious debt. Quaker doctrine demanded that Quakers not sue one another in court unless the meeting had first been consulted and permission been given to sue. Both the meeting minutes and the court records must therefore be used to assess the Quakers' economic performance. From 1714 to 1735, the success of tender, fond-fostering households is clear: only 25 percent of the Quaker families ran into debt compared to almost 50 percent of the Anglican families (see Table 2-4).

The remaining dispositions and executions also suggest the Quakers' care for their children's financial protection and the Anglicans' indifference. In over two decades only one Quaker family, the Simcocks, suffered a drastic fall from affluence because of debts, and only one poor Welsh Quaker had a lien placed on his land.[94] The other cases against Quaker families were less serious: they amounted to less than £50 and did not lead to the forced sale of land.[95] By contrast, debts ruined more Anglican families. During the

Table 2-4. Individual Debt Cases against Welsh Tract and Chester Quakers and Anglicans, 1714–35

No. of cases	Anglicans		Quakers	
	Percent	N	Percent	N
6+	7	3	3	2
5	2	1	3	2
4	9	4	1	1
3	0	0	5	4
2	5	2	3	2
1	19	8	10	7
0	58	25	75	54
Total	100	43	100	72

SOURCES: Chester Court of Common Pleas, Dockets, 1714–35, Chester County Court House, West Chester, Pa.; Radnor Men's Monthly Meeting Minutes, 1681–1735, Chester Men's Monthly Meeting Minutes, 1681–1735, Friends Historical Library, Swarthmore College, Swarthmore, Pa.

1720s Samuel Bishop was sued nine times for debts amounting to over £150.[96] Enoch Enochson, who left an estate of less than £150, was sued for a total of £204.[97] The land of John Wade was forcibly sold in 1731 in order to pay a £200 debt.[98] Charles Conner, a father of four children, was ordered to serve three years as a servant to his creditors.[99] The middling Anglicans' traditional habits helped neither their children nor the economic development of the Delaware Valley. The Quakers' modern fascination with private arrangements helped both.

Not surprisingly, though both Chester and Welsh Tract groups began with almost the same amount of resources, the Quaker families gathered significantly more wealth than did the Anglican families. Middling Quakers not only bought much more land but also gathered more taxable wealth and larger personal estates. The general wealth of the two communities can be compared by averaging tax assessments for each family from 1715 to 1735. Four to six assessments based on land and livestock were collected for each family and translated into Pennsylvania currency assessments according to the appropriate rate of each year. These assessments were then averaged for each family. Also, the personal estates (capital, livestock, and furnishings) were compared from probate accounts for sixty-seven families.

By 1730 the tender-hearted Quakers had developed a community of flourishing families. Though better off than they might have been in England and Wales, the Anglicans did less well than the loving Quakers in the Delaware Valley. Thirty-six percent of the Quakers were assessed more than £40, compared to only 7 percent of the forty Anglicans. Fifty percent of the Quakers died with personal estates of over £200, compared with 41 percent of the Anglicans. The Quaker community had also many fewer poor families and many more truly wealthy families (see Tables 2-5 and 2-6).

The Quakers also received a meaningful dividend in lower childhood mortality and greater fertility. The Radnor and Chester Monthly Meeting records are sufficiently detailed to allow an estimation of family size, and they can be supplemented by deeds, intestate records, and wills. Based on a total of seventy-two reconstructed Quaker families in Radnor and Chester Meetings in the first generation, the average number of Quaker children per family to reach twenty-one years of age was 4.73 in the Welsh Tract and 5.65 in Chester. By contrast, thirty-one Anglican families for which documentation can be provided had an average of 3.77 children

Table 2-5. Average Tax Assessment of Anglican and
Quaker Families in Chester and the Welsh Tract, 1715–35

£'s Assessment	Quakers		Anglicans	
	Percent	N	Percent	N
60+	27	14	0	0
40–59	9	5	7	3
20–39	41	21	48	19
0–19	23	12	45	18
Total	100	52	100	40

SOURCE: Chester County Tax List (microfilm), Historical Society of Pennsylvania, Philadelphia, Pa.
NOTE: Anglicans and Quakers from Merion township were excluded, since Merion was in Philadelphia County, where comparable tax lists do not exist.

who were born between 1681 and 1730 and who reached adulthood.[100]

Wealth satisfactorily explains this sliding scale of family size. The Chester Quakers were richer than the Welsh Quakers, and in the long run the Anglican families became poorer than both. Significantly, compared to family sizes in Cheshire and Wales, the Pennsylvania Anglicans did better; the Quakers simply did better still. Among forty-four middling families living in five Cheshire towns between 1660 and 1730, the average family had just 2.44 children reach twenty-one years of age.[101] The middling Cheshire families were far poorer on average than any of the Pennsylvania groups.[102] Additionally, the limited expectations the churchmen displayed in economic areas for their children may have seeped into early child care; doubtless the Quakers' deep concern for children did. Indeed,

Table 2-6. Personal Estates of Welsh Tract and Chester Anglicans
and Quakers, 1681–1740

Personal Estate in £'s	Quakers		Anglicans	
	Percent	N	Percent	N
400+	15	6	7	2
300–399	20	8	11	3
200–299	15	6	23	6
100–199	38	15	15	4
0–99	12	5	44	12
Total	100	40	100	27

SOURCES: Chester County Inventories, Chester County Court House, West Chester, Pa.; Philadelphia County Inventories, Philadelphia City Hall Annex, Philadelphia, Pa.

as Robert Wells has shown, Pennsylvania Quakers would later decide to control growing family sizes in order to have enough resources and time for each individual child. In the 1760s the resources of Pennsylvania finally appeared finite. But in 1740 it was clear which family system paid easily and bountifully.

The Quaker family system's success gradually affected local distributions of power and prestige and local ways of thinking. The vocal disgust traditional families initially displayed at the Quakers' radical style slowly faded. Anglican missionaries came to lose their popularity and role as saviors of a realizable traditional order.

Anglican missionaries, it should be remembered, were initially optimistic about the Church's place in the campaign to preserve a traditional society in the Pennsylvania countryside. Before 1720, unchurched English and Swedes long resident in Chester, Anglican Welsh and English immigrants, and Quaker refugees from the Keithian schism had filled Anglican benches and coffers. In 1704 Reverend Nichols had reported from Chester that "I do not want a considerable congregation every Lord's day, not withstanding my being seated in the very middle of the Quakers."[103] In 1707 Reverend Evan Evans had reported that "in Chester, twenty miles from Philadelphia, upon Delaware River, they have a good church built. . . . I preached the middle of December last in that Church to a congregation consisting of about 150."[104] This building, St. Paul's (the local Anglicans' major architectural accomplishment), had been completed by local Anglicans in 1714, outfitted with royal and aristocratic presents, and described by its vestry in a boastful report as being "one of the neatest on this continent."[105] Missionaries had cheered as satellite congregations grew in the 1720s at Radnor, Chichester, Concord, and Marlborough. In 1723 "The Clergy of Pennsylvania" had reported to the Secretary of the SPG that "the Church at Chester with those congregations that depend upon it are in a flourishing condition as appears to us from numerous and regular auditory that were present at our convention sermon in this place."[106]

But even skillful and optimistic Anglican ministers could not sustain this enthusiasm in the face of the Quaker success story. As early as 1712, Reverend George Ross despaired that "Quakerism has number and interest on its side and the true religion is crushed as unfashionable and impoverishing."[107] "This novelty [Quakerism] is so fashionable and prevailing in this place," he observed in 1712, "that some of those who own themselves Church people are strangely bewitched and lull'd into an indifferency about the baptism of their infants. . . . I baptized last quarter of a year but two adults, formerly Quakers," he wrote, "and eight infants."[108] Increasingly the local Anglicans' identification with the Church diminished into nominal loyalty and idle curiosity. Farmers and artisans would come to hear a sermon and watch the ceremonies on Sunday, but would do little else for or in the church. "I must beg leave to acquaint the Society," reported Reverend Currey in 1760 from St. David's, "that although my hearers are many in number . . . I cannot get them to meet on an Easter Monday to choose a Vestry." There were also maddeningly few communicants.[109] While the Quakers' discussions about the morality of slavery displayed their deepening loyalty to their sect, an angry Reverend Thompson reported from St. Paul's in 1752 that "when I entered the mission of Chester a twelve month ago, I found no Church wardens or vestry, only some who had been Church officers ten years ago; the Church ready to fall into ruin; the surplice that was a Royal present rotting under the reading desk, and a considerable part of the missionary's library spoil'd or lost."[110] Thompson's successor, Reverend Craig, told the same story in 1760: "In this village which is built on the River Delaware, wherein there are about thirty odd families, there are not three who can properly be said to be decent members of our church, and of them, if the husband comes to divine service, the wife perhaps and children go elsewhere." He suggested the mission be closed.[111]

The Anglican Church, of course, lost prestige and popularity in other places in early America. Internal weaknesses (the lack of an Anglican bishop in North America), the vastness of the land, and religious diversity enfeebled the Church generally. But the career of the Mother Church in Chester and the Welsh Tract was clearly tied to the response to local Quakerism. It owed much of its early liveliness to the rejection of the Quakers' social radicalism, and therefore part of its decline to the growing respect for, or at least acceptance of, the success of radical Quaker social style. Basically, the church's emphasis on honor, public display, and social hierarchy became increasingly lost to rural Pennsylvania farmers and artisans, watching Quaker families proving that contrary principles—privatism, denial of traditional rank, child-centeredness, respect for women, familial love and devotion—worked better in an empty and growing settlement. The ministers testified that many still often came to sit in church on Sunday, perhaps seeing the

Anglican minister's words and ceremonies as exotica in the quiet Pennsylvania summer, or perhaps as wistful reminders of grander places and days. Yet, as the ministers also testified, they had become almost as silent as their neighbors.

Many historians have told, of course, how the Quakers led the Delaware Valley settlers in the making of a successful province, which enjoyed almost spectacular economic growth, illustrated by the rise of Philadelphia, the largest city in North America by 1765. But with other things, the Quakers were clearly benefited by their radical, "modern" family system, which despite (really, because of) its emphasis on love and noncoercive controls, used the Delaware Valley's ample resources effectively, while maintaining adequate social discipline. In this way, the Quakers made the valley into a basic source of American culture: the first scene of a major, widespread, obviously successful assertion of the child-centered, fondfostering, nuclear family in early America and most likely in the Anglo-American world. Granted, the strategies of the modern family would prove influential elsewhere—in nineteenth-century cities, countrysides, even in New England. But despite the damage to prevailing interpretations, this family form was actually never more clearly workable, more visibly productive, nor more palpably triumphant than it was in the early, formative decades of William Penn's colony.

NOTES

1. The sociological and historical literature on the modern child-centered family is too extensive to cite here in its entirety, and, in any case, it presents problems. Until recently historians and sociologists defined the modern family primarily in terms of the structure of households. This definition proved too rigid, and historians have lately placed more emphasis on affection and sexuality. Though more interesting, the debate over who was really affectionate to whom, and when, is falling into some of the same problems of rigidity that plagued the old definition. By measures of affection and sexuality non-Western people with family systems all their own must be considered more modern than those of the modern, Western family, a classification that would do little justice to their family systems and cast little light on our own culture. I find the most useful definitions are those that stress the fact that the modern, Western, child-centered, conjugal family is an ideal type, a specific complex system of social relations characterized by a number of coexisting elements. See William J. Goode, *World Revolutions and Family Patterns* (New York, 1970), pp. 1–26; Talcott Parsons, "The Modern American Family," in S. M. Farber, P. Mutacchi, and R. L. Wilson, eds., *Man and Civilization: The Family's Search for Survival* (New York, 1965), pp. 31–50; Peter Laslett, *Household and Family in Past Time* (Cambridge, England, 1972); Rose Laub Coser, ed., *The Family: Its Structures and Functions* (New York,

1974); Carl Degler, *At Odds: Women and the Family in America from the Revolution to the Present* (New York, 1980), pp. 3–25.

2. See Philip J. Greven, Jr., "Family Structure in Seventeenth-Century Andover, Massachusetts," *William and Mary Quarterly*, 3d ser. 23 (1966): 234–56; Philip J. Greven, Jr., *Four Generations: Population, Land, and Family in Colonial Andover, Massachusetts* (Ithaca, N.Y., 1970); Daniel Scott Smith, "Parental Power and Marriage Patterns: An Analysis of Historical Trends in Hingham, Massachusetts," *Journal of Marriage and the Family* 35 (1973): 419–28; Nancy F. Cott, "Divorce and the Changing Status of Women in Eighteenth-Century Massachusetts," *William and Mary Quarterly*, 3d Ser. 33 (1976): 586–614; Nancy F. Cott, *The Bonds of Womanhood: "Women's Sphere" in New England, 1780–1835* (New Haven, 1977); Kathryn Kish Sklar, *Catherine Beecher: A Study in American Domesticity* (New Haven, 1973); Degler, *At Odds*, pp. 3–25. One historian sees a modern family emerging among planters in Virginia after 1750; see Daniel Blake Smith, *Inside the Great House: Planter Family Life in Eighteenth Century Chesapeake Society* (Ithaca, N.Y., 1981); though see also Michael Zuckerman, "William Byrd's Family," *Perspectives in American History* 12 (1979): 255–311, and Bertram Wyatt-Brown, "The Ideal Typology and Ante-Bellum Southern History: A Testing of a New Approach," *Societas* 5 (1975): 1–29. Two historians have also argued that the English aristocracy formed the vanguard of the modern family; see Lawrence Stone, *The Family, Sex, and Marriage in England 1500–1800* (New York, 1977), and Randolph Trumbach, *The Rise of the Egalitarian Family: Aristocratic Kinship and Domestic Relations in Eighteenth-Century England* (New York, 1978). I think the Quakers, who were rarely aristocrats, were more influential in America.

3. Chester County Tax Lists, 1715–1800, Historical Society of Pennsylvania, Philadelphia (microfilm copy). For 1715 the township lists of Chester, Marple, Ridley, Haverford, Springfield, Providence, and Radnor were collated with Anglican and Quaker church records. St. Paul's Church Records, Chester, 1701–1900, Historical Society of Pennsylvania, Philadelphia (hereafter cited as St. Paul's); St. Martin's Church Records, Concord, 1714–1860, Historical Society of Pennsylvania, Philadelphia (hereafter cited as St. Martin's); St. John's Church Records, Concord, 1724–1860, Historical Society of Pennsylvania, Philadelphia (hereafter cited as St. John's); Radnor Monthly Meeting Records, 1681–1765, Friends Historical Library, Swarthmore, Pa. (hereafter cited as RMMR); Chester Monthly Meeting Records, 1681–1765, Friends Historical Library, Swarthmore, Pa. (hereafter cited as CMMR).

4. Charles Browning, *Welsh Settlement of Pennsylvania* (Philadelphia, 1912), pp. 1–158; Thomas Allan Glenn, *Merion in the Welsh Tract* (Baltimore, reprint ed., 1970), pp. 1–72; Barry Levy, "Tender Plants: Quaker Farmers and Children in the Delaware Valley, 1681–1735," *Journal of Family History* 3 (1978): 116–35.

5. For a full discussion of these ideas, see Barry Levy, "The Light in the Valley: The Chester and Welsh Tract Quaker Communities and the Delaware Valley, 1681–1750" (Ph.D. diss., University of Pennsylvania, 1976).

6. Ibid.

7. *Conversation* was defined in the seventeenth century, according to the *Oxford English Dictionary*, as the "manner of conducting oneself in the world or society." See also Levy, "Tender Plants," pp. 117–19. Quaker ideas about language are discussed in Richard Bauman, "Speaking in the Light: The Role of the Quaker Minister," in Richard Bauman and Joel Sherzer, eds., *Explorations in the Ethnography of Speaking* (New York, 1974).

8. Radnor Removal Certificates, 1681–95, RMMR.

9. Ibid.

10. Removal Certificate of Griffith John, widdower, 8th Month, 6th day, 1690, Tyddyn Y Gareg Meeting, RMMR.

11. Removal Certificate of John ap Bevan and Barbara, his wife, Second Month, 7th day, 1683, Llantrisant Meeting, RMMR.

12. Alan Macfarlane, *The Family Life of Ralph Josselin, a Seventeenth Century Clergyman: An Essay in Historical Anthropology* (Cambridge, England, 1970), pp. 206–10; Laslett, *Household and Family*, table 4.13; Stone, *Family, Sex, and Marriage*, pp. 107–9.

13. See Christopher Hill, *Change and Continuity in Seventeenth-Century England* (Cambridge, Mass., 1975), pp. 3–75; J. S. Morrill, *Cheshire, 1630–1660: County Government and Society during the English Revolution* (Oxford, England, 1974); John Sheaill, "The Distribution of Taxable Population and Wealth in England during the Sixteenth-Century," *Transactions of the Institute of British Geographers* 55 (1972): 111–26; J. Howard Hodson, *Cheshire, 1660–1780: Restoration to Industrial Revolution* (Chester, England, 1978); David Williams, *A History of Modern Wales* (London, 2d ed., 1977); C. Stella Davies, *The Agricultural History of Cheshire, 1750–1850* (Manchester, England, 1960); G. Elliott, "Field Systems in Northwest England," in Alan R. H. Baker and Robin A. Butlin, eds., *Studies of Field Systems in the British Isles* (Cambridge, England, 1973), pp. 51, 88–92. For Quakers, see Barry Reay, "The Social Origins of Early Quakerism," *The Journal of Interdisciplinary History* 11 (1980): 55–72.

14. See Joseph Besse, *Collections of the Sufferings of the . . . Quakers* (London, 1756), pp. 99–112, 735–57.

15. William Penn, "Some Account of the Province of Pennsylvania," in Albert Cook Myers, ed., *Narratives of Early Pennsylvania, West New Jersey and Delaware 1630–1707* (Trenton, reprint ed., 1967), pp. 98–99.

16. Thomas Ellis to George Fox, June 13, 1685, *Journal of Friends Historical Society* 6:173–75.

17. See Cheshire Men's Monthly Meeting Minutes, Book 1, 1677–1702, Cheshire County Record Office, The Castle, Chester, England (hereafter cited as CCRO); Morley Men's Monthly Meeting Records, Book 1, 1677–98, CCRO.

18. Thomas Ellis to George Fox, June 13, 1685, pp. 173–75. For alternative views, see James Lemon, *The Best Poor Man's Country: A Geographical Study of Early Southeastern Pennsylvania* (Baltimore, 1972), pp. 98–101, 219–21.

19. George Fox, *The Journal of George Fox*, ed. Norman Penney (Cambridge, England, 1911), p. 152; Levy, "Tender Plants," p. 119.

20. Ibid.

21. RMMR; CMMR; Levy, "Tender Plants," p. 121.

22. Jack B. Marietta, "Ecclesiastical Discipline in the Society of Friends, 1685–1776" (Ph.D. diss., Stanford University, 1968), p. 138.

23. For insight into radical marriage practices in seventeenth-century England, see Christopher Hill, *The World Turned Upside Down: Radical Ideas during the English Revolution* (New York, 1972), pp. 247–60. A full statement of Quaker marriage doctrine has recently been discovered by the Penn Papers project under the direction of Professors Richard S. Dunn and Mary Maples Dunn. It clearly shows that Quaker marriage was to be based on uncoerced mutual affection and love that "naturally arises to engage them." Penn also noted that the consent of parents and relations "is not of that absolute force as either to make or unmake a true marriage and they ought to walk circumspectly towards their children in this matter"; William Penn, "Right Marriage, as It Stands in the Light and Council of the Lord God . . . ," c. 1671, in

The Birth of the "Modern Family"

Mary Maples Dunn and Richard S. Dunn, eds., *The Papers of William Penn*, vol. 1, 1644–79 (Philadelphia, 1981), pp. 232–36.

24. See Edmund S. Morgan, *The Puritan Family: Religion and Domestic Relations in Seventeenth-Century New England* (New York, 1966), pp. 78–86; Smith, "Parental Power and Marriage Patterns," pp. 419–28.

25. Chester Women's Monthly Meeting Minutes (hereafter cited as CWMMM), 7th Month, 28th day, 1713, Friends Historical Society, Swarthmore, Pa.

26. For a good example, see Morley Men's Monthly Meeting Minutes, Bk. 1, 5th Month, 26th day, 1681, CCRO.

27. Radnor Women's Monthly Meeting Minutes (hereafter cited as RWMMM), 7th Month, 3rd day, 1725, Friends Historical Library, Swarthmore, Pa.

28. Chester Men's Monthly Meeting Minutes (hereafter cited as CMMMM), 5th Month, 30th day, 1705, Friends Historical Library, Swarthmore, Pa.

29. For example, in 1728 the Chester men again reported that "the Friends appointed to attend the marriage of Edward Fell and Jane Kendal report it is not yet accomplished and that she doth not love him well enough to marry him. . . . therefore this Meeting expects our women Friends will take such measures as may bring her to make suitable acknowledgment for proceeding so far on that account." Actually, the suitable acknowledgment was only an informal apology about having a changeable testimony about the man. See CMMMM, 10th Month, 30th day, 1728.

30. Levy, "The Light in the Valley," pp. 103–8. A goodly proportion even of those disowned were later readmitted.

31. For the use of shame in southern child rearing from 1750 to 1860, see Bertram Wyatt-Brown, "The Honor of Fathers, the Burdens of Sons: Child-Rearing in the South, 1750–1860" (unpublished Armington Seminar Paper, April 3, 1980). See also Phyllis Vine, "Preparation for Republicanism: Honor and Shame in the Eighteenth-Century College," in Barbara Finkelstein, ed., *Regulated Children, Liberated Children: Education in Psychohistorical Perspective* (New York, 1979), pp. 44–59; Michael Zuckerman, *Peaceable Kingdoms: New England Towns in the Eighteenth Century* (New York, 1970), pp. 72–84; E. P. Thompson, " 'Rough Music,' Le Charivari Anglais," *Annales: ESC* 27 (1972): 285–312; Edward Shorter, *The Making of the Modern Family* (New York, 1975), pp. 218–27.

32. RWMMM, 12th Month, 5th day, 1720.

33. CWMMM, 3rd Month, 3rd day, 1713.

34. CWMMM, 1st Month, 28th day, 1715.

35. A collation of wills and deeds in families in which children disobeyed the marriage discipline shows that there was seldom any economic penalty. Although most male children who married out were not deeded land at marriage, most got land when their fathers' died; see Levy, "The Light in the Valley," pp. 121–27.

36. Cheshire Men's Quarterly Meeting, at Frandley, 8th Month, 10th day, 1689, Cheshire Men's Quarterly Meeting, Bk. 1, CCRO.

37. Greven, *Four Generations*, pp. 140–45. Interestingly, John Waters found differences between inheritance patterns of Quakers and Puritans in seventeenth-century Barnstable similar to the differing patterns between Andover and Delaware Valley Quaker families; see John Waters, "The Traditional World of the New England Peasants: A View from Seventeenth Century Barnstable," *The New England Historical and Genealogical Register* 130 (1976): 19. See also Levy, "Tender Plants," p. 127.

38. Greven, *Four Generations*, pp. 140–45.

39. Ibid., p. 145.

40. Mr. George Ross to Mr. Chamberlayne, Chester, Jan. 22, 1711, in *Historical Collections Relating to the American Colonial Church, Volume 2, Pennsylvania* (Hartford, revised from the edition of 1871, 1969), p. 68 (hereafter cited as *Historical Collections*).

41. The content of yearly meeting letters is discussed in J. William Frost, *The Quaker Family in Colonial America* (New York, 1973), pp. 74–75, 76–79, 221–24. This evidence, the removal certificates, and many of the letters and testimonies cited in this article contradict Frost's conclusion that until 1770 "a conception of childhood was not present among Friends" and that Friends' theology demanded "rigid control of small adultlike beings." (Frost, pp. 82 and 87). John Kelsall in John Kelsall's Diary, Manuscript, Friends' House Library, London, contains a description of the testimonies of traveling Quaker ministers in Montgomeryshire, Wales, during the 1690s; Kelsall was at this time a schoolmaster, and he recorded all the ministers' frequent advice about children and child rearing.

42. RWMMM, 12th Month, 5th day, 1720.

43. John Bevan, "John Bevan's Narrative," in James Levick, "Emigration of the Early Welsh Quakers to Pennsylvania," *Pennsylvania Magazine of History and Biography* 4 (1880): 336–44.

44. Edward Foulke, "Admonition to my Children," 1740, F-190, Cope Collection, Historical Society of Pennsylvania, Philadelphia.

45. Marylynn Salmon, "Equality or Submersion: Covert Status in Early Pennsylvania," in Carol R. Berkin and Mary Beth Norton, eds., *Women of America: A History* (Boston, 1979), pp. 114–33.

46. Removal Certificate of Cadwallader Morgan of Gwernfell and Family, 5th Month, 5th day, 1683, RMMR.

47. Removal Certificate of Ellis Pugh, Merionethshire, 10th Month, 5th day, 1685, RMMR.

48. Removal Certificate of John ap Bevan and Barbara, his wife, 2nd Month, 7th day, 1683, RMMR.

49. "An Epistle from Women Friends in London to the Women Friends in the Country, Also Elsewhere, about the Service of a Women's Meeting, 1674," in A. R. Barclay, ed., *Letters of Early Friends* (London, 1841), p. 345.

50. "George Fox to Friends, January 30, 1675," quoted in William C. Braithwaite, *The Second Period of Quakerism* (Cambridge, England, 2d ed., 1961), p. 274. For a slightly different view of Quaker women, see Mary Maples Dunn, "Saints and Sisters: Congregational and Quaker Women in the Early Colonial Period," *American Quarterly* 30 (1978): 582–601; Mary Maples Dunn, "Women of Light," in Berkin and Norton, eds., *Women of America*, pp. 114–33.

51. RWMMM, 12th Month, 2nd day, 1721.

52. RMMMM, 4th Month, 5th day, 1722.

53. Degler, *At Odds*, pp. 3–25.

54. Robert V. Wells, "Family Size and Fertility Control in Eighteenth-Century America," *Population Studies* 25 (1971): 73–82.

55. Mr. Robert Suder to the Governor, Nov. 20, 1698, in *Historical Collections*, pp. 9–12.

56. Mr. Ross to Mr. Chamberlayne, Chester, Jan. 22, 1711, in *Historical Collections*, p. 68.

57. Mr. Ross to the Secretary, Chester, Dec. 30, 1712, in *Historical Collections*, p. 69.

58. Mr. Ross to Mr. Chamberlayne, Chester, Jan. 22, 1711, in *Historical Collections*, p. 68.

59. Mr. Humphreys to the Secretary, Chester, Nov. 30, 1719, in *Historical Collections*, 119.

60. The Vestry of Chester, Alias Uplands, in Pennsylvania, to the Society, 1704, in *Historical Collections*, p. 23.

61. Address from St. Paul's Church in Chester, Pa., 1706, in *Historical Collections*, pp. 28, 29, 30.

62. Vestry of Chester to the Society, Sept. 1, 1709, in *Historical Collections*, pp. 53, 54.

63. Joseph New, *Anglican and Puritan* (London, 1964); J. H. Overton, *Life in the English Church, 1660–1714* (London, 1936); H. P. Thompson, *Into All Lands: The History of the Society for the Propagation of the Gospel in Foreign Parts* (London, 1951); John Calam, *Parsons and Pedagogues: The S.P.G. Adventure in American Education* (New York, 1962). For the founding of Pennsylvania churches see *Historical Collections*, passim.

64. W. G. Hoskins, *Provincial England: Essays in Social and Economic History* (London, 1963), pp. 151–60; Mildred Campbell, *The English Yeoman under Elizabeth and the Early Stuarts* (New Haven, 1942), chs. 3 and 4. For Cheshire, see Davies, *Agricultural History of Cheshire*, pp. 2–71.

65. "Gregory King's Scheme of the Income and Expence of the Several Families of England Calculated for the Year 1688," in Peter Laslett, *The World We Have Lost: England before the Industrial Age* (New York, 1965), pp. 33–34.

66. Notitia, 1684–1687, St. Asaph Collections, Miscellaneous 1303–1379, National Library of Wales, Aberystwyth, England.

67. William Penn, *Collection of the Works of William Penn*, vol. 1 (London, 1726), p. 901, quoted in Frost, *The Quaker Family*, p. 144.

68. *Historical Collections*, passim.

69. Ibid.

70. George Smith, *History of Delaware County* (Philadelphia, 1862), pp. 409, 468, 483, 489, 495, 507.

71. Based on an examination of 110 probate inventories, Chester County Inventories, Chester County Court House, West Chester, Pa.; Philadelphia County Wills and Inventories, Philadelphia City Hall Annex, Philadelphia.

72. For origins of Welsh Tract and Chester Quakers and Anglicans, see Walter Sheppard, ed., *Passengers and Ships, Prior to 1684* (Baltimore, 1970); RMMR; CMMR; Smith, *History of Delaware County*, p. 400 and passim.

73. "List of Landholders, 1689," in Gilbert Cope, *History of Chester County* (Philadelphia, 1912), 31.

74. "List of Taxables, 1695," in Cope, *History of Chester County*, pp. 32–34. See also manuscript tax assessments: 1693, Chester County, Miscellaneous Papers, Historical Society of Pennsylvania; Lemon, *Best Poor Man's Country*, p. 219.

75. For sampling procedures for the Quaker families, see Levy, "The Light in the Valley," p. 24; for the Anglicans, fifty-five families were reconstructed from a random sample of families mentioned in St. Martin's, St. John's, St. Paul's, and St. David's.

76. "Land Commissioner's Minutes of the Welsh Tract, 1702," mss., Land Bureau, Harrisburg, Pennsylvania; Chester County Treasurer's Book, 1685–1716, mss., Chester County Historical Society, West Chester, Pennsylvania; Philadelphia County

Deeds, Philadelphia City Hall, Philadelphia; Philadelphia County Wills and Inventories; Chester County Deeds, Wills, and Inventories, Chester County Court House. See also Levy, "Tender Plants," p. 122.

77. Levy, "Tender Plants," p. 128.

78. Chester County Wills and Inventories; Philadelphia County Wills; Philadelphia County Deeds.

79. Removal Certificate of Ralph Lewis, 6th Month, 18th day, 1683, RMMR; Will of Ralph Lewis, Sept. 19, 1712, E-313, Philadelphia County Will Books, Philadelphia City Hall, Philadelphia; Deed, Ralph Lewis to Evan Lewis, 6th Month, 8th day, 1705, F-202, Chester County Deed Books, Chester County Court House, West Chester, Pa.; Deed, Ralph Lewis to Samuel Lewis, Oct. 6, 1709, B-342, Chester County Deed Books; Deed, Ralph Lewis to Samuel Lewis, Sept. 6, 1712, C-326, Chester County Deed Books.

80. For the Wade family there are at least ten sales and rents, at very low rates, recorded in Chester County Deed Books, 1681–1735.

81. For example, Andrew Rawson died intestate, Feb. 2, 1731. He had a personal estate of £215-6-16, including a bond of £47. (Inventory of Andrew Rawson, Feb. 2, 1731, Inventory No. 931, Chester County Inventories.)

82. Deed, Thomas Dawson and uxor to Abraham Dawson, Nov., 1746, H-434, Chester County Deed Books.

83. Will of Thomas Dawson, July 11, 1748, E-18, Chester County Will Books.

84. Will of Abraham Dawson, Aug. 26, 1760, G-51, Chester County Will Books.

85. Chester County Wills; Philadelphia County Wills.

86. For a different view of familial values among seventeenth- and eighteenth-century Pennsylvania farmers, see Lemon, *The Best Poor Man's Country*. James Henretta, "Families and Farms: *Mentalité* in Pre-Industrial America," *William and Mary Quarterly*, 3d ser. 35 (1978): 3–32, is an elegant critique of Lemon's ascription of liberal values to Pennsylvania farmers and an assertion of the appropriateness of a model of the "lineal family" to Pennsylvania farmers and artisans. Henretta's criticism of Lemon is well taken, but his model fits the Quakers no better. Quakers were not liberals who consciously sought wealth for personal gain and status. But Quaker religious beliefs and community suasion dictated that each child, according to gender roles, be treated equally and that the successful spiritual socialization of all children take priority over the mere security and promotion of family line. Thus, the Quaker family represented a dramatic modification of the lineal family. For an interesting continuation of the debate between Lemon and Henretta, see James T. Lemon, "Comment on James Henretta's 'Families and Farms: *Mentalité* in Pre-Industrial America' with a Reply by James A. Henretta," *William and Mary Quarterly*, 3d ser. 37 (1980): 688–700. However, neither Lemon nor Henretta have closely studied the abundant surviving Chester County and Philadelphia County wills and deeds.

87. Gwynedd Men's Monthly Meeting Minutes, 12th Month, 13th day, 1730, Friends Historical Library, Swarthmore, Pa. The Gwynedd meeting was originally part of the Radnor monthly meeting.

88. For exact figures, see Marietta, "Ecclesiastical Discipline in the Society of Friends," appendix.

89. Inventory of Peter Eliot, Jan. 4, 1769, no. 1103, Chester County Inventories, Chester County Court House, West Chester, Pa.

90. Inventory of Morris Llwellyn, Oct. 4, 1749, Philadelphia County Inventories, Philadelphia City Hall Annex, Philadelphia, Pa.

91. Levy, "The Light in the Valley," pp. 107–20; Peter Bewind Schiffer, *The Chester County Historical Society* (Exton, Pa., 1971); George Vaux, "Rees Thomas and Martha Aubrey, Early Settlers in Merion," *Pennsylvania Magazine of History and Biography* 13 (1889): 292–97.

92. RMMM, 8th Month, 3d day, 1726.

93. CMMM, 6th Month, 4th day, 1723.

94. CMMMM, 5th Month, 3rd day, 1723; Executions, June 1, 1722, Chester Court of Common Plea Records, Chester County Court House, West Chester, Pa.

95. Chester Court of Common Pleas, Dockets, 1714–1735.

96. Indictments, Feb. 3, 1730, Chester County Court of Common Pleas Records; Dockets, May 27, 1718, Feb. 3, 1719, Docket Books, Chester County Court of Common Pleas.

97. Dockets, 1716, 1725, Docket Books, Chester County Court of Common Pleas.

98. Execution, Sept. 2, 1731, Chester County Court of Common Pleas Records.

99. Docket, 3d Month, 1732, Docket Books, Chester County Court of Common Pleas Records.

100. St. Paul's; St. David's; St. Martin's; St. John's; RMMR; CMMR. For sample, see Levy, "The Light in the Valley," pp. 10–45.

101. Ebenezer Worchester, ed., *Frodsham Parish Church (St. Lawrence) Register, 1555–1812* (Chester, England, 1913); Eccleston Parish Registers, 1593–1899, CCRO; L. M. Farrall, ed., *Parish Registers of the Holy and Undivided Trinity in the City of Chester 1532–1837* (Chester, England, 1914); Rev. G. E. Warburton, ed., *Warburton Parish Registers*, 1611–1752 (Chester, England, 1896); Rev. G. B. Sandford, ed., *Registers of the Parish of Church Minshull, 1561–1851*, 2 vols. (Chester, England, 1850); Robert Dickinson, ed., *The Registers of the Parish Church of Gawsworth in the County of Chester* (London, 1955); Ferguson Irvine, ed., *The Register of Bruera Church, Formerly in the Parish of St. Oswald, Chester County, 1662–1812* (Parish Register Society, London, 1910). The distribution of families sampled is five Church Minshull, fifteen Gawsworth, four Bruera, ten Frodsham, four Eccleston, thirteen Chester, four Warburton. Men with titles were excluded.

102. Conclusion based on examination of 142 Cheshire inventories of middling families, probated between 1660 and 1670. Fifty-two percent of the inventories, all of middling families, were under £100. (Cheshire Probate Records, 1660–1760, CCRO.)

103. Mr. Nicholls to Mr. Hodges, Chester, April 30, 1704, *Historical Collections*, p. 19.

104. Evan Evans, "The State of the Church in Pennsylvania, most Humbly Offered to ye Venerable Society . . . ," Oct. 18, 1707, *Historical Collections*, p. 36.

105. An Account or History of the Building of St. Paul's Church in Chester, June 21, 1714, *Historical Collections*, pp. 78–80.

106. The Clergy of Pennsylvania to the Secretary, Chichester, October 24, 1723. *Historical Collections*, p. 131.

107. Mr. Ross to the Secretary, Chester, Dec. 30, 1712, *Historical Collections*, p. 69.

108. Mr. Ross to Mr. Chamberlayne, Chester, Jan. 22, 1712, *Historical Collections*, p. 67.

109. Mr. Currey to the Secretary, Radnor, March 31, 1760, *Historical Collections*, pp. 281, 282.

110. He also noted, "I had 4 communicants on Christmas day and only 6 on Easter Sunday." Mr. Thompson to the Secretary, Chester, April 23, 1752, *Historical Collections*, pp. 185–86.

63

111. He also noted, "I was never more amazed than after a preparation sermon and six weeks' notice given them of the Sacrament to be administered on Christmas day I found but three communicants . . . : on Easter Sunday but four and two of them the same, and on Whit-Sunday at Concord the same." Mr. Craig to the Secretary, Chester, July 27, 1760, *Historical Collections*, pp. 290–91.

CHAPTER 3

The Scottish Proprietors and the Planning of East New Jersey

NED LANDSMAN

The middle colonies, according to an influential recent interpretation, were the prototypes of American liberalism. Founded in the latter part of the seventeenth century, later than the colonies of New England or the Chesapeake, the British settlements in the mid-Atlantic region were influenced by the economic expansion and the growth of individualism that had taken place in western Europe during the seventeenth century. The settlers were not restricted by the socially confining schemes of the Puritans or the hierarchical plans of the Virginia gentry. Even the religiosity of the Quaker proprietors of Pennsylvania and West Jersey imposed scant restrictions on the economic lives of the settlers.[1]

There was at least one middle colony whose development did not conform to this pattern: East New Jersey. Although that colony was organized at virtually the same time as its neighbors, East Jersey developed into a very different kind of society. As in the Delaware Valley colonies, East Jersey's principal sponsors were primarily Quakers, but unlike West Jersey and Pennsylvania, its leading founders were Scottish rather than English, and they derived their settlement plan from the society in which they lived. The conservatism of that plan stood in marked contrast to the more liberal schemes of the middle colonies' other Quaker proprietors and was to have an important impact on the development of the colony.

The settlement of East Jersey, and especially the Scottish involvement in that settlement, is among the least studied and least understood aspects of American colonization. Many historians have

65

viewed the whole endeavor as something rather quaint; several have made reference to such seemingly bizarre personalities as Lord Minevard, a Scottish gentleman who sold a fraction of his East Jersey proprietary share to one John Campbell, in return for which Campbell was to provide a "footman in velvet" to wait upon Minevard at the first meeting of the "parliament" in East Jersey. Told in this manner, the Scottish migration becomes merely a "fascinating episode" in the story of East Jersey's development. After discussing this interlude, most historians return to more conventional narratives organized around such standard themes as the growth of political divisions within the colony, almost as though the Scottish colonization had never taken place.[2]

Such a view of East Jersey's development overlooks some important aspects of the history of the province. Although East Jersey did not long remain a Scottish colony, settlers of Scottish descent formed a substantial minority of the population of the central belt of New Jersey. Their representation in the political affairs of the province was even greater, as the Scottish proprietors formed the predominant element in the powerful Perth Amboy elite, a major political faction throughout the eighteenth century.[3]

More than just the number and influence of the Scots made their settlement significant. The Scots derived from a social order very different from, and far more conservative than, that of their English counterparts, and they brought many elements of that society into the New World. Compared with the plans of the Delaware Valley proprietors, the Scottish plan was hierarchical in the extreme. And unlike many earlier attempts to impose a conservative social order in the New World, the Scottish plan, and Scottish influences generally, were to have significant long-term effects on the colony.[4]

East Jersey did not begin as a Scottish colony. Its origins were in a Restoration grant from the Duke of York (later James II) to two English gentlemen, John Lord Berkeley and Sir George Carteret. In 1676 their proprietary colony of New Jersey was divided, and Berkeley sold his interest—the western half of the colony—to a London-based Quaker group. East Jersey remained in the hands of Carteret. Under Carteret's proprietorship, East Jersey was settled by migrants from New England and Long Island, and by 1680 the colony contained six townships modeled on the New England town, with nucleated village centers, town meetings, and communally allocated shares of town lands.[5]

Following the death of Carteret, East Jersey was sold to a pre-dominantly Quaker English group headed by William Penn. This proprietory group had close connections with the proprietors of the neighboring colonies: three of the East Jersey proprietors were also first purchasers of Pennsylvania, and several others were involved in the colonization of West Jersey. As the original East Jersey proprietors drew more members into their group, these interconnections became even more pronounced.[6]

Despite the overlap among the proprietary groups of the three Quaker colonies, East Jersey was never of equal importance to the English Friends. They were turning most of their attention toward Pennsylvania, and they exerted little effort on behalf of East Jersey. Thus, in order to promote settlement in the smaller colony, the twelve English proprietors decided to take on twelve new partners, six of whom were Scots. These Scottish proprietors quickly became the most active members of the proprietary group.[7]

The leader among the Scottish proprietors was the Quaker Robert Barclay, the owner or "laird" of the estate of Urie, cousin of the Stuarts, and author of the famous *Apology for the True Christian Divinity*.[8] Like many members of his class, the laird of Urie was widely traveled; he had visited England on several occasions and had received a continental education. Barclay was well connected with the leaders of the Quaker movement in England, and it was William Penn who first persuaded the Scottish Friend to become involved in American colonization.[9]

When Penn and Barclay first discussed colonial affairs, it was the Englishman's intention to enlist Barclay's support for the Pennsylvania colony. From the beginning Barclay had other plans, and he sought to keep the Scottish interest separate from that of the rest of the Pennsylvania purchasers. In 1681, the Scotsman wrote to Penn that his countrymen could not be persuaded to join the new colony unless they were permitted to maintain direct trade connections with Scotland, using Scottish ships. He also asked to have the Scottish lands granted in a tract of 30,000 acres lying together.[10] When the possibility of acquiring a substantial and unified Scottish interest in the neglected East Jersey colony arose, that opportunity and the lower purchase price convinced the Quaker laird to invest in the Jersey colony.

From the time Barclay involved himself in the East Jersey enterprise, he was the most active member of the proprietary group. To obtain his support for the colony, the English proprietors appointed

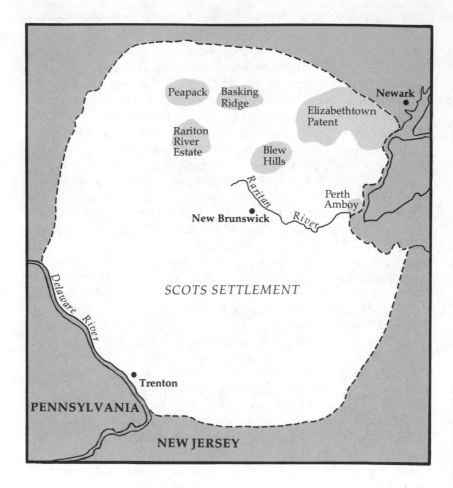

Barclay governor for life and granted him a free proprietary share, on the condition that he recruit four additional Scots as proprietors. The laird of Urie devoted much time and effort to East Jersey; the vast majority of the entries in his diary between 1683 and 1686 document his efforts on behalf of the colony, obtaining settlers and goods and persuading other Scottish gentlemen to join the venture.[11] His efforts did not cease when he had recruited four other proprietors, and by 1684 twelve proprieties, or one half of the colony's lands, were in Scottish hands. Under Barclay's direction, the Scottish proprietors sold off fractions of their proprieties to other Scots, so that more than fifty Scots eventually owned shares of East Jersey. Apparently Barclay was quite a salesman; John Forbes of Auchorthies wrote home in a letter from East Jersey that he had been so impressed by his friend's persuasion that he had left immediately for the new colony on a ship that was then in the harbor, without ever returning to his Aberdeenshire home.[12]

The original group of Scottish proprietors enlisted by Barclay were not all Quakers, but all were prominent gentlemen and close associates of Barclay. Included among this group were David Barclay, the governor's younger brother, and two cousins who were important Restoration politicians: James the Earl of Perth and his brother, John Drummond, later Viscount Melfort. Also included among the original proprietors were Barclay's uncle, Robert Gordon of Cluny, and Arent Sonmans, a Dutch-born Quaker merchant who lived in Scotland. Politically the proprietors were all conservatives and Royalists; three of the proprietors became Jacobites after 1689 (Sonmans and the two Barclays had died by 1690), and Barclay himself had a close relationship with James II.[13]

The shift of power in East Jersey to a predominantly Scottish proprietary group would have an important influence on the development of the colony. The social order from which the Scots derived was probably the most conservative in early modern Britain. As leading figures in that society, the proprietors worked to maintain essential elements of that social order within the colony they created.[14]

One of the most distinctive elements of the Scottish social order was the exclusivity of landowning. There was no class of small landowners in Scotland, except in a small area in the southwest of Scotland, and freeholding, as a status, did not exist. The vast majority of the countryside was dominated by large estates, and the bulk of the population worked as tenants or servants of the large landowners. The Scottish landed class was not only exclusive but powerful; there were no common rights in Scotland and no Scottish equivalents to the English systems of copyholding or customary tenancy. Leases, where they existed, were extremely short, often lasting for only a single year, and the landowner was under no obligation to renew a lease. Wherever leases did not exist, landlords could evict their tenants at will. Thus no Scottish tenant was able to establish a permanent stake in his farm, and the lower orders in Scotland were an unusually unstable and insecure group.[15]

East Jersey's Scottish proprietors did not represent a cross section of the Scottish upper class. All six of the original Scottish proprietors came from the east of Scotland, and the three most active proprietors—the two Barclays and Gordon of Cluny—came from the Lowlands of the northeast. Northeasterners, in fact, dominated the whole of the proprietary group. More than thirty of the early investors derived from that region, and another ten came from the Southeast; only a few had lived in the west of Scotland.[16]

The regional background of the Scottish proprietors was especially significant, for if the Scottish social order was the most conservative in Britain, the social order of the northeast was the most conservative in Lowland Scotland. In Aberdeenshire there was an average of only five landowners per parish, and in the other northeastern counties there were similar concentrations of landed property. Even these figures understate the close control of land in the northeast, since many wealthy gentlemen owned estates in more than one parish. And while the lower orders were far from stable anywhere in Scotland, in the northeast they were especially insecure; there was a turnover rate for tenants of almost 90 percent per decade in the latter part of the seventeenth century.[17]

Robert Barclay's Urie property is a good example of a northeastern estate. Located in Feteresso parish in Kincardineshire about a dozen miles south of the city of Aberdeen, Urie was one of two large estates in the parish. As the laird of Urie, Barclay controlled not only the economic administration of the estate but also its social life, which he administered through a local court of the estate, the "barony court." Despite his Quaker principles, Barclay was not averse to harsh discipline for infractions by his tenants, and the court minutes are filled with punishments meted out by the laird. For example, in 1667 the court evicted one David Watt of Woodhead from his tenancy for illegal shearing. A few years later, one George Hunter was fined £40 for "laboring a piece of controverted ground."

On another occasion, several residents of the farm of Glithno were fined £10 each for illegally taking peats from the ground, while a few years later two residents of the same farm were ordered to pay the laird £50 each for "mutual beating and striking of others." Procedures of this kind took place almost constantly in the Urie court.[18]

To aid in the administration of their Scottish estates, landowners such as Barclay called upon networks of neighbors, principally the sons of local gentlemen, to serve as clerks of the court, as bailiffs, or as factors on their estates. For example, in the Aberdeenshire barony of Logie Fintray, the four bailiffs listed in the court book were all sons of neighboring gentlemen. One bailiff, Alexander Gordon of Straloch, was also a member of an East Jersey proprietary family. When the laird of the estate died in 1722, the widow hired the son of an Aberdeen merchant to supervise the property. Estate records from other northeastern baronies demonstrate the existence of similar patterns.[19]

In recruiting colleagues for the East Jersey enterprise, Barclay and the other proprietors relied upon a very similar patronage network. Many of the purchasers of fractions of proprieties were younger sons of local gentlemen, particularly among those "fractioners" who moved to East Jersey. For example, three members of the family of Gordon of Straloch purchased fractions of the colony, but only the two younger sons traveled to the New World. Three Fullerton brothers also were involved in the proprietary scheme, but only the two younger sons purchased fractions. Several other fractioners can be identified as the sons of minor branches of landed families. Proprietor Robert Gordon of Cluny purchased a share with the intention of providing for his younger son Augustin, "since I had not estate whereby to make him a Scotch laird, that he might not hang on his elder brother."[20]

The Scottish proprietors employed their Old World connections to recruit not only fractioners but also proprietary agents. Only two Scottish proprietors moved to the New World: John Barclay, the governor's younger brother, and Robert Burnet of Lethenty. The rest employed agents to take control of their New World interests. Thus Burnet, an Aberdeenshire Friend, hired as his agent John Laing, a member of the same Quaker meeting to which Burnet belonged, while John Campbell of Edinburgh served as agent for several proprietors with connections in the Scottish capital.[21]

A good example of a proprietary agent was George Willocks, son of the Episcopal minister of Kemnay parish in Aberdeenshire. The families of Episcopal clergymen often maintained close ties to local landed families, and young Willocks used his connections to gain a position as agent for a prominent neighbor, Robert Gordon of Cluny. Once in the New World, Willocks used his position as agent to obtain a fraction for himself. Eventually he became the owner of one of New Jersey's largest properties.[22]

Willocks left no record of his motives for joining the East Jersey venture, but the extant letters of other fractioners and agents give some clue as to their motivations. Most striking in these letters is that none of the venturers described his motives as profit-making; their major goal was to acquire an estate or lairdship in the New World. For example, Thomas Fullerton wrote from East Jersey that his brother should not come over until "I have a good home, and entertainment to treat you with unbought; for you must not feel any of the inconveniences." Charles Gordon declared that "I intend to follow Planting myself, and if I had but the small stock here I have in *Scotland*, with some more servants I would not go home to *Aberdeen* for a *Regencie*, as was proferred to me." And James Mudie wrote to his cousin, heir to the family estate of Arbikie, that an "Earldom" could be bought in East Jersey "far below in pryce the vallue of what such pettie *Lairdships* as *Arbikie* is [sic] sold for in Scotland."[23] He continued,

> I hope to winn as much monie this year, as will buy a better Lairdship than *Arbikie*; and if ye resolve not to come over, I resolve to buy Land before I come from this, and title it *Arbikie*. But I shall be sorrie to take away your title, but if I do it, it will be your own fault. . . ."[24]

To provide homes and estates for these younger sons, the Scottish proprietors planned their colony on the model of northeastern Scotland. The Scottish plan was not the first settlement scheme for East Jersey, however. Before the Scots began investing in the colony, East Jersey's English proprietors had already devised a plan quite similar to that of Quaker West Jersey, based upon the sale of small farms and the collection of quitrents.[25] Such a plan held little appeal for the Scottish proprietors, and the Scots collectively issued a series of directives designed to alter the English plan to fit their own social models.[26] By looking at the alterations they made, we can gauge some of the social goals of the Scots.

72

One of the first goals of the Scottish proprietors was to establish a separate Scottish undertaking within the province of East Jersey, to create a colony within a colony. Even before Barclay had enlisted the support of any other Scottish proprietors, he already had drawn up a plan to have one-fourth of the colony's lands reserved for the Scottish proprietors. After more Scots had been drawn into the proprietary group, the Scottish proprietors instructed their representative, Gawen Lawrie, to see that all lands were divided into two lots, one of which was to be labeled the "Scots lot." And instead of relying on the colony's English surveyor to subdivide the Scottish properties, Barclay hired one of his countrymen to survey the Scottish lands.[27]

Under Barclay's direction, the Scottish proprietors embarked upon an ambitious campaign to populate their portions of the colony. Where the original English proprietors had published only one promotional pamphlet to advertise the East Jersey colony, the Scots published five, ranging from a one-page broadside to the massive *Model of the Government of East New Jersey*, which covered more than 270 pages.[28] Where the English proprietors had sent few settlers to East Jersey, the Scots chartered four ships to carry passengers and cargo to the new colony. Between 1683 and 1685, those ships carried approximately 400 Scottish settlers to the New World, about half of whom went as indentured servants.[29]

Most of the servants were imported by individual proprietors or fractioners, but the Scots also joined together in sending twenty-two servants and two families of tenants. The servants were set to work on two farms owned jointly by the proprietors and supervised by two overseers, John Reid and John Hampton. Both men were Quakers, and both had worked previously on the Scottish estates of members of the proprietary group. The two families of tenants settled on a third proprietary farm, where they worked as cotenants.[30]

In recruiting servants for the East Jersey colony, at least some of the Scottish proprietors used Old World connections. Unfortunately, very little can be determined about the former lives of most servants; the majority came from obscure backgrounds and their origins are almost impossible to trace. Of those we can identify, several can be traced back to the estates of members of the proprietary group. Included among them were two residents of Robert Barclay's Urie estate and one servant of the Fullertons at Kinnaber.

It seems that many of the twenty-two servants of the Scottish proprietors had prior ties to their patrons; at least six from this group were Quakers, and at least one other servant had lived on a proprietor's estate.[31]

That such a high proportion of East Jersey's Scottish settlers came as servants is indicative of the kind of society the proprietors were planning; it was to be based not on small farms but on landed estates. The village-based societies of small freeholders of the older English settlements had no place in the plans of the Scottish proprietors. Rather than granting large tracts of land to groups of settlers to be divided among themselves, the proprietors reserved all lands for large landowners, who would then reallocate the lands to their tenants and servants.[32]

As in the northeast of Scotland, East Jersey's landowning class was to be a wealthy and powerful group. In an early directive, the Scottish proprietors suggested that 2,000 acres lying together could be considered a "tollerable plantation" for each proprietor.[33] Interspersed among these estates were to be holdings of the "lesser fractioners," but even these were to be no smaller than 500 acres—very large farms by Scottish standards.[34]

While the large estate was planned as the fundamental economic unit of East Jersey society, the primary social unit was to be the neighborhood of large estates. Robert Gordon of Cluny, in a letter to his partner Gawen Lawrie, described his desire to settle in East Jersey with several other families, presumably as tenants or servants. "The chiefest thing for my settlement there," Gordon wrote, "is to get out the allottment of 10,000 acres to each proprietor, and of ours among the rest . . . at least betwixt us 2,000 acres continuous in one place, which I very much desire for our neighborhood." Gordon of Cluny was not alone in wishing to create such neighborhoods; several East Jersey fractioners wrote home that they had taken up land in clusters, where they soon set their servants to work. In one case the fractioners requested a minister for their new "neighborhood."[35]

East Jersey's Scottish proprietors were not the only middle colony investors to seek to create large properties in the New World; William Penn established a group of "manors" in colonial Pennsylvania, and the Quaker farmers of Chester County, Pennsylvania, acquired farm properties that averaged several hundred acres.[36] What was distinctive about the East Jersey plan was the intended function of the properties. Where Chester County Quakers acquired their lands in order to provide reserves of property for future generations, East Jersey's Scottish proprietors intended their properties to serve as landed estates that would be farmed by tenants and proprietary servants. Thus Deputy Governor Lawrie recommended that each proprietor import about thirty or forty servants initially and expect to bring more servants later.[37]

Another distinctive feature of the Scottish plan was the deliberate attempt to restrict the number of small properties that would arise in the Scottish sections of the colony. While East Jersey's English proprietors allowed settlers to purchase freeholds at the rate of two pence per acre, the Scottish proprietors forbade their agents from selling freeholds at any price and allowed only the sale of proprieties or fractions of proprieties. The Scots could not stop the English proprietors from selling freeholds, but they ordered that all such lands be taken from the portions of the English proprietors. The Scottish lands were to be preserved intact. Even the sale of fractions of proprieties was limited by the Scottish proprietors, so that no fractioner would end up with less than 500 acres. Unlike the proprietors of West Jersey, whose shares were continuously subdivided into smaller and smaller fractions, each of East Jersey's Scottish purchasers was to retain a sizable portion.[38]

Although East Jersey, like the other middle colonies, had adopted a "headright" system, granting a small farm to any settler who made his way into the colony, this was never a major feature of the Scottish plan. Instead, the proprietors hoped to bring in a substantial group of servants and tenant farmers. Thus the Scottish proprietors, in an early letter to their agents in the New World, wrote that "[we] incline to cleare our Lands by sending over People and Servants" rather than "by such Sale, and small quitrents." In another letter, the deputy governor wrote to a friend in England that "the *Scots* have taken a right course. They have sent over many servants and are likewayes sending more."[39]

According to proposals for settlement drawn up for the Scottish proprietors by Gawen Lawrie, any tenant who was willing to transport himself to the East Jersey colony would be granted both land and stock for fourteen years, paying half of the increase on the stock to the proprietors for the final seven years. As an inducement to attract settlers, the land was to be granted to the tenant outright at the end of that term, subject only to the payment of an annual quitrent. By offering such inducements, the proprietors were creating a social position, the quitrenter, that did not exist in the northeast of Scotland. Nonetheless, the creation of a class of quitrenters would require fourteen years' residence in the colony and did not pose an immediate threat to the proprietary plan.[40]

Even while allowing for the eventual creation of a class of quit-renters in East Jersey society, the terms offered to small purchasers by the Scottish proprietors were substantially more restrictive than were those granted by their English counterparts. The English proprietors allowed settlers to become freeholders by paying off their quitrents for a fee equal to twelve years of rent. The Scottish proprietors renounced this scheme and ordered that any quitrents sold within the colony be deducted from the English proprietors' lands, leaving intact the rents owed to the Scots. From the beginning, the Scottish proprietors paid close attention to the obligations of the quitrenters; in one of their first directives, the Scots instructed Deputy Governor Lawrie to undertake a complete survey of all quitrents owed to the proprietors and to seek an immediate settle-ment, but not to sell off any of the rents. Repeatedly in the first decade, the Scottish proprietors refused to sell their quitrents, even where they proved impossible to collect. As late as 1695 the Scots issued instructions to one of their agents that suggests the persist-ence of Old World attitudes towards quitrents and land ownership: if the proprietors could not let out lands on whatever quitrent they pleased, the proprietors asked, where was their advantage in pur-chasing the province?[41]

While the plan of the Scottish proprietors was considerably harder on the freeholders and quitrenters than was the plan of the English proprietors, the terms offered to servants were somewhat easier. At the end of his or her term of indenture, each servant was to receive thirty acres of land, subject to the payment of an annual quitrent. While several early contracts of service had allowed terms of service of up to seven years, Governor Lawrie's proposals recom-mended that all indentures granted by the Scottish proprietors be limited to four years, even where the proprietors held contracts for longer periods. As Lawrie explained,

[I]t is my judgement we should not abridge the poor, for it is the encouragement they have for their time and labor and venturing thither; and it is my mind that all servants after their time should be allowed by their masters a cowe and a sowe, and corn to sow an aker of ground. It was the law of Moses; a servant was not to go out empty-handed.[42]

Thus it is not surprising that the proprietors were more successful at recruiting servants than tenants.

The Scottish servants who arrived in the New World were set to work on a group of estates established by the proprietors primarily in the Raritan River Valley. The largest settlement was the group of estates established by eight fractioners along the Cedar Brook tributary of the Raritan, in an area known as the "Blew Hills." The families of these fractioners had many interconnections in the Old World, and once in East Jersey they took up lands "within half a mile or a mile of another." Together these eight fractioners sent fifty servants to the Blew Hills.[43]

Another large estate established by the proprietors was "Rariton River," the Somerset County plantation of Lord Neill Campbell, brother of the Earl of Argyll, who arrived in East Jersey in 1685 with a party of fifty-six persons. He immediately settled "22 men servants and 3 boyes" on that property under three year indentures and had them furnished with "corn, cattell and matterialls." Campbell remained in the colony only for a brief period, but he left his agent, James Campbell, to look after the 8,000-acre property.[44]

Most of the members of the proprietary group who came to East Jersey established homes not only on their estates but also in the new provincial capital at Ambo Point, which they named Perth Town after the most prominent of the Scottish proprietors. The town at Ambo Point was intended to serve as the colony's capital in every way. It was chartered as a free burgh, with weekly markets and fairs to sell the produce of East Jersey's hinterland. It was planned as the seat of East Jersey's government and of its prestigious Episcopal church, whose members included many Scottish gentlemen. And it was structured deliberately to reflect the colony's social order. The best lots in the capital—those facing the river or bay—were reserved for the landowners, while artisans, workers, and small farmers were routinely granted less desirable "back lots" away from the water.[45]

Despite the efforts of the proprietors, East Jersey did not evolve into precisely the kind of society the Scots had envisioned. Although the proprietors ruled the government until 1702, when East and West Jersey were joined together as a royal colony, it had become clear well before then that several aspects of the proprietary plan would not be fulfilled. By the end of the proprietary period, the large estate was no longer the predominant social unit even within the Scottish sections of the colony, nor had the proprietors been successful in limiting the number of small farms in East Jersey. In those important respects, the New World did have a liberalizing impact on the Scottish social order.

The transformation of the social order began quickly, as the proprietors in Scotland ceased to concern themselves so closely with the colony. One factor in their loss of interest was the changing political situation at home in the 1680s. The leading proprietors—Barclay, Gordon of Cluny, Perth, and Melfort—were all close associates of James II, who was deposed in the Glorious Revolution. As that Revolution approached, the dangers inherent in Old World politics probably seemed of greater importance than the promotion of a New World colony. Perth and Melfort both fled Scotland for the continent. Gordon of Cluny at one time considered fleeing to East Jersey. And when Barclay died shortly after the Revolution, the colony lost both its governor and its most active promoter.[46]

Another factor in the proprietors' loss of interest was that East Jersey, like most American colonies, did not produce the quick profits that the planners had anticipated. That was not of major importance to the fractioners and agents who came to the New World, most of whom acquired large tracts of land in the colony, but it did affect those proprietors who remained in Scotland. They had invested collectively in sending the first group of twenty-two servants to the New World, and for years afterward several Scottish proprietors sought unsuccessfully to collect a return on their original investments.[47]

As the proprietors in Scotland lost interest in promoting East Jersey, the real power in the colony devolved upon a new organization, the Board of Proprietors of the Eastern Division of New Jersey, the "resident Board of Proprietors," which had control over all allocations of land within the colony. Since very few representatives of the English proprietary group ever came to East Jersey, the resident Board of Proprietors was dominated by Scots throughout the colonial period. The Scottish members were primarily fractioners and agents rather than proprietors, and they used their positions to build up their personal fortunes. On one occasion in 1692, the members voted themselves an extra dividend in land as a bonus for their work on the board.[48]

A good example of the new breed of proprietor was John Johnstone, a fractioner from the southeast of Scotland. Born as a younger son of a minor branch of a powerful landed family, Johnstone first established himself as a druggist in Edinburgh, where he came into contact with several members of the proprietary group. After joining with his brother in purchasing shares of a propriety, Johnstone moved to East Jersey in 1685, took up residence in Perth Amboy, and obtained a seat on the resident board. Johnstone used his position to good effect, acquiring lands in many parts of the colony both individually and in partnership with George Willocks. Eventually Johnstone became one of the most prominent men in the East Jersey colony, served as mayor of New York, and founded an important Perth Amboy family.[49]

The changing composition of the proprietary group dramatically reduced the influx of servants into the colony. The proprietors in Scotland, busy with Old World affairs and still trying to obtain an accounting of their original investments, sent few additional servants to the colony. The resident proprietors lacked both the resources and the personal connections in Scotland to attract substantial numbers of servants. After 1690, only a trickling of Scots migrated to East Jersey as indentured servants.[50]

During the 1690s, the resident proprietors found themselves in possession of large and growing landed estates. But without a continuous supply of servants to work those lands, they came increasingly to rely upon land sales and the collection of quitrents to produce income, an important departure from the proprietary plan. By the end of the decade, more than twenty-five Scottish servants had completed their terms and acquired farms of their own.[51]

The story does not end there, however, for in other respects the social order was not liberalized. Even as individual Scottish servants took up farms in the colony, other remained on the proprietary estates. A precise calculation of their numbers is impossible, but the records do reveal that several of the larger manors continued to function even without new indentured servants. Those estates formed an important conservative element in the colony.

One such estate was Lord Campbell's Rariton River property. In an early directive to his agent, the proprietor described how even after the indentures of the servants had expired, some still resided at Rariton River, for he wrote that "all of them are under contract for Rent with us." Records from Rariton River beyond that date are scarce but revealing. To take but one example, they list the death in 1695 of one James Senzeour, a servant of Campbell's, six years after his term of service had been completed. Senzeour had never taken up his headlands; he still lived on the estate, although he possessed personal property of more than twenty-four pounds, a greater valuation than that of some persons who had purchased land. Moreover, Senzeour's inventory was drawn up by another servant, William Sharpe, who also continued to live at Rariton River.[52]

Exactly how many others remained at Rariton River is impossible to determine, although Campbell's directive to his agent suggests that there were many. At least six such persons appear in scattered East Jersey records. What can be ascertained is that only five of the male servants ever acquired land elsewhere in the colony. Even among this group, at least one remained on the estate long after the completion of his indenture: in 1700, servant Alexander Thomson purchased a farm in nearby Bound Brook. The deed issued to Thomson listed his residence as Rariton River.[53]

By the early years of the eighteenth century, several Scottish proprietors had accumulated vast tracts of land in eastern and central New Jersey, which would serve as the basis for estates far larger than Rariton River. In 1701, Johnstone and Willocks used their positions on the Board of proprietors to obtain a patent for a tract of land in Somerset County. The "Peapack Patent" originally was estimated at 3,150 acres, although recent estimates have placed it at about three times that size. Also in 1701, the Lyell family purchased 4,700 acres in central New Jersey, which they later supplemented with additional purchases. Another prominent Scottish family, the Alexanders, established a large estate at Basking Ridge, which eventually became the home of William Alexander, "Lord Stirling."[54]

While the proprietors frequently sold off parts of their estates to small purchasers, they continued to rent substantial portions to tenant farmers, many of whom were Scots. The Peapack estate, for example, grew steadily and was inhabited by more than fifty different tenants during the middle years of the eighteenth century. Scattered leases can be found among the papers of the Alexander and Lyell estates as well.[55]

It is, of course, true that the mere presence of colonial estates with tenant farms did not insure the existence of a truly conservative social order. Sung Bok Kim has demonstrated that on New York's manors tenancy could, under certain circumstances, be as favorable a situation as freeholding. The same was evident in Peapack, where the Johnstones sometimes had to strike disadvantageous bargains with their tenants.[56] Yet there are other aspects of estate life among the Scottish settlers that suggest that despite the more open land market of the New World, East Jersey was far from a "liberal" society.

One such aspect was the apparent lack of interest of Scottish servants and tenants in becoming landowners at all. In Scotland, people born into nonlanded families would hardly have encountered the possibility of becoming landowners. Economic success for a Scottish farmer ordinarily would have meant the achievement of a good tenancy or a secure place in the community. Even in the eighteenth century, it would not have been measured by the ownership of land.

In East Jersey as well, settlers could attain social status without acquiring estates of their own. A substantial majority of the Scottish settlers did not become landowners, even among those who held rights to the land. Every indentured servant transported to East Jersey during the 1680s was entitled to at least twenty-five acres of headland at the end of his or her term of service, yet it is striking how few took up those lands. Of 149 male Scottish servants whose indentures are recorded in the colonial records, only 32, or 21 percent, ever became East Jersey landowners. By comparison, almost 35 percent of a group of predominantly English male servants who arrived in Pennsylvania in the same years eventually acquired land in the colony.[57]

What happened to those servants who did not acquire land is difficult to determine. Some continued to work on the proprietary estates, and several others worked as tenants on the East Jersey farms of other common settlers. At least a few returned to Scotland, and a few others moved to New York, but very few obtained land in those places either. While our information on these servants is far from complete, it is clear that most did not acquire land either in East Jersey or the neighboring colonies.[58]

One reason so few Scottish servants took up their headlands may have been a lack of sufficient capital to stock their farms (although this consideration would have been as important in colonial Pennsylvania). But in some cases, Scottish servants evidently possessed sufficient capital to stock a farm and still chose not to do so, at least for a while. One such servant was Quaker John Hebron, who completed his term of indenture in 1687. After receiving a patent for his headlands, Hebron sold his land back to the Scottish proprietors and went to work on the farm of John Hampton, his former overseer. By 1693, Hebron had saved enough money to buy a 300-acre farm, but instead of moving there, Hebron sold the land and moved to Perth Amboy, where he was listed in the records as a tailor. Similarly, Thomas Ridford, another of the proprietors' servants, sold his headlands in 1688 and moved to Perth Amboy. In 1700, Ridford acquired the rights to 100 acres in Middlesex County, but he sold the land and continued to live in the capital. Both Hebron and Ridford eventually obtained farms, but they appear to have been in no great hurry to do so.[59]

The few extant letters left by Scottish servants also suggest that the main purpose of the writers in moving to the New World was not the acquisition of land. Peter Watson, a farmer, wrote to his cousin in Scotland that East Jersey provided the servant with many options, of which the acquisition of a farm was only one. Upon completing one's indenture, Watson wrote, servants could "gain abundance of work to other men; or if they desire to settle upon land of their own, they can have it reasonably cheap." John Cockburn, a mason from Kelso, wrote that he was glad to have come to East Jersey, "for I have abundance of imployment." Apparently Cockburn was more concerned with wage levels than with obtaining a farm, for he wrote that "Any who hath a mind to come here will get good wages; those who have a mind to come here will do better than in Scotland."[60] In neither letter was economic success equated with landowning alone.

Still another letter that suggested that landowning was not the primary motivation of the settlers was a note sent to East Jersey in 1718 by Thomas Paul of Edinburgh. Paul was writing to his cousin James Paul, one of the proprietors' servants who had arrived in the colony in 1683, and from Paul's letter it is evident that his cousin had not come to East Jersey with landowning in mind. James Paul's purpose had been to save his wages and return to Scotland; thus he had sold his headrights and gone to work as a laborer on an East Jersey farm. An earlier letter to Thomas Paul evidently had indicated that his cousin hoped to return home quite soon. Unfortunately, while working, James Paul had become crippled and been unable to save enough to return home. James Paul died in East Jersey in 1731.[61]

Another indication of the social conservatism of East Jersey's Scottish settlers was that many of those who did take up land requested that their farms be located near the estates of their former masters. In 1687, fifteen of the proprietors' servants joined in a petition to the Board of Proprietors for headlands near the proprietary estates in the Blew Hills, where they were joined by several other servants. Eleven of those servants sold their lands back to the Scottish proprietors, while six servants remained as neighbors of the proprietors in the Blew Hills. In the same year three other servants asked the Board for headlands in Monmouth County adjoining the estate of fractioner James Johnstone, the brother of John, and several servants who moved off the proprietary estates went to work on the farms of their former overseers.[62]

The existence of continuing economic and social ties between masters and former servants carried over into the political realm and may help explain the essentially conservative political behavior of the Scottish settlers. Where English settlers of all social levels participated extensively in the politics of colonial New Jersey almost from the beginning, participation among the Scots was sharply limited by social class. Throughout the colonial period, the proprietary group in Perth Amboy formed the most important political elite in the colony and controlled the Board of Proprietors, the Council, and often the governorship of the colony. They were opposed by factions of English proprietors or the inhabitants of East Jersey's English townships, but almost never by other Scottish settlers.[63]

A large part of the apparent disinterest of ordinary Scottish settlers in political affairs can be explained as a simple carry-over of Old World patterns. In most of rural Scotland, the dominant position of the gentry left the lower orders with very little room for political activity at either the local or the national level. Tenants occasionally were called upon to assist the political ventures of their patrons, as in the Jacobite rebellions of the eighteenth century, but aside from those cases there was no political institution that allowed for the political participation of the lower orders. Gentlemen such as Robert Barclay dominated not only the estate courts but also the shires, as Justices of the Peace. The relatively insecure position of the lower orders allowed them little leverage in the political realm.[64]

During the first decades of Scottish involvement in East Jersey, the proprietary group was subjected to a continuing series of attacks by English colonists over such issues as the validity of land titles and the payment of quitrents. The efforts of the proprietors to enforce their rights provoked petitions, law suits, and a series of riots in the colony. These protests involved the active participation of several hundred colonists over several decades, but virtually no Scots took active roles.[65]

The one case of active political participation by ordinary Scottish settlers in provincial politics—a petition by Middlesex County freeholders in 1710—constitutes the exception that proves the rule. The petition followed the assembly election campaign, in which Peter Sonmans, an opponent of the Scottish proprietors, sought to win the votes of English colonists with a speech that was explicitly anti-Scottish. In that address, Sonmans declared that "We will not go to North Brittain [Scotland] for Justice, No Turkish Government, No French Government," an obvious reference to the alleged Jacobitism of several Scottish proprietors. While the Scottish colonists previously had refrained from signing any of the petitions against proprietary rule that had circulated in the colony, more than twenty Scots joined other proprietary supporters in denouncing Sonmans's speech.[66] Thus the only time a significant number of Scottish settlers ventured into the political arena was in a petition in favor of the authority of the proprietary group.

The behavior of East Jersey's Scots in the first several decades in the New World raises questions about the extensiveness of the liberalizing influences that were brought about by the American environment, at least for one ethnic group. The Scots of East Jersey derived from an unusually conservative social order in which the rights of landowners were carefully protected. As members of the landed class, the Scottish proprietors used their power to plan a New World society in which the proprietors could maintain substantial landed estates and predominate in the political affairs of the colony.

Not all of the proprietary plan was instituted in the New World. The availability of land and the presence of a group of English colonists from a different social background increased the proportion of landowners in the colony and liberalized the terms of tenancy, just as in other American colonies. But in several respects the social order was not liberalized, as the proprietors retained control of much of the colony's land, and as the settlers, faced with a new, heterogeneous environment, often remained close to their patrons geographically and supported them politically.

The behavior of the Scots of East Jersey was conservative in both senses of the term. Scots displayed a remarkable fidelity to their social traditions, especially to the conservative social order of rural Scotland, and they exhibited a relative lack of interest in owning land and a relative acquiescence in hierarchical social order, even in a society in which the formal institutions of hierarchy were declining. It was in this second sense that Scottish patterns were distinctive, for the Scots were loyal to a set of social traditions that were quite different from those of the neighboring English colonists. These differences in social traditions were among the leading causes of political disputes in the colony and helped make East Jersey "the Rebellious Proprietary."[67]

NOTES

1. This interpretation of the middle colony social order can be found most explicitly in James Lemon, *The Best Poor Man's Country: A Geographical Study of Early Southeastern Pennsylvania* (Baltimore, 1972); but see also Stephanie Wolf, *Urban Village: Population, Community and Family Structure in Germantown, Pennsylvania 1683–1800* (Princeton, 1976). James Henretta has presented a somewhat different view of the middle colonies in "Families and Farms: *Mentalité* in Pre-Industrial America," *William and Mary Quarterly*, 3d ser. 35 (1978): 3–32. Lemon has used the term *liberal* to indicate an emphasis on individual freedom and material gain (p. xv); I have followed his lead and have used the term *conservative* to refer to that which is unliberal and emphasizes social traditions over individual freedom or material gain.

2. On the early history of the East Jersey colony, see William A. Whitehead, *East Jersey under the Proprietary Government* (Newark, 1875); George Pratt Insh, *Scottish Colonial Schemes, 1620–1686* (Glasgow, 1922), ch. 5, the only extant study of the Scottish colonization; Edwin Tanner, *The Province of New Jersey, 1664–1738* (New York, 1908); Donald Kemmerer, *Path to Freedom: The Struggle for Self-Government in Colonial New Jersey, 1703–1777* (Princeton, 1940); and John Pomfret, *The Province of East New Jersey, 1609–1702: The Rebellious Proprietary* (Princeton, 1962). Peter Wacker, *Land and People: A Cultural Geography of Pre-Industrial New Jersey* (New Brunswick, 1975), does examine the settlement of many ethnic groups in the colony, including the Scots, but makes little attempt to evaluate their impact on the overall development of the colony.

3. See the estimates of population in New Jersey in 1790 cited in Wacker, *Land and People*, pp. 160–63.

4. For a suggestive analysis of the failure of an early attempt to impose a hierarchical social order in the New World, see Sigmund Diamond, "From Organization to Society: Virginia in the Seventeenth Century," *American Journal of Sociology* 63 (1958): 457–75. That East Jersey may not have been the only hierarchical colonization plan in the latter part of the seventeenth century is suggested in Clarence Ver Steeg, *Origins of a Southern Mosaic: Studies of Early Carolina and Georgia* (Athens, Ga., 1975); and by implication, Sung Bok Kim, *Landlord and Tenant in Colonial New York: Manorial Society, 1664–1775* (Chapel Hill, 1978), although Kim probably would differ with my interpretation of his evidence.

5. See Pomfret, *Province of East Jersey*, chs. 2 and 3; Whitehead, *East Jersey under the Proprietary Government*, passim; and Edward Rindler, "The Migration from the New Haven Colony to Newark, East New Jersey: A Study of Puritan Values and Behavior, 1630–1720" (Ph.D. diss., University of Pennsylvania, 1977).

6. John Pomfret, "The Proprietors of the Province of East New Jersey," *The Pennsylvania Magazine of History and Biography* 76 (1953): 251–53.

7. Ibid.

8. *An Apology for the true Christian Divinity: being an explanation and Vindication of the Principles and dictums of the people called Quakers* (Aberdeen, 1687).

9. On Barclay's life, see David Elton Trueblood, *Robert Barclay* (New York, 1967).

10. Robert Barclay to William Penn, Dec. 17, 1681, Penn Forbes Papers, and Sept. 23, 1681, Society Collections, Historical Society of Pennsylvania.

11. Barclay's involvement in the East Jersey enterprise can be traced in two manuscript volumes in the Barclay of Bury Hill Collection in the Friends' Historical Library in London: "Notebook of Robert Barclay and Son, 1685–1689," and "Minutes of the Proprietors of East New Jersey, 1664–1683."

12. See the letter by John Forbes in George Scot, *The Model of the Government of East Jersey*, printed in Whitehead, *East Jersey under the Proprietary Government*, pp. 459–63. A good general discussion of the proprietary group can be found in Pomfret, "Proprietors of East Jersey."

13. Pomfret, "Proprietors of East Jersey," pp. 257–59.

14. Malcolm Gray, "Scottish Emigration: The Social Impact of Agrarian Change in the Rural Lowlands, 1775–1875," *Perspectives in American History* 8 (1973): 95–174; Ian Whyte, *Agriculture and Society in Seventeenth Century Scotland* (Edinburgh, 1979); and Ned Landsman, "Scottish Communities in the Old and New Worlds, 1680–1760" (Ph.D. diss., University of Pennsylvania, 1979), ch. 1.

15. Landsman, "Scottish Communities," ch. 1; and see T. C. Smout, *A History of the Scottish People, 1560–1830* (New York, 1969), chs. 5 and 6.

16. The estimates of the regional backgrounds of the Scottish proprietors are based upon my own research, cited in ch. 4 of Landsman, "Scottish Communities." For similar conclusions, see Pomfret, "Proprietors of East Jersey."

17. Landsman, "Scottish Communities," pp. 27–32. And see the *List of Pollable Persons in the Shire of Aberdeen, 1696* (Aberdeen, 1844), a mine of information on the social structure of one northeastern county; James Anderson, *A General View of the Agriculture of Aberdeenshire* (Edinburgh, 1794); and the descriptions of individual parishes found in Sir John Sinclair, comp., *The Statistical Account of Scotland*, 21 vols. (Edinburgh, 1791–99).

18. Rev. Douglas Gordon Barron, ed., *The Court Book of the Barony of Urie in Kincardineshire, 1604–1747* (Edinburgh, 1892), pp. 86–87, 89, 100–102, and passim.

19. "The Court Book of the Barony of Fintray, 1711–1726," in *The Miscellany of the Third Spaulding Club* (Aberdeen, 1930), 1:1–65; and see Henry Hamilton, ed., *Monymusk Estate Papers* (Edinburgh, 1945), pp. xxvi–xxxiii, 185–242.

20. Pomfret, "Proprietors of East Jersey," passim; and Robert Gordon to Gawen Lawrie, n.d., in "Some Unpublished Scots East Jersey Proprietors' Letters, 1683–84," *The Proceedings of the New Jersey Historical Society* (hereafter cited as *NJHS*), n.s. (1922): 10.

21. Pomfret, "Proprietors of East Jersey"; John Campbell to Lord Melfort, *An Advertisement Concerning the Province of East Jersey in America* (Edinburgh, 1685), pp. 2–4.

22. Pomfret, "Proprietors of East Jersey," pp. 282–83; *A Calendar of Records in the Office of the Secretary of State, 1664–1703*, in *Archives of the State of New Jersey* (hereafter cited as *NJA*) 21 (1880): 97–98, 152–56; and Robert Gordon's letter in "Unpublished Scots Proprietors' Letters," pp. 10–11.

23. Scot, *Model of Government*, pp. 440–42, 451–57, and see the other letters printed in the appendix.

24. Ibid., pp. 455–57.

25. See the English proprietors' pamphlet, *A Brief Account of the Province of East Jersey in America*, p. 545, printed in Samuel Smith, *The History of the Colony of Nova Caesaria, or New Jersey* (Burlington, 1765), pp. 539–46; and the early proprietary orders

in "Minutes of the Proprietors of East Jersey, 1664–1683." On West Jersey, see John Pomfret, *The Province of West New Jersey, 1609–1702: A History of the Origins of an American Colony* (Princeton, 1956).

26. The most useful documents for reconstructing the plans of the Scottish proprietors are "The Propositions of Gawen Lawrie," *NJHS*, n.s. 6 (1921): 229–33; "Some Unpublished Scots Proprietors' Letters"; and those proprietary orders published in vol. 1 of *NJA*, especially "The Proprietors to Deputy Governor Lawrie and Council," pp. 446–55.

27. "Propositions of Gawen Lawrie"; Robert Gordon to Gawen Lawrie, "Unpublished Scots Proprietors Letters," pp. 10–12; "The Proprietors to Deputy Governor Lawrie," pp. 448–49.

28. The one English tract was *A Brief Account of the Province of East Jersey in America*. The Scots published *A Brief Account of East New Jersey in America*, printed in Whitehead, *East Jersey under the Proprietary Government*, pp. 323–29; *An Advertisement Concerning the Province of East Jersey in America; An Advertisement to all Tradesmen, Husbandmen, Servants and others who are Willing to Transport themselves unto Province of New East Jersey in America*, printed in *The Bannatyne Club Miscellany*, vol. 3 (Edinburgh, 1858); Scot, *Model of Government*; and George Lockhart, *A Further Account of East New Jersey* (Edinburgh, 1685).

29. Pomfret, *Province of East Jersey*, pp. 186–88; and see the lists of servants printed in *Calendar of Records*, pp. 61–76.

30. "Account of a Shipment to East Jersey in August, 1683," *NJA* 1:463–69; Edith Mather, "John Reid of Hortensia," *NJHS*, n.s. 55 (1939): 1–26; and see Peter Watson's letter in Scot, *Model of Government*, pp. 438–40.

31. Scot, *Model of Government*, p. 458; "Robert Barclay's Account Book," ms. volume in the Barclay of Bury Hill Papers, p. 122. The backgrounds of some of East Jersey's Quaker servants were traced in "Records of Births, Marriages and Deaths of the Friends in Scotland," typescript in the Scottish Record Office, Edinburgh.

32. "Propositions of Gawen Lawrie," p. 230; "The Proprietors to Deputy Governor Lawrie," *NJA* 1:448–49.

33. "Propositions of Gawen Lawrie"; "Instructions to Deputy Governor Lawrie," *NJA* 1:427–28. The same goal was mentioned by a proprietor in a private letter; see Robert Gordon to Gawen Lawrie, in "Unpublished Scots Proprietors' Letters," pp. 9–11.

34. "The Proprietors to Deputy Governor Lawrie," *NJA* 1:448–49; "Instructions Relating to the Setting Out of Land in East Jersey," *NJA* 1:470–74.

35. Robert Gordon to Gawen Lawrie, "Unpublished Scots Proprietors' Letters," pp. 9–11; and see Scot, *Model of Government*, pp. 433–35, 440–42, 444, 459–68.

36. See Barry Levy, "The Light in the Valley: The Chester and Welsh Tract Quaker Communities and the Delaware Valley, 1681–1750" (Ph.D. diss., University of Pennsylvania, 1976), pp. 94–101.

37. "Propositions of Gawen Lawrie," p. 232.

38. The English proposals were offered in *A Brief Account of the Province of East Jersey*, p. 545. For the Scottish orders, see "The Proprietors to Deputy Governor Lawrie," *NJA* 1:449, 455; and the Scottish proprietors' instructions in "Unpublished Scots Proprietors' Letters," pp. 7–8. On West Jersey, see Pomfret, *Province of West Jersey*, especially ch. 6 and the appendix.

39. "A Letter from the Proprietors in Scotland," Dec. 15, 1682; "Minutes of the Proprietors"; and Gawen Lawrie to a Friend in London, March 26, 1684, in Scot, *Model of Government*, pp. 421–22.

40. "Propositions of Gawen Lawrie," pp. 229–30.

41. *A Brief Account of the Province of East Jersey*, p. 545; "Unpublished Scots Proprietors' Letters," pp. 7–8, 182; "Instructions to Deputy Governor Lawrie;" *NJA* 1:459–63; Robert Barclay to David Barclay, in "Notebook of Robert Barclay and Son"; "Instructions to Thomas Gordon, 1695," *NJA* 2:106–13.

42. "Propositions of Gawen Lawrie," p. 230.

43. Scot, *Model of Government*, pp. 459–63, 466–68; Pomfret, "Proprietors of East Jersey," pp. 283–88.

44. "Instructions for James Campbell from Lord Neill Campbell and Mr. Robert Blackwood Sr.," John Macgregor Muniments, Scottish Record Office, Edinburgh.

45. "Instructions for Laying out of Perth Town in East Jersey," *NJA* 1:434–37; William Whitehead, *Contributions to the Early History of Perth Amboy* (New York, 1856); *Minutes of the Board of Proprietors of the Eastern Division of New Jersey*, 3 vols. (Perth Amboy, 1949–60), vol. 1, passim.

46. "Unpublished Scots Proprietors' Letters," pp. 9–11; and see Pomfret, *Province of East Jersey*, pp. 134–38.

47. See John Campbell's letter in *Advertisement Concerning the Province of East Jersey*, pp. 2–4; and "Instructions for James Campbell."

48. See *Minutes of the Board of Proprietors*, passim, especially 1:196.

49. A. W. Savary, "Some Annandale Johnstones in America," *New York Genealogical and Biographical Record* 33 (1902): 246–49; and Pomfret, *Province of East Jersey*, pp. 287–88, 293.

50. *Calendar of Records*, passim.

51. Ibid., especially, pp. 120, 132.

52. *Calendar of Records*, p. 222 (and see pp. 164, 307); and "Abstract of Wills," 1670–1730, *NJA* 23:2.

53. *Calendar of Records*, p. 307, and see pp. 129, 278, for entries relating to servants John Pollocke and William Thomson.

54. The Peapack Papers are located in the Parker manuscripts in the New Jersey Historical Society. Included in the collection are three volumes of manuscript journals. The first two volumes have been published as "The Journal of Andrew Johnstone, 1743–1763," *The Somerset County Historical Quarterly*, vols. 1–4 (1912–15); the third volume is in a different handwriting and continues the story after 1763. See also *Calendar of Records*, pp. 155, 310, 333; "Extracts from American Newspapers Relating to New Jersey, 1704–1739," *NJA* 10:345, 356–57, 447–48; and Tanner, *Province of New Jersey*, pp. 51–54.

55. See the list of tenants in 1763 in the Peapack Papers, no. 11; see also "Journal of Andrew Johnstone," passim, and the other leases in the Peapack collection. Also see the "Rent Account Book 1758–1771," in the Stevens Family Papers, New Jersey Historical Society, microfilm reel 30; and the Alexander leases in the Alexander Papers, vol. 2, pp. 77 ff., also on microfilm in the New Jersey Historical Society.

56. Kim, *Landlord and Tenant*, passim; and see "Journal of Andrew Johnstone," 2:123 and passim.

57. This statement is based upon a comparison of the lists of indentured servants brought into East Jersey in *Calendar of Records*, pp. 61–76, with the land records in the same source and in the New Jersey State Library. For Pennsylvania, see Sharon Salinger, "Labor and Indentured Servants in Colonial Pennsylvania" (Ph.D. diss., University of California at Los Angeles, 1980). See also Russell Menard, "From Servant to Freeholder: Status, Mobility and Property Accumulation in Seventeenth-Century Maryland," *William and Mary Quarterly*, 3d ser. 30 (1973): 37–64.

58. West Jersey's land records to 1703 are published in *Calendar of Records*, pp. 339–684, while New York's can be found in *Calendar of New York Colonial Manuscripts Indorsed Land Papers . . . 1643–1803* (Albany, 1864). One group of settlers who returned to Scotland is discussed in Robert Wodrow, *History of the Sufferings of the Church of Scotland*, 4 vols. (Edinburgh, n.d.), 4:331–36.

59. *Calendar of Records*, pp. 61, 120, 148, 235, 241, 315, and passim.

60. Scot, *Model of Government*, pp. 438–40, 471–73.

61. Paule's letter is printed in Edwin Salter, *Old Times in Old Monmouth* (Freehold, 1887), p. 272.

62. *Minutes of Proprietors*, 1:156–57; and see *Calendar of Records*, pp. 92, 119, 241, 287, for references to the Cheesequake and Hortensia plantations. See also William Laing's 1709 will in "Unrecorded Wills of Monmouth County," New Jersey State Library.

63. Commenting on the power of the Perth Amboy elite in 1703, Colonel Robert Quarry wrote to the Lords of Trade:

> The Eastern Division [of New Jersey] hath been for a long time in the hands of a very few Scotch, the head of which party is now Coll. Morris, the Whole Number of them are not at most above Twenty, and yett they have always by the advantage of a Scotch Governour carryed it with a high hand ag' the rest of the Inhabitants.

See *NJA* 2.14. On New Jersey politics generally, see Tanner, *Province of New Jersey* and Kemmerer, *Path to Freedom*.

64. Landsman, "Scottish Communities," ch. 1; and see Smout, *History of the Scottish People*, ch. 6.

65. The petitions and lists of rioters can be found in *NJA* 2:332–39; 4:8–10, 15–17, 186–88, 306–10. Even on antiproprietary petitions signed by two hundred or more persons there were no more than two or three Scottish names.

66. *NJA* 4:8–10.

67. The phrase is Pomfret's, from *The Province of East Jersey: The Rebellious Proprietary*.

CHAPTER 4

The Roots of Episcopalian Authority Structures: The Church Of England in Colonial Philadelphia

Deborah Mathias Gough

Among the central themes of American religious history, few are more firmly established than the rise of the laity. According to conventional accounts, churches of all denominations departed from the hierarchical systems of the Old World and tended toward more democratic church governments in the New. Local autonomy supplanted regional or national control, and lay power displaced clerical authority.

Such theses are particularly prevalent in chronicles of the Church of England. These studies consistently hold that the absence of resident bishops compelled clergy to surrender much of their traditional and canonical authority and allowed the laity, as represented by the vestry, to exercise almost complete control over the local church.[1]

And indeed there is no question that the American environment had a profound effect on all religious denominations, nor doubt that it affected the Anglicans more than most. In the absence of a resident bishop as well as other elements of the ecclesiastical hierarchy, the distribution of authority within the Church of England evolved along lines almost inconceivable in the mother country. Nonetheless, to conclude, as many have done, that the laity quickly gained

I would like to thank Robert J. Gough and Jack D. Marietta for their helpful criticisms and suggestions in the preparation of this article.

control of the church throughout the colonies is to oversimplify the situation and to miss much of the dynamic involved in the adaptation of the church to its new environment. The Church of England actually faced vastly differing environments within different colonies and even within the same colony. Moreover, because there was no central authority or intercolonial leader, there was no guarantee that even those churches that faced the same environment would react in the same way. Therefore, if we are accurately to understand the development of new authority structures within the Church of England in America, we must look at the local churches. It is only at this level that we can determine the real effects of the absence of a bishop and see exactly what "lay authority" meant. It is only by examining individual churches that we can discover how quickly and with what degree of difficulty new authority structures were created.

If the history of the Church of England in Philadelphia is at all typical, it would appear that the church's adaptation to its new environment and its development of new governing structures occurred more slowly, were more complex, and were determined by many more factors than has generally been allowed. While the vestry of Christ Church, which was founded in 1695, and the vestries of its sister churches founded in the 1760s did grope for power, and did often act as if the hierarchical structure of the church had no bearing on them, their power was never as great as they wished or as historians have maintained.[2] The church in Philadelphia developed an ecclesiastical authority structure that was, in reality, neither "democratic" nor "hierarchical," a system that rejected both the episcopal system as it existed in England and the "lay control" that purportedly dominated the Virginia church. Slowly and painfully, through compromise and conflict, Philadelphia churchmen evolved a new system of government that combined elements of the democratic and hierarchical, a system that contained some elements of the English system as well as others resulting from the American environment.

In essence, Philadelphia churchmen created a horizontal authority structure within a hierarchical church. Instead of having a vertical line of authority where each person knew to whom and for whom he was responsible, different individuals and groups competed with each other for control of the affairs of Christ Church. Various issues brought out varying antagonists. But at no time during the colonial period did any person or group gain dominance.

The vestry was, indeed, one element in this complex arrangement. As the colonial period progressed, and the church in Philadelphia matured, the vestry increased its claims to power; more and more the vestry tried to control all aspects of church life. But its path to power was always strewn with obstacles. It had to contend with assertions of authority by both the rector and the bishop of London. It also had to compete with prominent laymen, the congregation as a whole, individual clergymen who attempted to play the role of surrogate bishop, and the Pennsylvania clergymen acting as a group in convention. When the authority structure of the Philadelphia church worked, it worked because all of these individuals and groups shared power in a horizontal fashion. When any one group or individual was not content to do so, conflict inevitably resulted.

The best way to understand the kind of ecclesiastical authority structure that developed in Philadelphia and how that structure affected the life of the church is to look at a specific incident in which most of the elements in that structure attempted to exercise their power. Such an incident occurred in Christ Church in 1715. The story is in itself intriguing and slightly bizarre, giving a graphic picture of the unruly nature of colonial life.

In 1714 Evan Evans, the pastor of Christ Church since 1701, left for England to settle some personal matters. During his absence, Francis Phillips, formerly a missionary in Connecticut, agreed to officiate, supposedly at the request of the vestry and with the approval of Evans. Phillips's career in America prior to his arrival in Philadelphia had not been too successful. Unhappy in the country town of Stratford, he spent most of his time in New York, upsetting his parishioners and leading to his dismissal from the service of the Society for the Propagation of the Gospel (SPG). While in New York he alienated Governor Robert Hunter, reportedly by making derogatory remarks about Scots. Despite these problems, he did nothing to portend the uproar he would cause in Philadelphia.[3]

During his first few months in the city Phillips seems to have been extremely popular. Robert Jenney, the priest whom the bishop of London had chosen to fill in for Evans, reported that upon his arrival he found Phillips had such a "good character" and "was so well beloved by the People that it was impossible to dispossess him."[4] But less than a year later Phillips sailed for England in disgrace, leaving behind him a badly divided congregation.

His problems began in February, 1715, when he was accused of slandering three prominent Philadelphia women. According to two men, John Smith and William Jones, Phillips had boasted that he had slept with the wife of William Trent, a wealthy Anglican who was a member of the Provincial Council and had been a friend of Phillips, with the daughter of John Moore, the collector of the customs, as well as with a Mrs. Neuman. At the same time Phillips was accused of propositioning Elizabeth Starkey, a servant of Reverend John Humphreys, the missionary to Radnor, Pennsylvania, with whom Phillips was staying.[5]

Understandably, these accusations caused a sensation. Trent and Moore had Phillips arrested at eleven or twelve o'clock on a Saturday night and "dragged . . . barelegged for near one half mile to the prison." Robert Assheton, another Anglican, set bail at 3,000 pounds and then refused to allow Phillips to send for that bail, although the law actually required no bail at all in such slander cases. To add to the insult, Peter Evans, the jailer who happened to be courting the slandered Miss Moore, refused to allow Phillips to stay in the under-sheriff's house, as was customary for persons of rank. Thus the members of Christ Church awoke on Sunday morning to find their church doors shut because their minister was in jail! Infuriated by this treatment of their beloved minister, 200 to 300 men and boys stormed the jail on Sunday, demanding Phillips's release. After achieving their goal, they went on to attack the house of John Smith. During the following two nights the crowds became more and more disorderly, breaking windows in the homes of Moore and Trent. According to Isaac Norris, a prominent Quaker, several Quakers "of best repute . . . were obliged to accompany the Watch for some Nights, to prevent mischief." And while the mob came to the defense of Phillips, Peter Evans became the champion of his fiancée, challenging the minister to a duel. Phillips wisely ignored the challenge, and Evans was indicted for his gallant efforts. The outcome of Evans's trial is unclear.[6]

Despite the efforts of the crowd, Phillips was brought to trial, found guilty of slander, and fined twenty pounds. The minister refused to acknowledge the authority of the court, maintaining that he could only be tried in an ecclesiastical court. Charles Gookin, the Anglican governor of Pennsylvania, supported the minister's position, first forgiving him his fine and then forcing the court to clear him of all charges. Unfortunately for Phillips, the bishop of London was not so magnanimous; in October of 1715, nine months after the controversy began, Phillips and Gookin received letters from the bishop ordering the minister to vacate Christ Church. Phillips followed this directive, leaving for England to plead his case in December, thus ending one of the most bizarre chapters in the history of Christ Church.[7]

While Phillips clearly had many supporters, by the time he left he had alienated part of his congregation and badly divided the church, demonstrating that, as he put it, while the churchmen "live in the midst of our enemies [the Quakers] . . . our greatest foes prove to be those of our own house."[8] With the aid of the governor, Phillips had been able to retain possession of the church building throughout the controversy. At the same time his opponents were worshiping at the Swedish Church with Robert Jenney or one of the area missionaries officiating. Phillips's opponents soon became so numerous that the services had to be transferred to the courthouse.[9] When Phillips was forced to vacate the church, leaving it in the hands of the missionaries, many of his supporters went elsewhere. John Talbot, the minister at Burlington, New Jersey, reported that Gookin began worshiping at the Swedish Church, "which he understands as much as I do Arabick," and John Newberry, a parishioner, commented that "some go to the Baptists; some the Presbyterians meeting, [and] some go nowhere."[10] Clearly the wounds caused by the controversy did not end with Phillips's departure.

At first glance this episode may seem like just another example of a scandalous minister causing havoc in a colonial church, a problem that many historians have overemphasized. But on closer look it becomes clear that because of the unique authority structure within the Philadelphia church, even dealing with a scandalous minister was no easy matter. A careful examination of the reactions of the various groups within the church to this controversy can tell us much about the workings of the horizontal authority structure and how it differed from the English system.

Had the situation occurred in England it would have been handled relatively quickly and easily: an ecclesiastical court would have either acquitted or convicted Phillips, and the bishop would have then taken appropriate action. In the absence of such machinery, the path was open for various groups to enter the fray. The vestry asserted its power for the first time, but it was not the only group involved. Individual laymen, the congregation, the surrounding clergy, and ultimately the bishop were all actively involved in the dispute.

The controversy involving Phillips provided the vestry with its first real opportunity to assert its rights in the selection of a minister. Because of the shortage of ministers in Pennsylvania, Christ Church had always had to accept whomever the bishop of London sent. Francis Phillips was the first minister of Christ Church who had not been sent by the bishop. Perhaps because of the fact that the vestry had itself selected Phillips, it strongly supported him throughout the controversy. In April of 1715 the governor and twelve of the fifteen vestrymen wrote to the bishop of London protesting the "unchristian and barbarous treatment, the reverend Mr. Phillips our worthy minister has met with." Maintaining that they spoke for three-quarters of the congregation, they argued that no minister was "more acceptable and serviceable to us" and blamed the accusations against Phillips on those who wanted to "distract and divide" the congregation in hopes of introducing "a Creature of their own." And four months later the same vestrymen again wrote to the bishop, proclaiming their faith in Phillips.[11]

The vestry did more than just affirm its support for Phillips. For the first time in the history of Christ Church, it asserted its power over the selection of a minister. In its April letter the vestry asked the bishop to license Phillips as rector of Christ Church. This move was particularly remarkable because Evan Evans had not yet resigned his rectorship; he had only taken a leave of absence to return to England to attend to family matters. This action starkly demonstrated the precarious position of the clergy in Philadelphia and the lack of concern for the church canons among the laity. More than that, it signaled the beginning of the vestry's struggle for control of the process of ministerial selection.[12]

However, while the vestry did try to assert its authority in this dispute, it is essential not to exaggerate the power of that body during the early years. It would be many years before the vestry would even claim supremacy in church affairs, let alone make its claim good. And some of the vestry's fiercest competition for power would come not from the bishop or the rector but from fellow laymen. For, contrary to the impression often given by historians, one cannot equate the interests and actions of the vestry with those of the laity as a whole. During the early years especially, prominent laymen, particularly those who held high political offices, often attempted to exert their influence independent of the vestry. Imitating the role the local gentry played in England, they expected to dominate both clergy and vestry. And while the problem of the proper role for prominent laymen was one that plagued the church in all the colonies, the situation was particularly acute in Pennsylvania because of the total separation of church and state and an especially unstable social order. In contrast to England and to certain southern colonies where the gentry were easily identified and their power over the clergy was relatively well delineated, the situation in Pennsylvania was chaotic. In the absence of a stable, accepted Anglican elite—either social, political, or economic—various prominent men vied for the power the local gentry would have had in England.

The vestry also had to compete for power with the congregation at times. Many historians have observed that the lack of institutional restraints in the New World led ordinary parishioners of all denominations to demand more say in the affairs of the church, and the Anglicans were no exception. While most laymen were willing to leave many of the affairs of the church in the hands of the vestry, they reacted with righteous indignation whenever anyone—vestrymen, bishop, governor, or other clergymen—denied them the minister of their choice. The congregation's demands for power increased as the colonial period progressed.

It was this competition among various lay groups, rather than lay control itself, which set the Philadelphia church apart from churches in England. For while the vestries in eighteenth-century England had little authority, individual laymen had great power over church life, both on the local level and in Parliament. Most significantly, over half of all clerical livings were controlled by lay patrons rather than by church officials.[13] But in England such lay power did not ordinarily cause problems, for which family would control which church was well established. Similarly, the cleric's relationship to his patron was also well defined. In Philadelphia no such clear lines of authority existed, and near chaos often resulted.

The kinds of problems competing laymen could cause can be clearly seen in the Phillips controversy. Prominent laymen were among the most important participants in, if not the root cause of, this dispute. But because they were not united they served as a disruptive rather than a stabilizing force. While Moore and Trent were using both secular and ecclesiastical structures to impose their will on the church—that is, to have Phillips expelled from the pulpit of Christ Church—Governor Gookin was doing everything in his power to support Phillips and, in so doing, establish his authority within the church.

The relationship between the governor of Pennsylvania and the Anglican community had always been uncertain and potentially troublesome. Unlike the governors of Virginia and South Carolina, where the church was established, neither the Penns nor their lieutenants had any legal powers in the religious realm. However, as the highest Anglican official in the colony, the governor usually expected to play an important role in the life of the church, especially in the absence of a bishop. This assertion of power was supported by the English authorities; the SPG generally made each governor a member, informed him when new missionaries were being sent, and expected him to look out for the interests of the church in any way he could. The reports he sent back were appreciated and taken seriously.

This leadership role was, however, often resented and challenged both by other laymen and by the clergy. The governor's position was made particularly difficult because at the same time that he was the defender of the faith he was also the agent of William Penn. As such, especially during the early years, he was at times forced to take positions opposed by most Anglicans, and as a result he was seldom totally trusted.

This situation, with its inherent potential for conflict, was aggravated by a succession of incompetent governors, including Charles Gookin, who took office in 1708. Gookin took his role as protector of the church particularly seriously, hoping that the ecclesiastical authorities at home would help him become royal governor if Penn or his heirs sold the colony.[14] However, at the same time that he was courting favor at home he was alienating many, if not most, prominent Anglicans in Pennsylvania by his overbearing attitude and arbitrary actions in both religion and politics. Gookin was on particularly bad terms with members of the Provincial Council, which included William Trent. And for unknown reasons he blamed the Anglican hostility toward him on John Moore.[15] Thus to Gookin the Phillips controversy must have offered a unique opportunity to retaliate against two of his worst enemies and to win support for his drive to become royal governor from members of the Anglican community who sympathized with Phillips. He also seems to have believed that by appearing as the champion of a persecuted clergyman and the defender of ecclesiastical privilege he could win the favor of the bishop. As we have mentioned, Gookin, emphasizing that he was only acting for the good of the church, refused to allow Phillips to be thrown out of Christ Church and reversed the ruling of the court. Attempting to demonstrate the importance of a diligent governor for the church, he conducted his own investigation of the charges, reporting his findings to the bishop and to the SPG.[16]

Gookin's efforts did succeed in winning him supporters. Phillips wrote to the bishop specifically suggesting that Gookin "should be confirmed under the Crown, when the Government is surrendered," and twelve of the fifteen vestrymen argued that the "potent fomenters of these unchristian Divisions" would have won out had it not been for "the Honorable Colonel Gookin our pious Governor."[17] Of course the strategy ultimately backfired; the bishop ruled against Phillips, and Gookin's efforts served only to increase the hostility between himself and the prominent people in Philadelphia of all religions. However, his actions clearly demonstrated the power a governor could wield, for his supporters were right about one thing: the controversy would have been much shorter and less intense if Gookin had stayed out of it or had sided with Trent and Moore. His behavior also showed how easily politics could become involved in a dispute in Christ Church, even when the original issue was not a political one.

The Phillips controversy also provided members of the congregation as a group with their first opportunity to voice their opinions and to test their strength. Refusing to stand idly by and let prominent men, the bishop, or even the vestry decide Phillips's fate, 104 members wrote to the bishop in March, 1715, decrying the "malicious insinuations" against their minister and affirming their support of Phillips.[18]

Not only did the parishioners refuse to allow the self-styled "gentry" to resolve the dispute, but there is evidence that they were consciously opposing these men. It appears that at least part of the dynamic of the Phillips controversy involved a power struggle between the prominent laymen and the rest of the congregation. Those opposing Phillips argued that the best people were being forced out of the church by Phillips's behavior, and John Humphreys, one of Phillips's firmest enemies, openly argued that the whole problem in Christ Church was caused by the "meaner people Acting in Opposition, and purely in opposition to the Better sort." While it may seem natural for Phillips's enemies, especially among the clergy, to blame everything on the "meaner sort," the accused's most adamant supporter, John Newberry, also saw the dispute in class terms. According to Newberry, the wealthy men, whom he called "Church papists," "whose conversations are so corrupt and vicious that they will not endure sound doctrine," objected because Phillips directed his sermons at all the members, rather than catering to the whims of the prominent men.[19]

While it is difficult to prove or disprove these assertions, there is some evidence that many of Phillips's supporters were of the "meaner sort." For one thing, the list of 104 names included thirteen women. Church authorities never gave Anglican women a voice in church affairs; their inclusion here suggests a protest against the traditional power structure. More important, the available economic evidence indicates that many of Phillips's male supporters were indeed far from wealthy. Of the ninety-one men who signed the letter, only twenty-nine appeared on the 1709 tax list, the only list remaining from this period. Among those twenty-nine, the mean value of estates was merely £59.9, whereas the mean value of estates for the entire city was £97.4. No less strikingly, considering the distorting effect of a few large properties on the mean, almost half of Phillips supporters had properties valued at less than £42, while little more than one-third of the population as a whole was so assessed. Similarly, while more than a quarter of the assessed had properties greater than £100, only one-tenth of the Anglican group were so blessed.[20]

It is possible that the overall membership of Christ Church was poorer than the general population, but the evidence that we have suggests that the wealth distribution of Anglicans during this period almost exactly paralleled that of the entire city. Of the 190 people who had their children baptized at Christ Church from 1709 to 1717, 39 appear on the tax list. The mean value of their estates was £97.3, significantly higher than the mean for Phillips's supporters. And the general distribution, as shown in Table 4-1, also indicates substantial differences between Phillips's supporters and the overall congregation.[21] Based on this information, it would seem that there is substantial validity to the charge that this particular dispute took on aspects of a struggle between the "better" and the "meaner" sort. And in any case, it would appear undeniable that in the Pennsylvania environment prominent men were not the only ones who felt a right to have a say in church affairs; men and even women of lesser means also thought they could and should make

Deborah Mathias Gough

Table 4-1. Tax Assessment in Philadelphia in 1709
(in Percentages with Cumulative Percentages)

Assessment in £	% Total Population	% Phillips's Supporters	% All Known Members of Christ Church
To 36	18.9 (18.9)	27.6 (27.6)	23.1 (23.1)
37–42	18.0 (36.9)	20.7 (48.3)	15.4 (38.5)
43–60	17.3 (54.2)	13.8 (62.1)	10.3 (48.8)
61–75	17.3 (71.5)	27.6 (89.7)	23.1 (71.9)
76–100	1.2 (72.7)	0 (89.7)	0 (71.9)
101–150	17.1 (89.8)	6.9 (96.6)	10.3 (82.2)
151–239	5.3 (95.1)	3.4 (100.0)	12.8 (95.0)
240+	4.2 (99.3)	0 (100.0)	4.9 (100.0)
Mean Assessment	£97.4	£59.9	£97.25

their opinions known to the powers in England. Though the Philadelphia parishioners exercised this right infrequently—only when their choice of a minister was denied them—the principle had potentially far-reaching consequences.

Laymen of all ranks were not the only ones who became involved in the Phillips controversy. As would be the case throughout the colonial period, the missionaries in the surrounding countryside considered it their duty to deal with this accusation against one of their brethren. The clergymen from Pennsylvania, Delaware and southern New Jersey had been meeting together four times a year since 1711 "to promote Brotherly Correspondence," and in both 1711 and 1712 they had sent letters home advising the SPG of the general condition of the church in the colony and asking favors for certain of their members.[22] But in this particular case they acted as more than mere informants of the bishop. In reality, they attempted to assume the powers of the ecclesiastical courts. As they informed the bishop, they felt it was more appropriate for them to determine Phillips's guilt or innocence than for him to have a "Public Trial before a Quaker Judicature."[23] And they clearly expected the bishop to follow their recommendation. While the clergy saw themselves as acting within the traditional hierarchical authority structure, they were actually adding one more element to the already complex horizontal authority structure that was developing in Pennsylvania.

Shortly after Phillips's arrest the clergy began their inquiry into his behavior. On March 10, 1715, they held a formal meeting to which Phillips and his accusers were all invited. Phillips, not surprisingly, did not attend, no doubt denying the authority of the clergy, but Smith and Jones must have told their story most convincingly. As a result, the clergy urged Phillips "quietly to withdraw himself," and when he refused to do so, they concluded that they "could do nothing but entirely disown him as unfit for the station which he holds." Reporting all this to bishop, they requested that he "purge the Church of so bad a member and rid us of so scandalous a Brother."[24] At the same time they began holding services for those Anglicans who would not worship with Phillips.

Not surprisingly, neither Phillips nor his supporters liked this outside interference. While the desire of the clergy to act for the good of the church is understandable, their assumption of authority was never really accepted by laymen, or by the clergyman under investigation. In a letter to the bishop, twelve vestrymen argued that the clergymen's "attendance upon their own cures, would have been much more commendable, then to Suffer themselves to be Sowers and Spreaders of Strife and Sedition, at least when they ought to have preached up peace and Unity." The vestrymen also suggested that the clergy themselves were interested in the Christ Church position. Phillips was more specific in his accusations, charging that Ross and Humphreys had been promised the church until Moore's son arrived, Talbot had two loans "forgiven," and John Clubb had been given money.[25] There is no reason to believe any of these accusations. It is much more likely that the ministers merely wanted to protect the reputation of their church and their calling. Knowing what a profound effect a scandalous minister could have on a church surrounded by dissenters and without a bishop, the clergy almost always acted quickly when rumors of scandal appeared, and generally believed the worst. Their strategy seems to have been to take no chances. This strategy inevitably created a context in which opponents of a minister were encouraged to charge him with immoral behavior, rightly or not. Several clergymen in Pennsylvania and the surrounding areas were later cleared of charges that their brethren had accepted at face value. Thus, while attempting to provide some order in the church and to increase their own power, the clergy may have actually encouraged divisions and increased the power of disgruntled laymen.

While the congregation, prominent laymen (including the governor), the clergy, and the vestry all tried to take the lead in resolving the Phillips controversy, they all realized that the bishop of London had the final say in the dispute. When Bishop Robinson ordered Phillips to return to England, no one challenged his authority. Francis Phillips sailed to England on the next ship.[26] And although some Anglicans at least temporarily left Christ Church, no further protest was made to the bishop.

As we will discuss later, Philadelphia Anglicans were generally content to ignore the bishop, or to treat him as merely one more element in the confused authority structure.[27] But when the crucial issue of who was to be the rector or assistant minister of Christ Church arose, the bishop's role inevitably loomed larger. Because all of the Anglican clergymen who served in Philadelphia until 1760, and all those who served the United Congregations until the Revolution, believed that the bishop's license was necessary for them to serve a church properly, the bishop of London had the ultimate power to determine who the ministers of those churches would be. And while this power of licensing has generally been considered to have been *pro forma* in Virginia and Maryland, the bishop's power was much more real in Philadelphia. Without an establishment to protect the interests of the church, bishops seemed to think they had to play an active role.[28]

Moreover, the competition for power within the church further increased the role the bishop played in the selection of a minister. When the local church was united on the choice of a minister, the bishop generally endorsed the decision. But when divisions occurred, as they did regarding Phillips, the prelate had to take a more active role. In these cases he served as the arbiter among the varying groups in the developing horizontal authority structure. And because it was difficult to arbitrate from the other side of the ocean, he ultimately had to make the final decision—as he did in the case of Francis Phillips. Despite the resentment this caused among many Philadelphia Anglicans, the bishop continued to utilize this power until the American Revolution.

But the fact that both Phillips and the congregation ultimately resigned themselves to the authority of the bishop—just as the ministers and congregations of the Philadelphia churches would continue to do in most cases throughout the colonial period— should not be seen as evidence of the smooth functioning of the hierarchical system. For this sense of ultimate powerlessness—the knowledge that the bishop controlled the most important decisions—may have actually increased both the intensity and the frequency of disputes within the Philadelphia church. As we have seen in the Phillips case, each individual and group did its best to influence the prelate's decision, both by stating its own case and by discrediting its opponents. Similar lobbying of the bishop would occur whenever there was any disagreement about who should be the minister of a Philadelphia church. As long as there was an outside authority to appeal to, dissident elements within the church would not passively accept the decision of any local authority, be it the governor, the vestry, or the area ministers. In this sense the one hierarchical element that existed in the Philadelphia ecclesiastical authority structure only added to the unstable character of the church.

Moreover, having little control over large decisions seems to have made the laity even more anxious to control smaller matters. For instance, when the rector of Christ Church, Evan Evans, returned in late 1716, the congregation took out on him its frustration with the system by failing to pay his salary.[29] And when poverty forced Evans to move to Maryland, it did not take the vestry long to come into conflict with the new rector, John Vicary.[30] The bishop of London could deny the vestry the minister that it wanted, but he could not stop Pennsylvania Anglicans from groping for power in other areas.

Unable to have either a truly localized, democratic church structure, or a properly functioning episcopal one, the Philadelphia church had to make do with a system that combined elements of each in a manner that almost ensured conflict. The Phillips controversy was the first one in which all the elements of the developing horizontal authority structure interacted, and as such it was perhaps the most chaotic. As the colonial period progressed, a degree of order began to emerge in the ecclesiastical structure of Christ Church. As a result of both conflicts and successful attempts at cooperation, the powers and authority of certain groups were delineated; that is, the competitors for power accepted the right of some elements of the authority structure, particularly the vestry, to assume specific powers, thereby narrowing the areas of conflict. At the same time, Philadelphia Anglicans gradually realized that no one group within the church was ever going to dominate; this realization further increased cooperation and reduced conflict. But as long as a horizontal authority structure existed within a hierarchical church, Christ Church would function smoothly only when all elements thought ecclesiastical peace was to their advantage.

The vestry was the group most intent upon establishing its authority over all aspects of church life. But while its power did increase as the eighteenth century progressed, at no time did it become the all-powerful force that historians have often portrayed.

The vestry's first target was the power of prominent laymen, particularly the governor. In 1719, apparently at the urging of the vestrymen, Governor William Keith was not reelected to the vestry. And while this was the first time on record that the governor did not sit on the vestry, it was not the last; never again during the colonial period would the chief executive serve on the vestry or be asked to play a leadership role in the church.[31] With the appointment in 1726 of Governor Patrick Gordon, a man who avoided conflict and never tried to dominate anything, the vestry's victory was complete. Future governors would continue to play a role in the life of the church, but only at the vestry's request.[32]

While the vestry was successful in limiting the influence of the governor, it never succeeded in totally eliminating the independent power of other prominent Anglican laymen. And in most cases such displays of power produced conflict rather than cooperation. Individual vestrymen themselves undermined that body's authority. Again and again vestrymen who found themselves in the minority would appeal to outsiders—local clergymen, members of the congregation, and ultimately the bishop—for support. For example, in 1741 dissident vestrymen were largely responsible for rallying people against the vestry's choice of a minister, Richard Peters—an effort that proved successful.[33] And as long as English officials would listen to the appeals of individuals, the vestry could never be totally powerful. In 1762, the SPG cut off its financial support for William Sturgeon, the associate minister of Christ Church, at least in part because John Ross, a prominent Anglican lawyer, reported that Sturgeon had not been catechizing the Negroes as his stipend required. The vestry investigated and assured the SPG that Sturgeon was performing these duties, but the SPG did not change its decision.[34] Since English authorities were used to the power of prominent laymen within the church and were not accustomed to dealing with vestries, it is not surprising that the vestry was unable to silence all other lay voices coming from America.

As the eighteenth century progressed the vestry discovered that its power was questioned not only by individual laymen but more and more by the congregation at large. As we have seen in the Phillips controversy, members of the congregation felt free to voice their opinions regarding certain ministers. But prior to 1759 their opinions had always supported the majority of the vestry. When the main foe was the bishop or the rector, no distinction was made between the rights of the vestry and those of the congregation. But in 1759, when the vestry gave only lukewarm support to the candidacy of William Macclenachan as assistant minister, a sizable proportion of the congregation openly asserted that the right of ministerial selection lay with the congregation, not the vestry. One hundred seventy-seven members, representing in all likelihood a majority of those who rented pews in 1750, endorsed the view that a minister's call was not legitimate unless he received a presentation from the congregation and that, once he received that call, neither the approval of the vestry nor a license was necessary.[35]

While most of Macclenachan's supporters left Christ Church to found St. Paul's in 1760, at least eight-one remained behind. Their influence can be seen in the bylaws adopted by the United Congregations in 1767. At this time the congregation refused to allow the vestry to choose a rector unilaterally, as it had done in the past and proposed to do in the future. The vestrymen were instructed by the congregation to rewrite the bylaws, requiring that no person be recommended to the bishop until at least one month after the vestry had voted, so that "if the major part of the Congregation . . . should have any reasonable objection to the Person so chosen, they may have an opportunity of signifying the same in writing to the Vestry."[36]

While the revision in the bylaws was only a small change, it clearly indicated the direction in which power was flowing: the authority of the congregation was slowly being increased at the expense of the vestry. The vestry did not willingly share its power with the congregation, but neither did it seem to resist. Once the will of the congregation was known the vestry approved Macclenachan's selection without much delay. And there is no recorded dissent from vestrymen to the new bylaws. Moreover, the new system seems to have worked well from 1767 through the Revolution. Three assistant ministers and three rectors were chosen during that time without any known problems. It would appear that during those years the vestry and the congregation both felt it was in their best interests and the best interest of the churches to cooperate rather than to test the potentially explosive procedure outlined in the bylaws.[37]

The vestry's struggles for authority were not, of course, limited to their fellow laymen. The conflicts with the rector, which many historians have emphasized, were also an important part of the history of the church in Philadelphia. But in these clashes as well, outcomes were inconclusive. Certain areas of authority were established yet neither side ever attained consistent dominance over the other. Their relationship alternated between conflict and cooperation.

Conflict between the rector and the vestry came to a head shortly after the Phillips controversy ended.[38] Unable to control the selection of the minister, the vestry seems to have focused its attention on controlling his conduct. The conflicts with Reverend John Vicary were comparatively minor, centering around such canonical questions as whether a lay reader could be used when a rector was ill and whether a vestry could meet without the presence of the rector. But these minor disputes began decades of intermittent power struggles between rector and vestry.[39] In 1737 several vestrymen asserted the vestry's right to choose an assistant minister without the rector's consent, going against canon law.[40] While this attempt to gain power failed to accomplish its goals, the vestry's struggles against the Reverend Robert Jenney during the 1740s were more successful. Ignoring canon law once again, the vestry in 1745 denied Jenney his right to choose the clerk of the congregation, the officer who led the responses and hymns, among other duties. The vestry's effort to deny the rector the right to choose one churchwarden proved unsuccessful but once again indicated its desire for power.[41] And perhaps most important in the long run, in 1750 the vestry withdrew Jenney's control over the pew rents. Rather than going directly to the rector, the money would henceforth go to the vestry, which would then dispense a salary to its minister. Such dependence upon the vestry decreased the rector's power in both obvious and more subtle ways.[42]

It would be wrong, however, to infer from these examples that the struggle between the vestry and the rector was entirely won by the vestry, or even that the relationship between vestry and rector was always one of competition and conflict. The degree of cooperation between the two varied depending on the rector, but in several instances the vestry reacted in a surprisingly docile manner to the actions of the ministers. In the 1760s, for example, when George Whitefield preached in Philadelphia, the vestry made no protest when Rector Richard Peters first allowed him to preach in the church, then denied him the privilege, and then once again allowed him the use of the pulpit. Given Whitefield's controversial nature, it is probable that some vestrymen disagreed with at least one of those decisions, but there is no hint of it in the minutes.[43] Even when Jenney was rector the vestry was not always hostile. In 1754, despite widespread support and a clear need for another church building, the vestry dropped the idea of constructing one when Jenney opposed it. And when Jenney finally agreed to the new building, the vestry quietly accepted the rector's unique plan for governing the two churches.[44]

Even when the choice of a minister was involved the vestry was not always aggressive. In 1768, despite the reported unanimous opinion of the vestrymen that John Porter, an evangelical minister, should be given a trial, the vestry bowed to the belief of Rector Peters and Minister Jacob Duché that such an action would be unwise.[45] And perhaps most important, when the bylaws were written in 1767 the rector retained his veto over the choice of an assistant minister.[46] The balance of power between rector and vestry was obviously more subtle than some historians have supposed.

Moreover, the Philadelphia vestries had to cope with other ministers besides their own. The missionaries from Pennsylvania, Delaware, and southern New Jersey continued to take an active interest in the affairs of Christ Church throughout the colonial period. In 1741 they wrote to the bishop urging that he not license Richard Peters as rector.[47] Peters, a young Englishman who had arrived in Philadelphia in 1736 and had already become a leading figure in Pennsylvania politics, was the vestry's choice. And in 1761 the local ministers were once again influential in persuading the bishop not to license a minister, William Macclenachan, who was the favorite of a large part of the congregation.[48]

Individual clergymen could also wield influence in the Philadelphia church. In 1726 Bishop Gibson appointed Archibald Cummings, the rector of Christ Church, as his commissary, or representative, in Pennsylvania. And while this position never attained the authority it had in some southern colonies, the bishop did pay special attention to the opinions of his commissary.[49] Then in the 1760s and 1770s William Smith, the controversial provost of the College of Philadelphia, succeeded in becoming the most influential clergyman in the colony, in many ways acting as a surrogate bishop. While his power was at times questioned, and often resented, his contacts in England made him a power with which all clergy and laity had to reckon.[50]

All the groups just described were important elements in the horizontal authority structure in Philadelphia. Prominent laymen, the rector, and the area clergymen all limited the power of the vestry. But the greatest obstacle to the vestry's hoped-for dominance, and in reality the factor that allowed all the other groups to have such influence, continued to be the power of the bishop of London. As long as dissident factions could appeal to the bishop, at times successfully, majority rule or even unanimous rule of the vestry was not going to be passively accepted by other individuals and groups within the confused authority structure in Philadelphia. And conversely, as long as there were competing groups and interests within the Philadelphia church, the bishop could not or did not relinquish his authority over ministerial selection.

The vestry did attempt to limit the bishop's power and objected to his interference in the life of the United Congregations. When in 1737 the vestry's choice of Peters for assistant minister was opposed by the rector, Archibald Cummings, and consequently by the Bishop, eighteen of the twenty vestrymen strongly condemned the bishop's interference and asserted their right to choose their own minister. Ignoring the canon that gave the rector a veto over his assistant, they preferred to emphasize a much more obscure legal point. They argued that because they built their own church and maintained their minister without any outside assistance, both the laws of England and the canons of the church gave them "the right of Patronage, that is, the right of presenting any Minister or Ministers, against whom there lies no legal objection to your Lordship for your Lycense."[51] While this bit of casuistry did not result in the approval of Peters, it did elicit an assurance from the bishop that he never claimed any power of selection, only that of licensing.[52]

This "moral victory" may have increased the vestry's sense of authority, but the victory turned out to be more apparent than real. When Cummings died in 1741 the vestry once again selected Peters, this time to be rector, and once again the bishop refused to license him. Furious at the bishop's intransigence, if not double-dealing, and by the local clergy's interference in the matter, the vestry came close to denying the bishop's authority altogether; Peters reported that it was only his insistence that prevented the vestry "from proceeding to an immediate appointment of me without leaving his Lordship any Choice."[53] And while the vestry eventually limited its protest to hiring a lawyer to present its case to the bishop, others went further; Peters suggested that Pennsylvania was not included in the diocese of London, and fifteen members of Christ Church wrote to England also questioning the bishop's authority and urging that no minister be accepted until the "Right of Nomination be settled between the Bishop and the Congregation."[54] Clearly Christ Church, and particularly its vestry, intended to increase its power at the expense of the bishop.

These disputes may seem merely like episodes in the familiar story of the rise of the vestry. But in reality the situation was much more complex than that. For in each case we have discussed the bishop turned out to be the winner; Phillips returned to England, and Peters returned to lay employment. Despite all its efforts, the vestry of Christ Church never gained complete control over the selection of a minister. It did not, indeed, deny the bishop of London the right to license its ministers until three years after the Declaration of Independence.[55] And, in the case of Pennsylvania, the bishop always considered his licensing as more than a rubber stamping of the vestry's decision.[56]

Time and again the vestry was forced to assume a subservient attitude in order to obtain a minister. In 1726, for example, Bishop Edmund Gibson had heard such negative reports about the church's treatment of ministers and its lack of respect for ecclesiastical authority that he was reluctant to send another minister to Philadelphia. It was only after Governor William Keith and vestryman Peter Evans assured his lordship of the congregation's loyalty to the church and good intentions toward its ministers that Archibald Cummings was sent.[57] Similarly, in 1741 after Bishop Gibson rejected Peters, the vestry not only gave up its search for power for the time but actually agreed to accept Bishop Gibson's choice of a rector without interviewing him first.[58] The vestry's desire to have a minister outweighed its desire to establish its power in these cases as well as in several others.

Thus, although the vestry did gain a degree of power over time, many of the same groups that were involved in the Phillips controversy were still competing for power to the very end of the colonial period. Ecclesiastical authority in the Philadelphia church remained horizontal; the vestry, the rector, prominent laymen, the congregation, area clergymen, and the bishop continued to share or compete for power. This unique authority structure caused or intensified many disputes within the churches over the years. But by the end of the colonial period both the parishioners and the clergy, most of whom had known no other system, had come to accept it as legitimate and even praiseworthy. Their support for this system was particularly encouraged in the 1760s and 1770s by the smooth functioning of the ecclesiastical structure; largely as a result of circumstances and personalities rather than changes in structure or principles, the United Congregations escaped major controversies during this period.

The development of this unorthodox system of church government proved to be more than merely an interesting footnote in church history. For, under the guidance of William White and William Smith, two Philadelphia clergymen, this horizontal authority structure served as the model for the government of the Protestant Episcopal church when it was founded in the 1780s. Mediating between the southern churches, which had already eliminated the power of the bishop and wished to further reduce the power of the clergy, and the New England churches, which believed that an Episcopal church without a strong episcopate was a mockery and that the laity should have no say in church government, the Philadelphia leaders were able to present a horizontal authority structure within an episcopal government as a viable alternative. As a result, for better or for worse, the government of the Episcopal church today—in which bishops, clergy, and laity share or compete for power—is a legacy of the Philadelphia colonial church.[59]

NOTES

1. For emphasis on the rise of the laity see, for example, Winthrop Hudson, *Religion in America* (New York, 1965), pp. 12–14; Timothy L. Smith, "Congregation, State and Denomination: The Forming of the American Religious Structure," *William and Mary Quarterly*, 3d ser. 22 (1968): 155–76. For discussions of the power of the vestry and the laity in the Church of England see, for example, George Maclaren Brydon, *Virginia's Mother Church and the Political Conditions under Which It Grew* (Richmond, Va., 1952); Borden W. Painter, "The Vestry in the Middle Colonies," *Historical Magazine of the Protestant Episcopal Church* 47 (1978): 5–36; Gerald Hartdagen, "Vestry and Clergy in the Anglican Church of Colonial Maryland," *Historical Magazine of the Protestant Episcopal Church* 37 (1968): 371–96; Hartdagen, "The Anglican Vestry in Colonial Maryland, a Study in Corporate Responsibility," *Historical Magazine of the Protestant Episcopal Church* 40 (1971): 315–35, 461–79.

2. For the founding of Christ Church, St. Peter's, and St. Paul's, see Deborah M. Gough, "Pluralism, Politics and Power Struggles: The Church of England in Colonial Philadelphia, 1695–1789" (Ph.D. diss., University of Pennsylvania, 1978), pp. 27–30, 215–23, 243–63.

3. Phillips to Secretary, Sept. 9, 1713, Society for the Propagation of the Gospel, Letters (hereafter cited as SPG Letters), ser. A, vol. 8, pp. 481–83. For Phillips's career in Connecticut, see E. Beardsley, *History of the Episcopal Church in Connecticut*, 2 vols. (New York, 1866), 1:26. The Society for the Propagation of the Gospel in Foreign Parts (SPG) was a missionary organization founded by a group of lay and clerical Anglicans

in 1701 to provide missionaries and churches in the colonies. The SPG supported all the ministers in Pennsylvania except for those in Philadelphia.

4. Jenney to Secretary, Jan. 4, 1714/15, in William S. Perry, ed., *Historical Collections Relating to the American Colonial Church*, 5 vols. (Hartford, 1871; reprint ed., New York, 1969), 2:81.

5. It is unfortunately impossible to determine whether the charges against Phillips were true, but there are grounds to doubt their validity. Elizabeth Starkey, the servant girl who testified that Phillips had propositioned her, later swore that she did so only because her master, Reverend John Humphreys, promised her her freedom and twenty pounds. Moreover, Phillips had a good point when he argued that the words he allegedly spoke were "so ridiculous and groundless that no man in his wits could ever be guilty of such scandalous folly." It is curious that the main charge against Phillips was only *saying* he had slept with three women, a charge that was almost impossible for him to disprove, and that the only two people who heard him were not men in whom he would have confided. Neither the vestry in Stratford nor Governor Hunter found any moral failings in Phillips, even though both had good reason to try. See Phillips to Reverend Dr., May 16, 1715, Fulham Papers, American Colonial Section, Lambeth Palace Library, microfilm, Van Pelt Library, University of Pennsylvania, 7:59–60; Phillips to Reverend Sir, Aug. 15, 1715, ibid., 7:73–74; Phillips to Secretary, March 23, 1714/15, in Perry, *Collections*, 2:90–93. For the affidavit of Elizabeth Starkey and others backing her up, see Fulham Papers, 7:61–64.

6. For accounts of these bizarre events, see John Newberry to Mr. Vesey, Nov. 30, 1715, in Perry, *Collections*, 2:94–97; Phillips to Secretary, March 23, 1714/15, in Perry, *Collections*, 2:90–93; Isaac Norris to Benjamin Coole, July 18, 1715, Norris Letter Book, Historical Society of Pennsylvania (HSP), 1:267–268. Evans's challenge and the court proceedings can be found in Perry, *Collections*, 2:512.

7. John Newberry to Vesey, Nov. 30, 1715, in Perry, *Collections*, 2:94–97. For a good narrative account of this controversy see Charles Keith, *Chronicles of Pennsylvania . . .* (Philadelphia, 1917), pp. 564–67.

8. Phillips to Reverend Sir [probably the bishop], May 22, 1715, Fulham Papers, 7:65–66.

9. "Extracts from the Journal of Reverend Andreas Sandel, 1702–1719," *Pennsylvania Magazine of History and Biography* 30 (1906): 448–49.

10. Talbot to Bishop Robinson, Oct., 1715, Fulham Papers, 7:74; Newberry to Vesey, Nov. 30, 1715, in Perry, *Collections*, 3:94–97.

11. Gookin, Vestry and Wardens of Christ Church to Bishop Robinson, April 20, 1715, Fulham Papers, 7:51–52; Vestry of Christ Church to Bishop, Aug. 12, 1715, Fulham Papers, 7:69–70.

12. Vestry to Bishop, April 20, 1715, Fulham Papers, 7:51–52; while the vestry records do not exist prior to 1717 there is no evidence in the letters to the bishop or the SPG that would indicate any previous efforts of the vestry to assert its rights.

13. Daniel Hirschberg, "A Social History of the Anglican Episcopate" (Ph.D. diss., University of Michigan, 1976), p. 4.

14. For examples of Gookin's attempts to ingratiate himself with the English authorities and to explain his actions, see Gookin to Secretary, Dec. 1, 1711, SPG Letters, A7, p. 497; Gookin to Bishop Robinson, May 2, 1711, SPG Letters, A6, no. 92. These letters also illustrate his quarrels with other Anglicans. Gookin was actually the lieutenant governor appointed by William Penn. But in 1715 there was much specula-

tion that Penn, who was paralyzed by a stroke and would die in 1718, or his heirs would sell Pennsylvania to the crown.

15. For the best account of Gookin's political career, see Gary Nash, *Quakers and Politics* (Princeton, N.J., 1968), pp. 312–19. For Gookin's relations with John Moore, see Keith, *Chronicles of Pennsylvania*, p. 557.

16. See Gookin to Secretary, Aug. 12, 1716, SPG Letters, A11, p. 231.

17. Phillips to Reverend Dr., May 22, 1715, Fulham Papers, 7:65–66; Twelve members of the vestry to Bishop, Aug. 12, 1715, Fulham Papers, 7:69–70.

18. Members of Christ Church to Bishop, March 7, 1714/15, Fulham Papers, 7:43–44. The area clergy claimed that the people had later forsaken Phillips, but there is no way to confirm this. See Clergy to Bishop Robinson, March 17, 1714/15, in Perry, *Collections*, 2:86.

19. John Humphreys to Secretary, n.d., SPG Letters, A10, p. 139; Humphreys was missionary to Radnor, Pa. John Newberry to Mr. Vesey, Nov. 30, 1715, in Perry, *Collections*, 3:94–97. See also Jenney to Secretary, Jan. 4, 1714/15, in Perry, *Collections*, 2:81; Sandel's "Journal," pp. 448–49.

20. The names of Phillips's supporters are found in Members of Christ Church to Bishop, March 7, 1714/15, Fulham Papers, 7:43–44. The tax list itself and the distribution for the total population are found in Peter J. Parker, comp., "Rich and Poor in Philadelphia, 1709," *Pennsylvania Magazine of History and Biography* 99 (1975): 3–19.

21. The records of Christ Church baptisms are found in the Genealogical Society of Pennsylvania Collections, HSP.

22. Missionaries to Secretary, April 12, 1711, SPG Letters, A6, no. 86; Clergy of Pennsylvania to Secretary, n.d. [1712], in Perry, *Collections*, 2:70–73.

23. George Ross and John Humphreys to Bishop of London, March 10, 1714/15, in Perry, *Collections*, 2:86.

24. Clergy to Bishop, March 17, 1714/15, in Perry, *Collections*, 2:84–87. They sent the same report to the SPG: April 20, 1714 [1715], SPG Letters, A10, pp. 141–43.

25. Vestry of Christ Church to Bishop, Aug. 12, 1715, Fulham Papers, 7:69–70; Phillips to Rev. Sir, Aug. 15, 1715, Fulham Papers 7:73–74.

26. Keith, *Chronicles of Pennsylvania*, p. 567: James Logan to Johnathan Askew, Oct. 7, 1715, Logan Letter Book, 1712–15, p. 324 (HSP). The bishop's order is not extant.

27. For a discussion of the authority of the bishop of London in America, see Simeon E. Baldwin, "The American Jurisdiction of the Bishop of London in Colonial Times," American Antiquarian Society, *Proceedings*, n.s. 13 (1899): 179–222; Arthur L. Cross, *The Anglican Episcopate and the American Colonies* (New York, 1902), ch. 1.

28. A full accounting for the differences between the bishop's role in Pennsylvania and his role in Maryland and Virginia is beyond the scope of this essay. Part of the explanation lies in the fact that procedures and traditions governing the church in those colonies had been established before the authority of the bishop of London was extended to the colonies. The fact that the first commissary in Virginia, James Blair, established a strong position and from that position espoused the power of the vestries also decreased the power of the Bishop. The existence of well-established gentry families during the later years no doubt decreased conflict within parishes. But the main difference seems to have been the existence of an established church in both these colonies. The bishops of London looked to the proprietors in Maryland and the governors and the Assembly in Virginia to protect the church and direct its activities. No such protection or direction could be expected in Pennsylvania. Unfor-

tunately, the role of the bishop in other colonies without state churches has not been fully explored.

29. Christ Church Vestry, Minutes, Feb., 1717/18, Christ Church Archives.

30. Gough, "Pluralism, Politics and Power Struggles," pp. 112–14.

31. William Keith had served as chairman of the vestry and had performed several tasks at the request of the vestry. See Christ Church Vestry, Minutes, March 11, April, May, 1718; May, June, 1719. For a discussion of his ouster, see Peter Evans to Bishop Gibson, n.d. [c. 1725], Smith mss., Archives of the Protestant Episcopal Church, Austin, Texas, 3:2–3 (Perry, *Collections*, 2:516–17).

32. Governors James Hamilton and John Penn both demonstrated their desire to help rather than dominate Christ Church and St. Peter's by aiding in the United Congregations' efforts to obtain a charter. See Christ Church Vestry, Minutes, April 21, 1749; Vestry of the United Congregations, Minutes, Dec. 27, Dec. 28, 1762, June 28, 1765, Christ Church Archives.

33. Gough, "Pluralism, Politics and Power Struggles," pp. 167–77.

34. See Ross to Secretary, July 2, 1762, SPG Letters, B21, no. 219; Ross to Secretary, July 6, 1763, SPG Letters, B21, no. 22; Sturgeon to Secretary, Nov. 20, 1763, SPG Letters, B21, no. 281; Sturgeon to Secretary, Aug. 15, 1764, SPG Letters, B21, no. 282; Vestry of the United Congregations, Minutes, March 30, April 27, 1763.

35. The only list of pew renters prior to the Revolution that is extant is from 1750: 31 percent of these men signed one of the letters supporting Macclenachan and asserting the rights of the congregation. Given mortality and mobility rates in eighteenth-century America this probably represented at least 50 percent of those pew renters who remained in 1759. For the letters expressing these views see Members of Christ Church to Jenney, Nov. 1, 1759, Smith mss., 3:44; Members to Archbishop, received Aug. 23, 1760, Lambeth Papers, 1123, 2, no. 194, transcripts, Library of Congress; "Articles of Agreement of St. Paul's Church," Norris Barratt, *Outline of the History of Old St. Paul's Church* (Philadelphia, 1917), pp. 29–32. For a discussion of the controversy surrounding William Macclenachan, see Gough, "Pluralism, Politics, and Power Struggles," pp. 224–63.

36. Vestry of the United Congregations, Minutes, April 20, April 27, 1767.

37. For a discussion of the selection of Peters as rector in 1762, see Gough, "Pluralism, Politics and Power Struggles," pp. 265–81. For the selection of Thomas Coombe and William White in 1772 see Gough, pp. 354–60. The selections of Jacob Duché and later William White as rectors, as well as the choice of Robert Blackwell as assistant minister, were all void of any known controversies.

38. Since there are no vestry records prior to 1717, it is impossible to be sure of the nature of earlier conflicts. However, the letters to the SPG seem to indicate that Evan Evans's problems were primarily with prominent laymen, particularly government officials.

39. See Christ Church Vestry, Minutes, Jan., Feb., 1721/22.

40. See Gough, "Pluralism, Politics and Power Struggles," pp. 136–58; Some Vestrymen of Christ Church to Bishop, n.d., Fulham Papers, 7:204–5.

41. Robert Jenney to Secretary, June 20, 1751, SPG Letters, B19, no. 103–4; Christ Church Vestry, Minutes, May 14, 1745.

42. Christ Church Vestry, Minutes, Feb. 23, March 5, April 24, July 25, 1750; Jenney to Secretary, Oct. 13, 1750, SPG Letters, B18, no. 151.

43. Peters to Archbishop, n.d., in Perry, *Collections*, 2:392–93; Hugh Neill to

Secretary, Oct. 18, 1764, SPG Letters, B2, no. 121 (Perry, *Collections*, 2:363–66); Coombe to Smith, Aug. 11, 1770, Hawks Papers, Smith Section, no. 27, Archives of the Protestant Episcopal Church.

44. Rather than establishing the new church, St. Peter's, as a separate parish, or setting it up as a chapel-of-ease subordinate to Christ Church and presided over by an assistant minister, Jenney's plan called for the two churches to be completely equal, governed by the same vestry and served by the same ministers. For the reasons behind this arrangement see Gough, "Pluralism, Politics and Power Struggles," pp. 214–23.

45. Ibid., pp. 354–57; Duché to Peters, Oct. 18, 1768, Peters Papers, HSP, 6:65.

46. Vestry of the United Congregations, Minutes, April 20, April 27, 1767.

47. Clergy to Bishop Gibson, April 23, 1741, Smith mss., 3:17; Ferdinando Paris to Peters, July 7, 1741, Penn Papers, Official Correspondence, HSP, 3:181. Part of the opposition to Peters was a result of his having unwittingly committed bigamy as a young man. But his supposedly overly rationalistic theology and his strong support for the proprietor were also held against him. For an account of the controversy, see Gough, "Pluralism, Politics and Power Struggles," pp. 166–79.

48. Missionaries and other Clergy of the Church of England to Bishop Sherlock, Oct. 21, 1759, Lambeth Papers, 1123, 2, no. 153.

49. For a discussion of the position of commissary in Pennsylvania, see Gough, "Pluralism, Politics, and Power Struggles," pp. 128–32.

50. For a discussion of the role Smith played in the Philadelphia church, see Gough, "Pluralism, Politics and Power Struggles," chs. 6–11, particularly pp. 300–305.

51. Christ Church Vestry to Bishop Gibson, n.d., Fulham Papers, 7:242–43. For a discussion of the entire controversy, see Gough, "Pluralism, Politics and Power Struggles," pp. 136–58.

52. Cummings to Bishop Gibson, Aug. 12, 1738, Fulham Papers, 7:238–41; Bishop Gibson to Vestry, Oct. 19, 1738, Fulham Papers, 7:230–31.

53. Peters to Ferdinando Paris, May 7, 1741, Penn Papers, Official Correspondence, 3:161.

54. Peters to John Penn, Oct. 4, 1741, Peters Letter Book, 1739–1743, 36–37, HSP; Members of Christ Church to "Gentlemen," n.d., Peters Papers, 1:26.

55. As late as 1778 the vestry had not declared its independence from England. In April it received a letter from the bishop of London, dated March 8, 1776, confirming Jacob Duché as rector. "In consequence of the above approbation," the vestry agreed to "Confirm & Establish the Reverend Jacob Duché rector of said United Churches." This was particularly interesting since Duché had already fled to England. It was not until June, 1779, after a Whig vestry had been elected, that the charter was changed, leaving out the clause requiring the bishop's approval. See Vestry of the United Congregations, Minutes, April 27, 1778, June 18, 1779.

When the dissident congregation of St. Paul's was founded in 1761, its charter did not require the license of the bishop for its minister. But even this independent church eventually acknowledged the bishop's authority, at least in part, asking for and receiving a license for its minister in 1773. See Gough, "Pluralism, Politics and Power Struggles," pp. 224–64, 312–15.

56. In 1760 Bishop Osbaldeston denied William Macclenachan a license as assistant minister because of his behavior while an SPG missionary and because of the disapproval of the Pennsylvania ministers. Then in 1763 he almost refused to pro-

mote William Sturgeon from assistant minister to minister. See Gough, "Pluralism, Politics and Power Struggles," pp. 224–44, 282.

57. See Keith to Bishop Gibson, April 8, 1726, in Perry, *Collections*, 2:147. Peter Evans to Bishop Gibson, n.d. [c. 1725], Smith mss., 3:2–3. This is another example of a governor working in cooperation with the vestry, rather than dominating it.

58. Jenney had been in Philadelphia during the Phillips controversy, but this was twenty-five years earlier. For the negotiations that brought him to Philadelphia in 1741 see Vestry of Christ Church, Minutes, July 6, July 14, 1742; Thomas Penn to Jenney, Dec. 23, 1741, Fulham Papers, 7:291–92; Jenney to Bishop Gibson, Jan. 14, 1741/42, Fulham Papers, 7:293; Vestry to Gibson, Nov. 17, 1742, Fulham Papers, 7:298–99; Jenney to Gibson, Dec. 8, 1742, Fulham Papers, 7:300. The vestry's action is particularly interesting in that it acted despite the objections of forty-four members of the congregation who wrote asking that Jenney's appointment be delayed until "Diverse other necessary matters are Settled" (Vestry of Christ Church, Minutes, July 14, 1742).

59. Gough, "Pluralism, Politics and Power Struggles," pp. 564–92.

CHAPTER 5

Power Challenged: Rising Individualism in the Burlington, New Jersey, Friends Meeting, 1678–1720

VALERIE G. GLADFELTER

This study examines the changing power relationships between an authoritative group and its individual members. The object of this study is the Burlington (West Jersey) Friends Meeting from its formation in 1678 to 1720.

Within these forty-two years, three periods emerge. In the first period, 1678–94, the Burlington Monthly Meeting held *acknowledged power*. It demanded and obtained general conformity. Its disciplinary sanctions were infrequent and effective enough when employed to extract effusive apologies from miscreants. In the second period, 1695–1709, the Meeting experienced *challenged power*. Events occurring inside and outside the Meeting weakened its control over members' behavior and made it susceptible to individual challenges. Nonconformity with some previously accepted behavior standards became more frequent, the number of disciplinary actions taken by the Meeting increased, and condemnations of misbehavior became on occasion more perfunctory. During the third period, 1710–20, a new balance developed. The Meeting held *conditionally acknowledged power*. Its monitoring of members' behavior was acknowledged within more narrowly defined boundaries, outside which individuals had more personal freedom. The rate of disciplinary actions decreased to levels of the first period, and condemnations were routinized.

Under conditions of acknowledged power, the group is authoritative and is accorded obedience. The group has the power to influence, or require, specific standards of behavior. When this power is acknowledged, conformity is automatic and authoritarian controls are unnecessary. In the situation of acknowledged power, the group rarely needs to discipline its members. Therefore, it is benign in its behavior management strategies. When members of a group acknowledge the group's collective controls, it is often because there are compelling reasons for individuals to maintain their affiliation with the group. Affiliation includes the individual in the group's power and resultant privileges. Nonconformity entails exclusion from power. A group with acknowledged power can afford to remove the stigma of deviance and restore offenders to status positions within the group.

Under conditions of challenged power, the group handles disciplinary questions differently. In response to the stress produced by loss of power and internal dissent, a group experiments with alternative strategies to maintain its survival and to accommodate change. It may increase the kinds of member behaviors for which it is willing to impose discipline. It may be less willing to overlook departures from the accepted norms. It may permit a wider range of nonconformity to exist. It may mete out discipline more perfunctorily, giving the appearance of disapproving nonconformity that it has become powerless, in reality, to control. When its power is challenged, the group must respond to substantial nonconformity with previously accepted values and behavior, and to loss of consensus among members on important norms.

With conditionally acknowledged power, a new balance between the individual and the group comes into play. Members acknowledge the group's authority to regulate certain behaviors, especially when they want recognition of their membership status from the group. Procedures are developed that permit an individual to keep membership even if norms are violated. Self-condemnations are perfunctory and discipline trivialized for many behaviors. However, the group develops its right to extrude members who fail to give prompt apology for wrongdoing, even if the apology is ritualized and indifferent. Discipline is routinized and bureaucratized. It takes on a *pro forma* quality in which both the group and its members expect to go through the motions of disciplinary proceedings. Individuals who are reluctant to follow this practice are disowned.

This is how the Burlington Friends Meeting came to have acknowledged power. In 1677, a group of English Quakers, encouraged by

George Fox and William Penn, bought shares in the new proprietary colony of West New Jersey, emigrated, and created the Burlington settlement. Anticipating both economic opportunity and political autonomy, the earliest settlers expected to control their own destiny.[1] They believed Burlington would be the major center for trade in the Delaware Valley and a potential exporter of agricultural products as well. They also thought the West Jersey proprietary accorded them the right of government. In that first flush of colonization, a prosperous and self-governing Quaker commonwealth seemed a plausible prospect.

From the time of settlement through the early 1690s, the English population in Burlington and the membership of the Burlington Monthly Meeting of the Religious Society of Friends were virtually identical. The non-Quakers in Burlington had no place of worship, no strong representation in the provincial government or court, and no forum for their concerns that was not directly under the control of Friends who were members of the Burlington Monthly Meeting. All inhabitants lived under laws that were written and enforced by Quakers.

The town of Burlington was the center of West New Jersey life. It was the "head" of the province, the seat of the Assembly and the court, the provincial market, and the mercantile and population center for the area; and it was also the location of the Friends Yearly Meeting. Burlington Quakers knew themselves and their town to be weighty in West New Jersey.

Indeed, even when the settlement of Philadelphia a few years later eclipsed Burlington in the Delaware Valley, Burlington Friends retained real power. Members of the Meeting played consequential roles in the life of the province. The Meeting continued to have a remarkable capacity to sanction and control the behavior of its constituent members in a late seventeenth century world that still allowed little individualism. Within the intimate scale of face-to-face encounters, the Burlington Friends Meeting's power was acknowledged by its constituency.

By the mid-1680s, the Meeting had established certain important supports for Meeting activities and for individual members. It established procedures for marriage and recorded births and deaths. It systematized collections for the poor and provided a place for the burial of the dead. It built meetinghouses to furnish places for worship and for the transaction of other Quaker business. It decided what was an appropriate length of time for remarriage after widowhood; that rum should not be sold to the Indians; that everyone was obliged to support oneself and one's family financially; and that Quaker orphans were to be raised in a Quaker family.

While creating the Meeting organization, Burlington Friends served as members of the West Jersey Assembly and the Council of Proprietors. In the Burlington court, the justices, juries, and constables were all Quakers in the early years. During this first period, Friends were the arbiters of social behavior both inside and outside the religious community. Even if a settler left the Meeting, he was still subject to the courts, which were controlled by the Quakers.[2] If a Friend was disowned by the Meeting, there was no alternative place for him in the social structure. This condition alone must have been a powerful incentive to individuals to acknowledge the Meeting's power and to accept the good order used by Friends.

There are many signs of the Meeting's power in this first period. Friends who violated the norms of the group were visited by a committee designated by the Meeting, and committee members were often leaders of the province as well as of the Meeting. The first disciplinary committee appointed in Burlington had both the governor and the deputy governor as members.[3] The Women's Meeting also appointed leaders' wives to such committees, and by such appointments offenders knew that the Meeting took their misbehavior seriously.

Thomas French was such an offender. Burlington Meeting kept after him continually from 1682 to 1695 for his "hasty words," his "abrupt and rude behavior in ye Monthly Meeting," his "rebellious spirit" (which greatly displeased Friends), his "slandering and very grossly abusing" another member of the Meeting, his "behaviour in Court contrary to Truth," and his "haste and passion."[4]

Reputation did not exempt an individual from the surveillance and control of the group, and neither did community standing nor even high public position. Daniel Leeds, one of the Meeting's earliest settlers, was Burlington's almanac writer, the provincial surveyor, and a justice in the Burlington court. The Meeting reprimanded him twice for un-Friendly use of language and also reproved him for his public criticism of conduct in the Men's Meeting. Prodded by the Meeting, Leeds condemned his own misbehavior publicly, apologizing for using words that offended Friends and for publishing material that was "too light and airy for one that is a Christian." He also submitted his writing to censorship. In order to assure itself that Leeds would change his behavior, the Meeting decreed that two Friends "speak with Daniell Leeds yt he lett ye Meeting have ye perusal of any Book . . . he may Write before it go to the Press."[5] Though known to be outspoken, short-tempered, and protective of his privileges, Leeds still conformed to the demand of the group.

Even more revealing was the Meeting's extraction of a public confession of misbehavior from John Skene. Skene's appointment as deputy governor in 1687 did not save him from being summoned to "answer" his "outgoings" in 1688. And though he did not do so until 1690, Skene did ultimately make public apology to the Meeting for having shot his servant in the legs, declaring his sorrow "for having done anything yt might have given offense and notwithstanding yt my Provocation was Great yet upon more deliberate consideration do wish I had forborn ye Shooting of ye Gun in ye case."[6]

Another sign of the Meeting's power is evident in the contrite language offered in such confessions. One Friend who had married a non-Quaker called herself a "miserable sinner" and said she hoped "that through repentance and a humble heart God will forgive me that wicked sin I have committed."[7] Another couple who had dared to marry with a provincial license, instead of in the Quaker fashion, described that misdeed as "ye greatest exercise yt ever came to us that wee should bring a blot and scandall upon God's truth."[8] A bulwark of the Meeting who had breached a contract with his servant acknowledged: "My soul hath been weighed for ye time and ye hour that I might feal deliverance from ye unclean spirit which subtilly led my soul into trancegression . . . for which my soul hath been sorrowful and gon bowed down many an hour."[9] A Friend wrote of her "suffering condition" at having been accused of marital infidelity,[10] and another claimed to feel "much Broakeness of heart" since she had "brought dishonour to God and Greeved his people."[11] After repenting of a wrong, the miscreant Quaker usually indicated to the Meeting that he "received Friends love" and stated his willingness to do as the Meeting wished.

Members of the Meeting could escape its discipline only by changing their behavior in time. Those who gave up their provocation before the Meeting intervened were not required to write self-deprecating letters.

Either implicitly, by alteration of his misbehavior, or explicitly, by making effusive apology, the wrongdoer recognized the group's right to control his conduct and cooperated in his own constraint. And even when men and women of the Meeting did no wrong, they acknowledged the right of Friends to monitor their day-to-day behavior, as was typical of closely joined traditional communities. Though there was no formal appointment of overseers in this first period, the model of Friends spying on each other to keep members' behavior in check was well established informally.[12]

From the time the Meeting was settled to 1694, a total of twenty-nine men and ten women were disciplined by it. Of the disciplinary actions initiated during the Meeting's first forty-two years, the period of this study, 18 percent were initiated during this sixteen-year period, at a rate of two or three a year.[13] In conjunction with the quality of the confessions, and the consistency with which they were secured, this relatively modest level of disciplinary action is an indication that during this initial period the membership acknowledged the group's power. Since the Meeting was willing and able to chastise even the influential nonconformist, most members avoided castigation by controlling their behavior, thus preventing the calling of attention to themselves. In the 1680s and early 1690s, there were no alternative social structures to those of the Meeting and, therefore, no avoidance of its behavioral norms. Conformity was readily obtained.[14]

The Burlington Monthly Meeting's disciplinary actions focused around five behavioral concerns: familial and sexual behavior; disorderly behavior; relationship to the Meeting and its discipline; aggressive behavior; and doctrinal differences.[15]

Both men and women were concerned about the reputation of Friends. Since Friends set the behavioral standards for the community at large, the Meeting could not afford to allow its members to misbehave in public. The Men's Meeting, which included the most prominent standard-setters in its membership, was particularly concerned about public misbehavior. Nearly three-fourths of its disciplinary actions in the first period (twenty-one of twenty-nine cases) involved offenses in the family, disorderly behavior, or aggression codes. For women, public misbehavior meant violation of the Meeting's familial and sexual mores.[16] Overwhelmingly, offenders were disciplined for acts easily noticed by the community at large: bastardy, marriage by a magistrate, drunkenness, unauthorized publications, or other intemperate behavior.

The Men's Meeting had another major concern: relationships within the Meeting.[17] Here, the issue was ostensibly compliance

121

with and acknowledgement of the Meeting's power. But because the Meeting was so powerful, and its power so widely acknowledged, compliance was not the real issue. Only one person was disciplined for failure to comply with a Meeting directive in this first period.[18] The real issue inside the group during this first period appears to have been maintenance of intragroup peace and love. Cohesion or solidarity is necessary to the continuation of power. Internal disputes lead to subgroup formation, shifting alliances, questioning of established norms, and fragmentation of power. When the cohesiveness of a group deteriorates, challenges to its authority are the logical outcome. It is not surprising, therefore, that the real concerns of the Burlington Meeting during this first period were the management of public misbehavior and the maintenance of intramural peace.

The years from 1695 to 1709 were dramatically different for Burlington Friends. Though there had been certain signals of incipient challenge in the first period, the Meeting was strong enough to disdain, ignore, and override them. However, these matters laid the groundwork for trouble in the second period, when the power of the Meeting in the early years could no longer be sustained.

One of the reasons for acknowledgment of the Meeting's power in the first period was, as we have seen, Burlington's peculiar situation as a virtually homogeneous Quaker world. But Quaker isolation and dominion were short-lived. Greater numbers of non-Quakers soon settled in the province, diversifying the religious composition of the population.[19] The West Jersey proprietors' right to rule was disputed. A non-Quaker, Dr. Daniel Coxe, became the chief proprietor and governor of West Jersey in 1687, and all the governors who followed after him were non-Quakers as well. One, Jeremiah Basse, a former Anabaptist preacher, was a virulent anti-Quaker during whose tenure Friends were pushed out of the judiciary in 1698 and 1699. With the court as well as the executive taking on a distinctly anti-Quaker cast, crucial civil functions were detached from Quaker leadership.[20]

Inside the Society of Friends, a major controversy began in 1691 when George Keith and his followers broke from the Philadelphia Yearly Meeting, ostensibly over questions of ministerial authority, hierarchy, and the democratization of the Meeting for business. The Burlington Monthly Meeting Minutes record no involvement of local figures in the controversy at the outset, but after 1695 the dispute did reach Burlington and cause dissension there.

The growing non-Quaker population in the province, the decline of Quaker civic leadership in Burlington, and the religious discord within the Meeting made the challenges of the second period possible.

In the first period, a disobedient Friend was forced to accede to the Meeting because there were no alternative social structures. If he wanted high status or power in the Burlington community, conformity was the price. But as the demographic shifts, changing leadership structure, and emerging religious options gathered force in the second period, they offered Burlingtonians opportunities they had not had before. Now the world outside the Meeting seemed more attractive to some. Indeed, the non-Quaker world offered possibilities of status and power too. The rising anti-Quaker faction was happy to engage the Quakers in a struggle for provincial control, thus offering dissatisfied Friends an alternative path to status and power that did not require them to capitulate to standards of behavior they did not share with the Meeting. Perhaps even more important, life outside the Meeting afforded possibilities of a life of one's own according to other values than those of the Meeting, even if the person never achieved high status or power. The attraction of the outside world was relatively greater individual freedom. Burlingtonians embraced the new opportunity, and as they did they challenged the hegemony of the Meeting. They forced the Meeting to react as it had not had to do earlier.

The Keithian controversy was one of the first events that obliged the Meeting to address the issue of membership under these altered conditions. For in the Keithian controversy the Meeting was not in charge. The individual member elected to withdraw; the Meeting did not decide to expel him.

Daniel Leeds, the writer, became one of Burlington's most prominent Keithians. He was especially concerned with the issue of ministerial authority, having been its victim on several occasions. Leeds wrote pamphlets to support the Keithian cause. This controversy gave him a forum to attack the Meeting. His attacks on Samuel Jenings, a former West Jersey governor and speaker of the Assembly and probably Burlington Meeting's most powerful member, pleased the anti-Quakers in the community.[21] Leeds eventually became the spokesman for almost every anti-Quaker cause and,

123

with the opportunity presented by the Keithian controversy, a spokesman for individualism as well. He wrote:

> So I also find, the Good Things are Good things within or without the Pale, that matters not; for Scripture and Church History shews, that many times Single Persons have been in the right, when gathered Churches and Congregations have been wrong; Examples of this we have in all ages.[22]

The Meeting called Leeds an "evil Malicious Instrument,"[23] but it did not disown him. Leeds withdrew, renouncing Friends' practice, as when, in the Court of Common Pleas on May 8th, 1700, "being called to his Attestation," he "refused that and was willing and desired to have the Oath administered to him according to the Law of England which was done accordingly by order of Joshua Newbold."[24]

Leeds had a special role among the separatists in Burlington. He had ambivalent attachments to Quakerism, but to get the status and freedom he wanted, he had to withdraw from the group. Merton claims that if a member of a group has not developed a full affective attachment to the group, then if he becomes an ex-member, he may look at his former friends as a negative reference group toward which he will be dependently hostile rather than merely indifferent. Parsons says that such individuals suffer a "compulsive alienation," rigidly rejecting the norms of the repudiated group.[25] Leeds became Burlington Meeting's most articulate, hostile ex-member.

Leeds and others had shown that it was possible to challenge the authority of the Meeting and not only survive but prosper. They provided role models for defiance. How to respond was now the Meeting's problem. Would members withdraw if the Meeting acted authoritatively? Could the group prevent membership losses? Was there a way to maintain authority and, at the same time, retain members?

At the end of the seventeenth century, the original ruling structures of the province of West Jersey disintegrated. Even as the proprietors' right to govern continued at issue, the opposition to their prerogatives was reinforced by internal discord verging on anarchy, reflecting the inability of the proprietary government to maintain order.[26] East Jersey proprietors faced similar problems. The unrest in both Jerseys coincided with changes in colonial policy, when the crown decided to bring all of New Jersey into the royal colonial system. The creation of the Board of Trade in 1696 helped extend the crown's authority.

Dreams of Quaker rule in West Jersey ended when the proprietors of both East and West Jersey surrendered their pretensions to the right to govern. In 1702 they yielded to Queen Anne the power to "correct, punish, pardon, govern and rule" the inhabitants of East and West New Jersey and the right to "nominate, constitute or appoint, revoke, discharge, change, or alter any governor or governors, officers, or ministers."[27]

In exchange for their giving up the government to her, Queen Anne promised Friends that they could practice their religion in peace and that their faith and its practices, such as affirmations instead of oaths, would not bar them from full participation in the public service, the courts, or the government.[28] But in spite of these guarantees, the first royal governor, Edward Lord Cornbury, the Queen's cousin, disregarded her instructions and persecuted Quakers. When Cornbury got to New Jersey, he immediately joined the anti-Quaker faction in the colony. He tried to disenfranchise the Quakers and nullify their power. He prohibited the seating of Quaker members of the Assembly, insisted on oaths rather than affirmations, and demanded that Friends support the military, contrary to Quaker conviction. He removed Quakers from the judiciary.[29]

As the proliferation of groups continued, new associations were formed. The Keithians allied themselves politically and socially with the rising anti-Quaker faction. At the end of the century, George Keith had joined the growing Anglican population in Burlington. He became a missionary for the Society for the Propagation of the Gospel, an Anglican group, and worked to establish an Anglican church in Burlington, recruiting Friends as members. Many Keithian defectors from the Meeting did indeed become Anglicans.

St. Mary's Church was established in Burlington in 1703, with the Reverend John Talbott as its rector. The parish register lists many names which previously appeared in the Burlington Monthly Meeting Minutes—Leeds, Budd, Woolstone, Peache, and Silver, to list just a few.[30]

In the first period (1680–1694), discipline was meted out only once for failure to comply with a Meeting directive.[31] By comparison, during the first five years of the second period (1695–1699), 58 percent of the disciplinary actions initiated by the Meeting were against individuals who had disregarded the Meeting's authority.

Half of these authority-challenging actions involved individuals who had failed to comply with the Meeting's directives. The Monthly Meetings for both men and women initiated thirty-one disciplinary actions between 1696 and 1699, nine of which were for failure to comply with a Meeting directive,[32] five for doctrinal disputes, three (all involving women) for flouting the Meeting's authority, and one for failure to give adequate satisfaction as defined by the Meeting. Rebellion was evidently in the air. In the late 1680s, even Daniel Leeds, the combative Thomas French, and Deputy Governor Skene complied with the Meeting's demands. In this second period, it was not just the eccentric individual who refused to do the Meeting's bidding. Challenges came from many places in many ways.

Young people refused to accept the Meeting's counsel about marriage. Young women defiantly married Keithian husbands against the advice of the Meeting. The Women's Meeting tried to routinize the advising process but had only partial success.[33] One young woman, after being visited, said that "she took kindly friends care of her," and agreed to follow the Meeting's advice; but a second disciplinary committee reported that it "found nothing but that she would proceed in her marriage."[34] Other disciplinary committees also came back "disatisfied" from visiting young women. The Women's Meeting was told that its "advice came too late" or that the Friend visited "had nothing in her mind to take their advice."[35] Even Ann Jenings, Samuel's wife, was unable to persuade such persons to heed the Meeting's counsel. Increasingly, young women unwilling to be bound by the Meeting's decisions about suitable husbands told the group that their marriage was not the group's concern.

Other misdoers also told the Meeting that their behavior in the community was beyond the sphere of Quaker control. When the proprietary disintegrated and unrest swept West Jersey in 1701, John Woolstone, an active member of Burlington Meeting, was indicted as a leader of a riot in Burlington.[36] Other Friends participated in the rioting, too, breaking down the prison door, releasing political prisoners, and demanding that the governor deal personally with their grievances.[37] The Meeting vehemently protested this disorderly behavior. It activated disciplinary committees and demanded satisfaction. The Yearly Meeting also issued strong injunctions against this violent, antigovernment behavior.[38] Yet individuals maintained that their participation in the riot was not the

Meeting's business. One of the rioters declared "yt ye Meeting in his opinion hath nothing to do with it."[39]

The "prison dore riot" in 1701 was concerted action in defiance of Quaker precepts in the public sphere. In 1702, a group of Friends acted together to thwart the authority of the Meeting in the domestic arena. Thirteen young women and men of the Meeting, as well as the bride's mother, who was a Women's Meeting overseer, "were aiding and assisting to Tho Branson in ye night seson in ye stealling of John Days daughter and clandestinely marrying her unknown to ye said John Day her father."[40] By 1703, the Meeting was being challenged by both individuals and groups. Though it tried to prevent unruly behavior, its attempts at authoritative control were thwarted because its power was no longer acknowledged unequivocally by the entire membership.

The increasingly heterogeneous character of the community also affected Quakers as they continued to participate in the affairs of the colony. The paradoxical result of such pluralism was to bolster the authority of the Meeting in the short run. One of the first concerns of the royal government was the establishment of a militia. Quakers were unable to prevent passage of "an Act for Settling the Militia of this Province" in 1704, but they added several important items to it. The act required all males between sixteen and sixty years of age to sign up for service in the militia and made failure to serve punishable by fine. However, Quakers had enough power to gain a concession

> For the Ease and Benefit of the People called *Quakers*, that if any Person shall produce unto the Capt. of the Companys, within whose District the said Person shall inhabit, a Certificate under the hands of six or more Members of the Monthly or Quarterly Meetings of the People called *Quakers*, within the County where such Persons do inhabit, testifying that such Person producing the same, is and was at the time of passing this Act one of the People called *Quakers*, that from thence forth until such Certificate be retracted, such Persons shall not be lyable to the Penalty for not listing.[41]

Quakers were not let off military service entirely. They had to pay a twenty-shilling penalty for not appearing and doing service and a twenty-shilling tax to support the militia, under threat of seizure and sale of their chattels and goods.[42] But the privilege accorded to Quakers was significant for the control it gave to the Meeting over membership. Individuals wishing to claim membership to get exemption from military service had to have the Meeting affirm that they were members. Before granting such certification, the Meeting required individuals to submit to its authority.

Appointing committees to inquire into the "behavior and conversation" of any who wanted a certificate for the captain of the militia, the Monthly Meeting could count a man's every misdemeanor adversely if he wanted a certificate. Understandably, under the circumstances, it paid particular attention to offenses involving violence or the threat of violence. Ten men condemned themselves before the group for carrying arms, and another three apologized for fighting and hasty words. But the Meeting went beyond insistence on condemnations for serious misdoing such as violent behavior. It used the Militia Act as an excuse to require self-condemnation for petty misconduct such as "playing chuckfarthing or shuffleboard."[43]

Nonetheless, even the lure of exemption from military service was insufficient to secure ready compliance from all Friends. In the disorderly milieu of the second period, some Friends became less ready to yield to the Meeting's sense of their behavior. Instead of expressing sorrow or a sense of sinfulness, some accused members were more defiant or belligerent than contrite. One Friend wrote, "As for any thing yt I am guilty of I am willing to condemn & take more care, but to condemn that I am not guilty of I am not willing to it."[44]

As a result of the Militia Act, condemnations were written by 19 individuals who produced twenty-two separate letters.[45] All those who condemned their misbehavior were acknowledged as members by the Meeting. At the end of this long investigatory process, the Meeting had a list of 150 men who "for conscience sake . . . could not bear nor use arms to ye destruction of ye lives of men."[46]

In effect, the Militia Act generated a new agreement between the Meeting, its members, and the community at large. Individuals agreed to submit to enquiry into their behavior and judgment of it by the Meeting. The Meeting protected its members by attesting to their good behavior. And even as it did so, it acknowledged that it was no longer the *only* salient group in the community. Instead, it had become a mediating social structure between the individual and a larger, increasingly pluralistic society.

With the passage of the Militia Act, Quaker concern for the public reputation of the group became even more acute, since the Meeting saw itself as responsible for the public behavior of members. Faithful Friends were offended by a particularly unsavory and public altercation in 1705, which shows the heightened sensitivity of both the Meeting and the members to this issue. Christopher Wetherill, a leading Friend, sought permission to marry for the third time. By so doing, he precipitated a violent reaction from his son Thomas, who was also a well-known and highly regarded Friend. Thomas strongly demonstrated his displeasure with his father's proposed match.[47]

These proceedings, and the "scandalous reports" they generated, were investigated by a Monthly Meeting committee, which found

> that the said Thomas Wetherill hath been very abusive to them both but especially to ye said Mary Whitten [his father's intended wife], violently Thrusting her out of the house of Thomas Scattergood in doing of which she received some hurt on her head *And that which makes the abuse of her & ye scandal to Truth ye Greater was that it was don openly in ye faire time in the yew of many people and not content there with did afterwards in the open street rail and revile her in such terms as modesty forbids to mention* Wee therefore hereby declare it to be our sense and judgement that he ought to condemn his irreverant and unduafull behaviour to his father and abuses to ye young woman in such a manner as ye Meeting shall think fit.[48]

Since the prime actors in this event were both well known, weighty Friends, the group was doubly shamed over their having come to public blows.

Though Thomas Wetherill apologized profusely, saying,

> *I am hartyly sorry that I should be ye occasion of bringing so much trouble and exercise to friends by my unseamly and unsavory words and actions which hath brought such reproach and scandall upon ye profession which I make* Especially in that unseamly action of turning Mary Whitten out of Thomas Scattergood House *in so violent a manner* and also giving the occasion of provoking my father at such a *public time as the fair* which I am truly sensable was very ill for which I am very sorry and do utterly condemn all unseemly actions and do desire to be forgiven by my father and Mary Whitten and all persons whom I have . . . otherwise abused,[49]

and though more problems were to come in the Wetherill family dispute, the greatest damage to Burlington Friends had already been done. The mechanisms designed to keep peace, resolve disputes, make equitable property settlements, and keep the Meeting's business private had all failed. The consequence of those failures was greater sensitivity to public shame on the part of the Meeting. Concern grew with the appearance of behavior to the non-Quaker world rather than with the behavior itself.

The Meeting had reason to be concerned about its reputation. The ever-hostile Daniel Leeds, whose behavior the Meeting had monitored, now monitored the Meeting's behavior. He had access to information about the Meeting's internal affairs, and he published what he obtained.[50] As Quaker transgressions were publicized by the group's own members and by hostile outsiders, the Meeting must have wished for some privacy and the opportunity to close ranks. But diversity precluded such privacy.

Diversity brought another problem to the Meeting as well. It invited attrition of members, especially young members, to St. Mary's Church. In 1706, for example, five young men "acknowledging ymselves to be of our profession and having received a certificate accordingly . . . have of late been to hear ye priest . . . which is great dissatisfaction to this Meeting."[51] Upbraided about it, "ye young men appeared and acknowledged their weakness in it and declared yt it were not through any dissatisfaction that thay had to friends But from an unadvised curiousity and hoped thay should do so no more AND friends beleaving what thay said was true were tender to them AND advised them to be more cautious in the futur."[52] To survive, the Meeting had to permit members to assess the Meeting as well as require them to submit to the Meeting's discipline. Eventually, some young people went to St. Mary's because of "unadvised curiosity" and got "sprinkeled according to ye form of ye Church of England."[53]

Diversity drove individuals and the group alike to new strategies. Individuals challenged the Meeting as they never had before. The Meeting responded, first, by increasing the number of disciplinary actions it initiated. Two-thirds of all discipline initiated in the Meeting's first forty-two years was initiated in the second period, 1695–1709. Only 39 disciplinary actions had been begun in the first period, while 145 were undertaken in the second. The Women's Meeting and the Men's Meeting showed similar increases, reflecting their common recourse to discipline to contain the Meeting's sense of chaos.[54]

Another result of diversity was the pressure on the Meeting from the world that it manage its members' behavior successfully. Forty of 145, or 28 percent, of the disciplinary actions initiated in the second period were clear responses to outside pressure from such sources as the Militia Act or Leeds's publications. In fact, these outside pressures, and the sheer volume of disciplinary business they created, were one force pushing the Meeting to extend its dealings with offenders. The many requests for Militia Act certificates led to appointment of an investigating committee for each preparative meeting (local worship group) within the monthly meeting structure.[55] A similar procedure was used when the Monthly Meeting ordered "yt there should be friends appointed out of each perticuler Meeting belonging to this Meeting to speak to every friend belonging to their respective Meeting for to bring in an account . . . of ye goods strained from them for their refusing to pay to ye upholding of ye Militia."[56] Similarly, in response to the greater opportunity to marry out created by the Keithian schism and a growing non-Quaker population, the Women's Meeting "agreed that inquiry be made at every monthly Meeting concerning irregular proceedings in marriage."[57]

At the same time, the Meeting tried to make membership more attractive to individuals by being more "tender," as in the instance of the young people visiting St. Mary's, and by giving individuals repeated opportunities to make amends for wrongdoing.[58]

The Meeting's new patience combined with individuals' resistance to produce disciplinary actions that dragged on and on. Peter Fretwell, William Gabitas, Samuel Gibson, and the Hollingshead brothers took years to come to terms with the Meeting and its requirements.[59] And though these were unusual episodes, ordinary disciplinary cases also took considerably longer to settle in the second period than in the first. From 1680 to 1694, all disciplinary actions but six were settled in three months or less. Of those six, four cases took from four to six months, and the other two took one year and one and one-half years. From 1695 to 1709, routine cases required six to twelve months, and, as indicated above, there were several instances of disciplinary efforts extending for more than two years. Foot-dragging is a good example of the result of the interaction between an individual's perception of a milieu that opened the door to challenges and a group's need to survive.

Individuals also took advantage of this new milieu to express outright defiance. Women in particular simply refused to do what the Meeting asked.[60] And, as shown by the "prison dore" riot, the

Wetherill family dispute, and other events, some Friends actively created disorder or scandal in the community at large.[61] Though some Friends were sincerely contrite for transgressions, the Meeting seemed, on the whole, to be trying and failing to maintain control.

By the end of the second period, there were signs of a new accommodation between the group's authority and the individual's freedom. Certainly individuals were less willing to conform and comply, but membership in the Meeting was still attractive to some. Individuals who hoped to retain Meeting membership had to be prepared to condemn their misdeeds, no matter how minor or ancient, if they wanted anything from the Meeting. For example, in his attempt to gain a Militia Act certificate, Charles Woolverton was made to condemn his denials of Quakerism quite abjectly. Not only that, the following month he was told "that this Meeting expects yt he should condemn his carriage in being present at ye pretended Marriage of Tho Branson & John Day's daughter & also his contribution to ye same."[62] That marriage had occurred nearly two years before. Other Friends were refused permission to marry, removal certificates, or traveling minutes until they "satisfied" the Meeting for their follies.[63]

The period from 1695 to 1709 was a time of crisis for Burlington Friends. They were reduced to ineffective grumbling inside the Meeting and became significantly less powerful outside it. Whatever success other West Jersey Friends Meetings may have had in maintaining discipline during these chaotic years it seems clear that, though the Burlington Meeting was expending considerable effort in trying to regulate behavior and maintain discipline, the effort produced mixed results at best. A considerable extent of individual independence emerged anyway.

Such independence appeared as Burlington Friends attempted to adapt to their loss of power in the proprietary, the growth of a hostile non-Quaker population, the divisiveness of the Keithian schism, the presence of hostile ex-members in the community serving as role-models for rebellious youth, the coming of age of a native-born generation, the development of new opportunity structures for economic and social success, the emergence of other churches, the surrender of the province to the crown, the rise to power of an antagonistic governor, the removal of Quakers from the courts, and the shift of power in the Delaware Valley from Burlington to Philadelphia.

That the Meeting managed to survive these simultaneous stresses and pressures indicates that it adjusted to fragmentation, diversity, and the challenge of rising individualism. The milieu gave members the courage to make challenges. Each successful challenge forced further accommodation and change. The group strategies that emerged during this second period enabled the Meeting to maintain a measure of influence while individuals became more free.

In changing and unsettled times, groups use many strategies simultaneously. Social change does not happen linearly with a single cause producing the new circumstance. Neither do groups change their patterns of interaction singlemindedly. The unsettledness in the wider community is reflected in the search for a new balance within the group, as it reacts to bubbling from within and pressures from without. There is a time of multiple and almost conflicting responses. The group that is haughty and demanding one moment is nurturing and tender the next. The defiant individual thinks better of it and apologizes profusely for the defiance. The hostile, rejecting, competing community become accommodating and finds ways to use the group's skill and expertise in its ongoing life. The interacting reciprocities between the individual, the small group, and the community at large create new social stuctures out of the disorderly milieu.

The third period, 1710–1719, was inaugurated with major changes in the leadership of both the colony and the Meeting. In New Jersey, Governor Cornbury was recalled in 1708 by Queen Anne, when at last she concluded that she "should not Protect him in Oppressing her Subjects," and Cornbury's replacement died in 1709. The following year Robert Hunter was appointed governor, and order began to return to New Jersey. During Hunter's tenure, Quaker participation in the affairs of government was welcomed. His support of the Quakers blocked strong Anglican attempts to disenfranchise them.[64] The Burlington Meeting had more time for concerns other than fighting with its enemies.

Within the Meeting, important changes took place as well. After the death of Samuel Jenings in 1708, his power was diffused throughout a larger and changing leadership group. There were requests that the Meeting appoint new overseers because the old ones were "removed out of this town," "aged & not so capable," "antient," or dead.[65] The membership of the Meeting changed as families returned to England or relocated in Pennsylvania and other parts of New Jersey, and as new families arrived and settled within the bounds of the Burlington Monthly Meeting.[66] New residents moved quickly into leadership roles as individuals with established status in the wider Quaker world came into the Burlington community.[67] Some members of the community entered the Meeting by "convincement," sometimes in order to marry a Meeting member.[68] During this period, the Meeting's official membership was vague and unsettled. Even important members who carried frequent Meeting responsibilities might not know everyone who was deemed a member of the Meeting.[69] With the change in leaders, the rise of a native-born generation, immigration, exodus, convincement, and uncertainty about the membership of nonparticipant children of active Friends, Burlington Meeting had a substantially different membership than it had in the second period of this study.

The challenges of the second period, both from inside the Meeting and from the community at large, had disorganized the Meeting's response to infractions of discipline. When the homeostasis of the first period was disrupted by the chaos of the second, the Meeting could only try to reestablish a balance. The third period was the period of reorganization.

The reorganization was characterized, in part, by a shift in power relations between individual members and the corporate structure. Conditions were placed on the Meeting's power and the acknowledgment of it by members. The definition of rights, responsibilities, and authority of both individuals and the group was increasingly formalized.

One reaction to the disorganizing force of the Keithian controversy and other challenges of the second period was a codification in writing of the *Discipline* of the Society of Friends. The *Discipline* specified acceptable and unacceptable behavior. It delineated procedures to deal with offenders, who were given the right to appeal decisions made by local meetings. It defined levels of meetings—monthly, quarterly, yearly—and outlined the role of each hierarchical level. The *Discipline* also spelled out the specific duties of offices to be held by meeting members. Altogether, this process of formalization enabled the Meeting to control individuals, but it also placed conditions on the power of the group.[70]

The starting place for discipline—for the management of members' behavior—was the monthly meeting. With formalization, the way in which disciplinary actions were initiated underwent important changes. In the first period, 1680–94, the meeting appointed particular Friends to monitor specific behavior problems as such oversight seemed needed. In this third period, the surveillance of members' behavior was institutionalized in the office of the overseer. Overseers were appointed to "take care to instruct, advise and admonish the Friends that walk disorderly amongst us."[71] The overseers' task was a difficult one. They were instructed to protect the meeting's reputation and the miscreant's soul simultaneously. They were told to deal with those "that raise scandall more publickly to others not of our communion," but they were also warned

> that in speaking or dealing with any it be done in a Christian Spirit of love and tenderness, labouring in meekness, by laying the evil before them, to bring such persons to a sence of it in themselves, that they may be restored if possible—And altho such as transgress, or loose their hold of Truth, are apt to oppose or be Testy while they are in that condition, yet wee ought patiently, and Meekly to Instruct and advise them—So that we may not only have a Testimony of peece in ourselves, but that it may also, so affect the spirit of ye Friend spoke to as that he may be sencible we have performed a truly Christian Duty and an office of Brotherly Love towards him.[72]

But neither the local meeting nor its overseers had final authority without the acquiescence of the disciplined member. An individual who was not reconciled to the judgment of the monthly meeting and the perceptions of its overseers had the right, spelled out in the *Discipline*, to appeal its decision to quarterly and, ultimately, yearly meetings. Even in the absence of dispute, overseers of men's and women's monthly meetings alike were required to report on their success in the maintenance of good order to the loftier levels within the hierarchy. Overseers from each preparative meeting would report to monthly, quarterly, and yearly meetings on the behavior of their charges.[73]

Just as the institution of overseers substituted highly structured and official controls for the informal constraints of the traditional community that had prevailed in the first years of settlement, so the institution of meeting-initiated family visiting represented another transformation of informal ways of dealing with people into official interventions with prescribed procedures. In 1710, the Philadelphia Yearly Meeting directed that Substantial Friends be appointed to visit every Family amongst us, where they think there is occasion to suspect they are going backward in their worldly estate & to enquire & see how things are with them, & if they will not take the advice of Friends, then to give them Gospel Order, & proceed Therein against them.[74]

Though the Burlington Monthly Meeting was never fond of the strategy of family visiting, it was repeatedly required to account to the Yearly Meeting for its failure to institute the practice with vigor.

An important result of such proliferation and specialization of disciplinary duties was that the control of members' behavior shifted from the mutual concern of all members for each other—an expression of friendly care—to the task of a few officially designated social controllers who had clear jurisdiction, authority, and responsibility. The *Discipline* did not excuse the membership as a whole from admonishing the disorderly, but it directed "that [though] the same may not be overlooked or neglected it ought to be more particularly the business and service of the Overseers."[75] Though a solicitous Friend could bring a concern to the meeting about another member's behavior, disciplinary issues were generally brought to the meeting by the overseers.[76]

In such ways as prescribing tasks for monthly meetings, delineating the role of overseers, and weighting behavioral monitoring in the direction of officials, the expansion of the sphere of hierarchy reduced the power of the individual and put more formal controls in the hands of the group. But this same formalism prescribed rights for individuals that helped keep the group's power under control.

The right of appeal was not the only thing that helped sweeten compliance for individual Friends. Other factors had changed which also encouraged conformity. In the first period Friends complied because it was expected, because most were traditional creatures in a traditional world, and because the social price of noncompliance was too high. In the second period individuals embraced new opportunities, and the Meeting adopted an experimental attitude toward disciplinary tactics. In the third period, members conceded the claims of the Meeting in a more instrumental and calculated manner. The Meeting was able to get deference from wrongdoers in instances where they wanted something from the Meeting. In a way, this was a continuation of the tendency that developed during the second period, when the Meeting required members desiring a certificate, permission to marry, or some other documentation of membership to confess first their past transgressions.

Joseph Haines was not given authorization to marry until he apologized for "some hasty words that past by."[77] Joshua Humphries was required to settle "ye difference [that] still remains between him and Nathaniel Cripps" before the meeting would give him permission to marry. His simple statement that he was "always redy to end" the dispute satisfied the Meeting enough that he and his betrothed were given "their liberty to solemnize their intentions when they shall see meete."[78] In order to get back in good standing with the Meeting, Joan Brown had to produce her certificate from England and to "condemn her disorderly practices since she came to these parts."[79] Susanna Marriot took care to "present to friends a writing wherein she condemns all such actions that she have had which have been a dishonour to Turth and a grief to Friends" two months before requesting permission to marry.[80] As in the second period, the individual member had the initiative and could decide to comply with the Meeting's requirements or take his membership elsewhere.

The person who wanted to marry under the care of the Meeting had to clear up disciplinary questions in advance of the wedding. But young people could marry whomever they pleased without consulting the Meeting and retain their membership in the Meeting by purely *pro forma* apology unless they had irritated the Meeting in some other way. Elinor Cutler, Mary Naylor, Sarah Rowland, Martha Dickson, and Jane Green were all reproved for marrying contrary to discipline and were all retained in membership when they condemned their wrongs.[81] John Wetherill was similarly chastised in the Men's Meeting and continued in fellowship when he condemned his behavior in the next Monthly Meeting.[82] Daniel Leete alone declined to provide the Meeting the perfunctory apology it required, and even he was treated with extended circumspection. Leete first claimed sickness, then refused to appear, then promised to write his condemnation for the next Meeting, and then failed to show up once more. When he did finally appear with a condemnation, the Meeting found that "his paper . . . did not give satisfaction." But a month later he "brought in a paper the second time in order to condemn his outgoings in taking a wife contrary to ye good order & discipline, established amongst us, which was red & accepted."[83] When Leete married a second time, he again married contrary to discipline and again was asked to condemn his misbehavior.[84] The overseers asked for and obtained extra time for him to make a satisfactory condemnation, but in 1720 found that "he still refuseth and rather justifies himself in his outgoings." As a result of his recalcitrance, the Meeting finally "disowned him to be of our Society of Church fellowship with us until he do make satisfaction for his outgoings."[85] As in the second period, marriage was one of the key barometers of individualism and the group's response to challenge.

Leete's foot-dragging response to the Meeting's attempt to discipline him was a technique typical of the third period. Individuals whose conduct displeased the Meeting increasingly responded to its discipline with passive resistance, a strategy well chosen to frustrate its victims. The Meeting would note its dissatisfaction with a member's "dallying with them so long," or lament that a Friend "still neglects to observe the order of this Meeting though tenderly and carefully advised thereto,"[86] and threaten or actually carry out disownment proceedings.

Disownment was potentially one of the few controls left to the Meeting, but disownment was rarely used. In the period from 1695 to 1709, individuals withdrew to enjoy newly developing social opportunities; the Meeting did not often expel them. Before 1710 there were only two disownments.[87] And in the third period, there were but three additional expulsions.[88] In every instance, disownment, or the threat of it, was only imposed until the individual was willing to "satisfy" the Meeting.

The individual's willingness to satisfy the Meeting was an important issue in this third period. As in the first period, surveillance and informal discussion with the misbehaving person may have been a more effective means of control over the member's behavior in this third period than the threat of disownment. Good behavior was not entirely obtained by the individual's free choice of conformity. Surveillance and the process of oversight used the persuasion of the face-to-face relationship along with the threat of institutional controls.

At the same time, a new formalism particularized offenses and disciplinary enforcement, reducing the role of whim, personal animosity, or an ever-changing definition of what constituted a disciplinary infraction.

Together this augmentation of personal choice and this proliferation of formal offices and structures worked to reduce the incidence of discipline in the third period. The Meeting appears to have been aware of its inability to sustain its controls except over individuals volunteering for discipline in order to escape conscription or to gain some other positive advantage. Its very sensitivity to the volitional aspect of membership further reduced its recourse to discipline. The Meeting's power was conditionally acknowledged, with individuals deciding where and under what circumstances they would submit themselves to group controls.

In the third period, then, the rate of discipline returned to that of the first period, when the Meeting's power was fully acknowledged. Only 14 percent of all the disciplinary actions initiated in Burlington's first forty-two years were initiated during the years from 1710 to 1719. In the Meeting's first forty-two years, it initiated 215 disciplinary actions. Discipline was initiated most frequently during the second period, 1695 to 1709. Sixty-seven percent of all persons disciplined during the period of this study were disciplined during the time of challenged power, at a rate more than three times that of the third period (see Table 5-1).

There was another important change in disciplinary patterns in the third period, in the ratio of actions initiated by the Women's Meeting to those begun by the Men's Meeting. From 1678 until 1709, the Men's Meeting inaugurated three disciplinary cases for every one started by the Women's Meeting. After 1709, the women's meeting assumed substantially more authority. In the period of conditionally acknowledged power, three men were disciplined for every two women (see Table 5-2).

The dawning of diversity not only gave women more power over discipline but also broadened the scope of their authority. In the earliest years, 90 percent of the disciplinary work of the Women's Meeting focused on family issues. In the second and third periods, domestic offenses accounted for only 64 percent and then 58 percent of Women's Meeting discipline, with the other categories accounting for the rest. The result of heterogeneity and challenged hegemony in Burlington was a measure of relative freedom. With freedom came some control for women over important issues in their lives.

Table 5-1. Disciplinary Cases Initiated, by Period

1678–94		1695–1709		1710–19	
Number of cases	Cases/Year	Number of Cases	Cases/Year	Number of Cases	Cases/Year
39	2.4	145	10.4	31	3.1

Table 5-2. Disciplinary Cases Initiated, by Sex

	1678–1694		1695–1709		1710–1719	
	N	%	N	%	N	%
Men	29	74	106	73	19	61
Women	10	26	39	27	12	39

Friends had come to Burlington with hopes of founding a Quaker world, with Burlington Meeting at its center. In only 40 years, those hopes had proven false. Philadelphia had eclipsed its short-lived leadership among American Friends; Anglicans and others had constricted its political power; and its own unruly youth had successfully challenged its right to govern without their consent. The experience of such stress in the years from 1695 to 1709 made clear that the Meeting could not manage those who would not accede to its authority. Energy shifted from organizing the Meeting and caring for individuals to defending and protecting the Meeting's organization, somehow freeing or abandoning individuals to care for themselves. Burlington Friends had learned to live in the world.

NOTES

1. Samuel Smith, *The History of the Colony of Nova-Caesaria, or New Jersey; containing an Account of its First Settlement, Progressive Improvements, The Original and Present Constitution, And Other Events to the Year 1721, With Some Particulars Since; and a Short View of its present State* (Spartanburg, S.C., 1975), pp. 103–4, 111, 114.

2. For example, John Skene, deputy governor and justice, was prosecuted by one of his servants for breach of contract in the June, 1680, Quarter Sessions Court. Skene's five colleagues, all Friends, found for his servant and ordered Skene to honor the agreement. Skene threatened to appeal the decision, but the other justices "took noe notice of him" (H. Clay Reed and George J. Miller, eds., *The Burlington Court Book: A Record of Quaker Jurisprudence in West New Jersey, 1680–1709* [Washington, D.C., 1944], pp. 101–2 [hereafter cited as *Court Book*]).

3. Minutes, Burlington Monthly Meeting (Men) (hereafter cited as BMM), 6/1680.

4. BMM, 12/1682, 1/1683, 3–5/1683, 7/1692, 8/1693, 11/1693, 3–4/1695.

5. BMM, 11–12/1682, 1/1687–88.

6. BMM, 2/1690.

7. Minutes, Burlington Monthly Meeting (Women) (hereafter cited as BWM), 6/1686, 12/1686.

8. Noted in BMM, 10/1706, as "Read in Meeting," 9/1683.

9. Noted in BMM, 10/1706 as "given forth 5th 4th mo 1682."

10. BMM, 10/1706.

11. BMM, 10/1706.

12. The Minutes show frequent concern with tale-bearing, back-biting, and scandal-mongering. See A. D. J. Macfarlane, *Witchcraft in Tudor and Stuart England* (New

York and Evanston, 1970), for an intriguing study of the use of rumor in social control.

13. Instances were counted only when an action or inquiry was initiated, no matter how long it took to resolve the episode.

14. While there was no book of discipline in these early years, meetings created consensus around prescriptive documents such as Fox's *Advices*, and the Yearly Meeting itself used a consensual process to develop its own *Advices* to constituent monthly meetings. Most Meeting members were in apparent agreement with the Meeting's stated behavioral norms and standards.

15. Offenses coded in the *family* category included such behavior as keeping company with a non-Quaker, allowing a child to keep company with or marry a non-Friend, using a marriage procedure not approved by the Meeting, marrying too soon after being widowed, assisting at or attending a disorderly marriage, and sexual offenses such as fornication and bastardy. *Disorderly behavior* included those acts that brought the offending Quaker into the view of the larger society in a presumably shameful fashion. Coded in this category are all instances where the Meeting chastised an individual for "scandals" or "disorderly walking" without further specification. When court records or other documents gave more specific information, the best available information was used for coding. Also, offenses such as breaking a public law, failure to honor a contract with a non-Quaker, drunkenness, indebtedness, and gambling were coded in this category. *Relationship to the Meeting*, or discipline that focused on intragroup issues, included actions such as failure to attend Meeting, failure to follow the directives of the Meeting, failure to "answer" the Meeting, falsely accusing Friends of misbehavior, failure to resolve differences with other Meeting members, and unauthorized preaching. *Aggressive behavior* included a range of activities that were seen by the Meeting as violating the basic peace testimony, such as "hasty words," fighting, physical violence, carrying and/or using weapons, and rioting. Offenses coded as *doctrinal disorders* included such behaviors as joining with Keith, denying Quakerism, going to hear a priest, becoming a member of the Church of England, complying with the Military Act (1704) by paying fines for failure to serve, and failure to obey "hat honor."

16. Of the 29 men disciplined in the first period, nine were disciplined for family code offenses, 10 for disorderly behavior codes. One case, Robert Young, 1684, for "hasty words," coded aggression for this analysis, is grouped below with private offenses. Nine of the ten women were disciplined for family code offenses, and the remaining woman for unspecified disorderly behavior.

17. Twenty-four percent of men's discipline in the first period (seven of twenty-nine cases) was for Intrameeting relationships, in addition to the Young case cited in note 16.

18. BMM, Thomas French, 1683.

19. Unfortunately, there are no demographic sources for Burlington in this period, but local records such as the *Burlington Town Book* and the *Court Book* do name increasing numbers of non-Quaker inhabitants.

20. *Court Book*, pp. xxxiv, xxxv, xxxvi.

21. It was never a good idea to oppose Jenings in the Meeting. Disputes with him were nearly certain to induce at least an inquiry for disciplinary purposes.

22. Daniel Leeds, *News of a Trumpet Sounding in the Wilderness or the Quakers Antient Testimony Revived, Examined and Compared with itself, and also with their new Doctrine. Whereby the ignorant may learn Wisdom and the Wise advance in their Understandings.*

Collected with Diligence, and carefully cited from Their Antient and Later Writings, and Recommended to the Serious Reading and Consideration of all Enquiring Christians (New York, 1697), preface.

23. Abraham Heulings' disownment paper, BMM, 7/1698.

24. *Court Book*, p. 233. Other Keithians were similarly ignored by the Meeting, which instituted only two disownments for association with the Keithian cause. Abraham Heulings was disowned in 1698 for "shattering unity" and, more, for feeding Leeds material for his writings. Henry Burcham was disowned for disunity over Keith in 1700. See BMM, 6/1700, and William Wade Hinshaw, *Encyclopedia of American Quaker Genealogy* (Ann Arbor, 1938).

25. Robert K. Merton, *Social Theory and Social Structure*, enlarged ed. (New York, 1968), p. 349; Talcott Parsons, *The Social System* (New York, 1951), p. 254.

26. Richard P. McCormick, *New Jersey from Colony to State, 1609–1789* (New Brunswick, N.J., 1964), pp. 41, 49.

27. New Jersey Proprietors' Surrender to the Crown, quoted in Smith, *History of New Jersey*, p. 217.

28. Instructions from Queen Anne to Lord Cornbury, quoted in Smith, *History of New Jersey*, pp. 246–47.

29. McCormick, *From Colony to State*, pp. 64–65; *Court Book*, pp. liii–liv; John E. Pomfret, *Colonial New Jersey: A History* (New York, 1973), pp. 122–26.

30. St. Mary's Parish Register.

31. See page 122.

32. All coded Intrameeting.

33. In 10th month 1695, BWM "agreed that enquiry be made at every monthly meeting concerning irregular proceedings in marriage."

34. BWM, 12/1695; BWM, 7/1698.

35. BWM, 9/1700.

36. *Court Book*, pp. 252–53.

37. John E. Pomfret, *The Province of West Jersey, 1609–1702* (New York, 1976), pp. 207–9.

38. Minutes, Philadelphia Yearly Meeting (hereafter cited as PYM), 1701.

39. BMM, 4/1701.

40. All of these Friends were between the ages of 18 and 28, according to the birth and marriage records of the Meeting and Hinshaw (BMM, 1/1703).

41. *New Jersey Archives*, 3d ser., vol. 2, Bernard Bush, comp., *Laws of the Royal Colony of New Jersey 1703–1745* (Trenton, 1977), pp. 15–21.

42. Ibid.

43. BMM, 11/1704.

44. Thomas Atkinson's letter, BMM, 11/1704. Atkinson's name was not among those listed by the Meeting for the militia captain.

45. BMM, 11/1704.

46. BMM, 11/1704.

47. BMM, 5,6/1705. Thomas was joined in his displeasure by his sister Phoebe Scattergood and her husband Thomas Scattergood.

48. BMM, 7/1705 (my italics).

49. BMM, 8/1705 (my italics).

50. See, for example, Daniel Leeds, *The Mistery of Fox-Craft Discovered and the Plainness & Sincerity Demonstrated First in their great Apostle George Fox 2ndly In Their Late Suscribing the Oath or Act of Ajuration* (New York, 1705; reprinted Tarrytown,

N.Y., 1923), pp. 180–83, 166–67. See also BMM 4,5/1705, and letters of condemnation, BMM, 11/1704.

51. BMM, 7/1706.

52. BMM, 10/1706.

53. See, for example, BMM, 3–5/1709, and BWM, 10–12/1708.

54. Of the total number of disciplinary actions initiated by the Men's Meeting, 19 percent were initiated in the first period, in contrast to the second period where 69 percent of the disciplinary actions initiated by the Men's Meeting took place. Likewise in the Women's Meeting, 16 percent of all disciplinary actions were initiated in the first period, and 64 percent in the second.

55. BMM, 11/1704.

56. BMM, 3/1706.

57. BWM, 10/1695.

58. See, for example, the case of Abraham Heulings, BMM, 3/1698.

59. Peter Fretwell, BMM, 2/1700 to 4/1702; William Gabitas, BMM, 11/1697 to 2/1700; Samuel Gibson, BMM, 10/1696 to 3/1704, when the Meeting dropped the matter, and 1/1706 to 6/1709, shortly after which Gibson died; and the Hollingshead brothers, BMM, 8/1700 to 8/1704.

60. For just a few examples, see the cases of Rebeckah Cole, DWM, 2, 3/1704; Sarah Evens, BWM, 6, 7/1698; Elizabeth Day, Jr., and her accomplices, BWM, 12/1702 ff.; BMM, 1/1703 ff.

61. See, for example, the Wetherill family dispute, BMM, 1705 and 1706; participants in the "prison dore" riot of 1701; and the "French Army Affair," BMM, 5/1705.

62. BMM, 11, 12/1704.

63. See, for example, the cases of Joseph Parker and William Petty and his wife, BMM, 5–7/1704.

64. Pomfret, *Colonial New Jersey*, pp. 123, 130–38.

65. See, e.g., BWM, 5/1713; BMM, 2/1712, 4/1718.

66. There are many references to the sending and receiving of certificates for traveling and relocating Friends throughout the minutes.

67. For example, Marmaduke Coate's certificate from England was received in 4/1718, and in the same month he was appointed an overseer to replace the "antient" John Day. Richard Smith arrived from England in 6/1712, and he was appointed a representative to Quarterly Meeting in 9/1712.

68. The earliest example of BMM accepting a convincement is the case of Tho Middleton, 3/1710.

69. One such Friend, Richard Smith, was chastised by the Meeting because he arrested a fellow Meeting member. He defended himself by saying that if he had known the person "had been owned as a friend he would not have dealth with him after that manner to cause any trouble or exercise to the Meeting" (BMM, 7/1719).

70. Edwin Bronner, "Quaker Discipline and Order, 1680–1720," Philadelphia Yearly Meeting and London Yearly Meeting (Spring, 1981), typescript p. 10 (cited with the permission of the author).

71. BWM, 5/1713.

72. PYM, *Discipline*, 1719.

73. BMM, 6/1714, 4/1717, 6/1717, 6/1718; BWM, 6/1714.

74. PYM, Men, 1710.

75. PYM, *Discipline*, 1719; see also H. H. Gerth and C. Wright Mills, eds., *From Max Weber: Essays in Sociology*, reprint (New York, 1975), pp. 199–244.

76. Disciplinary issues were also brought to the disobedient members themselves by the same overseers, and one Friend whose behavior had been disorderly tried to persuade the Meeting that "he had given satisfaction to ye overseers, and therefore thought this meeting had no further business with it." But specialization had not gone that far, and the man was still required to satisfy the Meeting (BMM, 12/1718).

77. BMM, 1/1714.

78. BMM, 11/1716.

79. BWM, 7/1715.

80. BWM, 5/1714, 7/1714.

81. BWM, 1/1717, 3/1717, 3/1718, 5/1718, 6/1718, 12/1718, 1/1719.

82. BMM, 5/1715.

83. BMM, 4,5,6,7,8,9,10/1715.

84. BMM, 12/1719.

85. BMM, 2/1720.

86. BMM, 3/1711.

87. Edward Hardman, whose "life and conversation appears . . . to be exceeding wicked," was prohibited from preaching and "pretending to exort people to godliness & contrariwise he appears to be a lewd liver" (BMM, 1,2/1707). Joseph Parker was disowned after investigation of the "scandalous reports" about him. The Meeting found them to be accurate, "although shifted and avaided by ye said Parker, although the Meeting laboured to bring him to a sense of his evill, but of little purpose, his hardness & wickedness being such that they see no hopes for his coming to repentance for it" (BMM, 5,6,7/1707).

88. Charles Woolverton, who had been intermittently denying Quakerism since 1704, and had long-standing disagreements with the Springfield Preparative Meeting and "ye bitterness of some members of itt," was disowned and readmitted to membership in 1737 (BMM, 11/1704, 3/1712, 1737). Jacob Lamb was threatened with disownment for "destraining the Indian's Law" and behaving in a way that was "a reproach & Scandall to Truth & ye professors of itt" (BMM, 5/1714). He failed to condemn his actions. After repeated requests from Lamb that the Meeting extend its time limit for condemnations, he was disowned 12/1714. The third disownment was Leete's, discussed above.

CHAPTER 6

Quaker Tribalism

Susan S. Forbes

In his classic essay on the American national character, J. Hector St. John Crèvecoeur, using a metaphor that was to become famous, observed that Americans were "melt[ing] into a new race" as former ethnic and religious identities evaporated. One group, however, Crèvecoeur saw as holding itself aloof from this new order: "The Quakers are the only people who retain a fondness for their own mode of worship; for be they ever so far separated from each other, they hold a sort of communion with the society, and seldom depart from its rules."[1] While Crèvecoeur's prescience may be debated, his observation about Quaker communion reveals a deep understanding of the theory and practice of the Society of Friends. Because the group life of the Quakers was their witness to the world, the Quaker meeting may be seen as a candle that sheds light upon the very nature of Quakerism. This paper will discuss the corporate nature of the Society of Friends with particular reference to the patterns of participation of Friends in colonial New Garden, Pennsylvania.

The Society of Friends, despite its strong emphasis on inner revelation and the unique relationship between the individual and God, sees man as essentially a social being who requires contact with others of the same persuasion. The basic precept of Quakerism is the presence of an Inner Light within each individual, given by a merciful God who wished to present to man his means of salvation. But because the individualistic, antinomian thrust of this theology soon disclosed a prospect of anarchy, early Quakers were impelled to emphasize the spiritual authority of the group. They therefore founded their religious order upon the bedrock of a system of meetings whose decisions were binding upon members.

Such members would bear witness in their meetings to a corporate testimony of the principles and practices of the group. Though each individual was entrusted with an Inner Light, by which to seek the Truth, all Friends had to test their leanings against those of others seeking the same truth in meeting. Quakers saw a vital difference between the lonely individual listening to the divine voice within and the member of a gathered meeting in which all of those present searched for the voice of God in separate but converging channels.[2] The great Quaker theologian, Robert Barclay, likened the gathering of believers to "many candles lighted and put in one place." As the many candles

> greatly augment the light, and make it more to shine forth, so when many are gathered together into the same life, there is more of the glory of God and His power appears, to the refreshment of each individual; for that he partakes not only of the light and life in himself but in all the rest.[3]

While at first there might be disagreement among those attending a meeting, as the candles may flicker out of time with each other, through patient discussion all should come to see the matter in the same bright glow of God.

Majority rule, hence, had no meaning for the Quakers, since there was no guarantee that a lone dissenter might not be reading the word of God with more success than all the others. As Edward Burroughs advised, Friends were to proceed

> not in the way of the world, as a worldly assembly of men, by hot contests, by seeking to outspeak and overreach one another in discourse, as if it were controversy between party and party of men, or two sides violently striving for dominion, . . . not deciding affairs by the greater vote, . . . but in the wisdom, love and fellowship of God, in gravity, patience, meekness, in unity and concord, . . . all things to be carried on; by hearing and determining every matter coming before you, in love, coolness, gentleness, and dear unity.[4]

The Society of Friends realized that it would be impossible for all Quakers to gather in any one meeting but also wished for men and women of a great variety of interests to meet together to discuss the problems facing the religious community. George Fox, the founder of Quakerism, bequeathed to the Friends a system of meetings based on the representative ideal. The smallest geographic unit held the meeting that encompassed the greatest proportion of Friends of that unit. Each town with a sufficient number of Quakers established a worship meeting to be attended by all those professing the faith. This was to be a silent meeting broken only by the revelations of those who received the word of God during their meditation. Adults and children alike were expected to attend regularly on Sundays and frequently on weekdays.

One or more worship meetings formed one business meeting. The members of a worship meeting, joining together under the title of a preparative meeting, selected several representatives to attend the monthly business meeting and then report back to the worshipers. These persons were joined by any other Quaker adult who wished to attend. In business meetings, men and women met separately, each having full jurisdiction over the members of their sex. The two groups dealt with a large range of affairs. Each monthly meeting within a larger geographic area, such as a county, was required to send representatives to a quarterly meeting, which acted as a court of appeal from the decisions of the lower meetings and as the institution through which the decisions of the yearly meeting were transferred to the monthly meetings and from them to the public. The yearly meeting, composed of representatives from the various quarterly meetings in one or two colonies, decided all questions of theology. As the author of the *Rules of Discipline*, it established the code of conduct accepted by all Quakers. It also served as a final court of appeal for those accused by the lower meetings of breaking the discipline. While the word of each yearly meeting was final for the area it represented, all remained in close contact with the London Yearly Meeting and usually took its advice even if it ran counter to the original opinion.[5]

Apart from the mainstream of meetings were two others of great importance. The first was the meeting for ministers and elders, a gathering of those who, because of a special gift of prophecy and revealing to others the Word of God, were named ministers and were therefore welcomed to speak in any meeting. These ministers, often itinerants who traveled the length of the American colonies, served to forge the Quaker community by carrying news from one family to another and from one meeting to another. The preparatory meetings nominated men for the position of minister, while the monthly meetings made the final decision on their acceptability.

The second meeting was the meeting for sufferings, established in London in 1676, at first to help persecuted Quakers but later extended to help the needy of all religions and races.

The monthly meeting was considered by all Quakers, including George Fox, who established the idea, to be the real foundation of the church government.[6] Although its decisions could be overturned by the quarterly meeting and it could not establish itself without the permission of the quarterly meeting (just as the latter needed the consent of the yearly meeting), the monthly meeting exerted an influence over the everyday activities of the Quakers that the more remote meetings could not match. A brief examination of the duties of the monthly meeting as detailed in the *Book of Discipline* will suffice to indicate its importance. Its duties came under five main categories: the supervision of behavior; the punishment of breaches of discipline; the arbitration of differences between Friends; the protection of members against adversity; and the collection of funds for its own use and that of the higher meetings.

The monthly meeting began the regulation of an individual's life when it recorded his or her birth in its records. Parents were instructed to ensure their children's attendance at meetings, their good conduct, and their plainness of speech, dress and gesture. Quakers were instructed to marry other Quakers at a wedding supervised by the meeting. An adult Quaker wishing to move to another town or to join another meeting closer to his dwelling was required to apply for a certificate of removal, without which he could not be admitted to the new meeting. The meeting continued its supervision after a member's death, when it regulated his funeral. Refreshments were permissible but only if served with the gravity that became the occasion.

The monthly meeting also had authority to punish those breaching its rules of conduct. The punishment at its disposal was the disownment of those who refused to testify to, and sincerely repent, their misconduct. A great number of offenses were thus punishable: excessive drinking, swearing, cursing, lying; unlawful or unseemly keeping company with women; negligence in attending meetings; immoderation in gesture, speech, apparel, and furniture; marriage outside of the meeting, either to a non-Quaker or performed by a minister or justice; trading of liquor to the Indians; and, eventually, keeping of slaves. Any person involved in a public scandal who did not publicly claim all responsibility for himself and clear the meeting completely was to be speedily disowned. Those committing offenses solely against the church did not have to repent publicly but were required to testify in the meeting.

When two or more members of the Society of Friends disagreed about their worldly affairs, the monthly meeting discouraged any recourse to the provincial courts of law. Instead, Quakers were urged to submit their problems to the meeting for arbitration after following a series of prescribed steps. First, the aggrieved party was to speak calmly and in a friendly way to the other, to obtain what he believed was his right. This failing, he was to ask several neutral Friends to accompany him when he again made his claim. After hearing both sides, if the case appeared to be clear, the Friends were to urge immediate settlement. If there were grounds for debate, they were to urge the appointment of arbitrators who would determine the outcome of the case. Should either party refuse to accept the judgment of the referees, the other would report to the monthly meeting, which would appoint arbitrators of its own. Their decision was then binding upon the parties, with disownment the penalty for disobedience (the disowned party having the right of appeal to the quarterly meeting). So successful was this method of arbitration that many non-Quakers, as they settled in eighteenth-century Pennsylvania, submitted their quarrels to a monthly meeting rather than take them to a civil law court.

The monthly meeting also helped those of its members struck by adversity. Friends who found themselves unable to pay their debts could apply to the meeting for financial help. The meeting would provide a loan and also appoint a committee to advise the unfortunate member, suggesting means of recouping his losses and conducting his farm or business affairs with more success. The monthly meeting was designated by some Quakers as the executor of their estates and guardian of their children. The meeting would appoint a committee of Friends to fulfill the duties demanded of the gathering. The committee had full powers to make decisions concerning the operation of the farm or business and the discipline of the children, subject, of course, to the approval of the meeting as a whole in case of controversy. If the children were young, they were sent to live with a Quaker family or to apprentice with a Quaker craftsman or merchant. If old enough, they might be allowed to operate their father's means of livelihood with the advice of their guardians. Failure to comply with the wishes of the meeting could result in disownment from the meeting. After the disownment proceedings, the meeting could authorize the committee of guardians to institute a private suit against the recalcitrant in a civil law court.

Cases in which the meeting had to help unfortunate Friends led to the need to raise funds amongst the members. The monthly meetings were also authorized to collect funds to ensure the continued operation of the quarterly, yearly, and ministers and elders meetings. Again, a committee would be appointed to collect money or needed goods, while another committee would be responsible for safeguarding the funds. Still another might be assigned the task of distribution.

The monthly meeting served a purpose beyond the sum of these specific functions. Its primary function was to reinforce the faith of the Quakers under its tutelage. During its earliest days, when Quakerism was marked by a strong evangelical urge, all men were considered to be potentially under the authority of a meeting. During the first quarter century of the existence of the Society of Friends, Quakers tried to convert those about them to their theology and their way of life. While not all Quakers martyred themselves to the cause, many were willing to risk physical hardship in their efforts to convert men unreceptive to their ideas. And all used their rules of discipline as a manual of behavior that would teach others to lead a godly life.

As meetings became more uniformly organized, they often lost their original sense of mission. Instead, their goal became the preservation of the existing group. Throughout the 1660s and 1670s, Quakers facing insurmountable opposition from governmental authorities found their only solace in the convocations of fellow sufferers. Withdrawing from the hostile world of the Restoration, they took refuge in their own meetings. Fox himself saw the organization of all Quakers into uniform monthly meetings as a source of energy for the service of the community of believers—not of the whole human community.

Those Quakers who settled in Pennsylvania in the years after 1680 found themselves in a very different situation. No longer were they members of a persecuted minority struggling to save their neighbor's soul or life. Most of their neighbors were already Quakers and shared in the religious toleration of the Holy Experiment. At first, Quaker leaders in the American colonies expected to make their religion prevail throughout the colonies, through political as well as religious means. Yet, after the first wave of enthusiasm passed, Quakers mellowed in their new surroundings and found business and political pursuits as pressing as religious ones. Soon they became content to concern themselves with their own members rather than the conversion of outsiders. The meeting maintained its demand that Quakers live exemplary lives and shield their transgressions from the world, but its reason was not the hope of conversion. Friends wished to have good reputations so that those who might oppose their economic and political hegemony would have no arguments to use against the Society.

By the 1750s, however, change had again taken place within the Quaker community. Pennsylvania was clearly divided into three camps: the 'worldly' Quakers, who paid lip service to the ideals of their fathers but left the religion whenever this adherence proved too difficult; the moderates, who were troubled by the conflict between worldly pursuits and religious principles but were willing to give up neither; and the reformers, who wished Friends to give up any interests that prevented their full commitment to the religion.[7] The reformers inherited the fervor of the founders but directed it inward at their own members. As the worldly group left the fold and the moderates wavered, this minority of extremists obtained control of the meeting structure. While few were disowned because of theological differences, many were disowned because of their actions. This cleansing process, left to the monthly meeting, served to reinforce the faith of those who chose to remain within the community of believers. Once again, the meeting as the agency of corporate testimony made an effort to cement the Quaker fellowship.

This general discussion of the Quaker monthly meeting and its functions has left unanswered many questions about the purpose and operation of meetings which can only be approached through careful examination of the records of individual monthly meetings. As a start, I have examined the minutes of the New Garden Monthly Meeting in Chester County, Pennsylvania.[8] The New Garden meeting was established in 1718 by Irish Friends attracted to the religious freedom of the Quaker commonwealth. These late arrivals eschewed the comforts and civilities of the established areas, preferring the Pennsylvania piedmont of southeastern Chester County, with its rich soil and possibilities for agricultural success. Although not a central area, since it was located some thirty miles from Philadelphia and twenty miles from Chester, the New Garden area was nevertheless important as a supplier of the foodstuffs that the growing urban center required. By 1720, roads connected its farming communities to both the Brandywine Creek and the city of Philadelphia. In addition, the main road between Philadelphia and Baltimore passed nearby. Local farmers soon produced far more than was necessary for their own subsistence and joined the ranks of the commercial farming communities that dominated Chester County during the colonial period. As the area became more prosperous, its population also increased. In New Garden, for example, the number of landowners increased from thirty-three in 1730 to fifty-nine in 1750 and seventy-five in 1770, an increase of 127 percent. Despite the population gains, the area retained its basically rural complexion, although some artisans and shopkeepers supplied the farmers with needed products and services. As the population grew and diversified somewhat occupationally, so, too, did the religious composition of the New Garden area change. While almost all of the names of the residents on early tax lists could be located in Quaker records, many of the later arrivals, farmers and artisans alike, were strangers to the Society of Friends.[9]

With the growth in population and diversification of resident groups, the New Garden area became more stratified. Though the land distribution among owners remained remarkably equal relative to the older settlements of eastern Pennsylvania, a new body of paid laborers and transients appeared during the second half of the eighteenth century. Many were non-Quaker, but even within the Quaker community many of those entering the area never appeared on tax lists as landowners, while others soon moved on to different communities.[10] Thus, in New Garden, as elsewhere in Pennsylvania, major demographic changes occurred: the all-Quaker haven of the first generation changed to a heterogeneous community in which families of various economic, social, and religious backgrounds lived together as neighbors.

As the environment of New Garden changed and the meaning of Quakerism became less clear in a community becoming yearly more heterogeneous, Quaker residents looked to their monthly meeting for guidance. Through participation in the affairs of the meeting, individual Quakers gained a sense of attachment and even subservience to group needs. The meeting, through its supervision of marriages and treatment of breaches of discipline, provided standards of conduct by which Friends could judge their own behavior. The remainder of this paper will examine the New Garden patterns of participation and decision-making in order to understand the corporate nature of the Quaker system of meetings in action and the role of the individual and family within that system.

The decision to be a Quaker left open to the individual the amount of time he would devote to the Society of Friends. All Quakers were required to attend meetings for worship, but they were only urged to attend business meetings. Mere attendance was, in any case, only the beginning of the activities one could perform in the meeting. The monthly gathering appointed a clerk to moderate at meetings and to keep minutes of the activities of the assembly; ministers and elders who were recognized for their spiritual and temporal author-ity, respectively, and who were asked to attend the general meeting for ministers and elders; and overseers who were to speak to each of those breaking the rules of discipline and, it was hoped, obtain a testimony of guilt and sorrow before the matter reached the monthly gathering. In addition to the appointment of these perma-nent officers, the monthly meeting appointed members to help the overseers, approve certificates of marriage and removal, collect funds, and perform the myriad of other duties required of the meeting.

Since anything important enough to require the oversight of the meeting required the presence of at least two Quakers, these appointments can be considered to be ad hoc committee assign-ments. Such appointments—recorded in the meeting minutes—are a useful indicator of the pattern of participation and help us identify the central members.[11]

The New Garden Monthly Meeting may be divided into three distinct groups of members based on their levels of interaction. About 60 percent of the town Quakers attended the meetings but performed none of the business tasks delegated by the gathering. Although we find these members listed in the minutes, they appear as petitioners for certificates or financial help. This group I will refer to as the *general congregation*.

Forty percent of the members were given committee assign-ments, ranging from 1 to 200 during a lifetime of activity. Eighty percent of these committee workers, or 32 percent of the total population, were assigned to less than 50 percent of all the commit-tee positions. These men were the "backbenchers" of the meeting. The other 20 percent of officeholders, or 8 percent of the total population, shared among themselves the majority of available positions and were thus the central members. They may also be considered the meeting elders. Although the Quaker meetings reserved the title *elder* for those appointed to attend the meeting for ministers and elders, the term, used in the congregational sense of the weighty, important members to whom the rest of the group defers, may as well be applied to these central figures of Quakerism, who interacted more frequently than any of their fellow members.[12] The elders, with the help of the backbenchers, furnished the congregation with the information necessary to make decisions and, in so doing, influenced the decisions made.

The actual distribution of committee assignments among the backbenchers and the elders may be demonstrated through the use of Lorenz curves that measure the degree to which a distribution departs from the ideal of complete equality. In order to determine if the meeting went through any changes during the years studied— 1718–1774—I have plotted the curve for intervals of five years and then superimposed the curves. The horizontal axis of each curve represents the accumulated percentage of members, while the vertical axis represents the accumulated percentage of appointments. The diagonal straight line represents the ideal of complete equality. Figures 6-1 through 6-3 give this graphic representation of the distributions, and Table 6-1 shows the numerical distribution derived from the graphs.

From 1718 until 1722, forty-one men received at least one appointment at the New Garden Monthly Meeting. In all, 172 assignments were made.[13] The smallest number of men capable of controlling a majority of appointments was eight, or 20 percent of the total. The thirty-three backbenchers accounted for 80 percent of the population and 49 percent of the appointments. Of these, twenty-eight men could be considered underrepresented in that they received less than the number of appointments they would have had if the distribution had been equal.

By the period 1728–32, the last in which residents of both Nottingham and Sadsbury were present, the number of participants had grown to seventy-seven, and the number of appointments to 461. The Lorenz curve indicates that the degree of inequality had increased. The percentage of the population that can be called elders had decreased to 18 percent, while the backbenchers now accounted for 82 percent of the population. Sixty-two percent were underrepresented. As the monthly meeting became settled into a routine of expanding membership and expanding work, it also became settled into a pattern of expanding inequality.

After Nottingham and Sadsbury formed their own monthly meet-

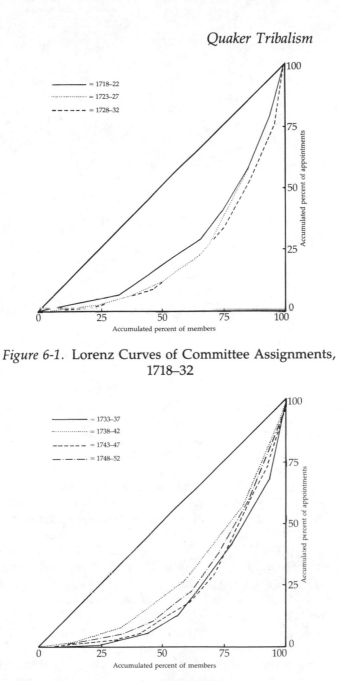

Figure 6-1. Lorenz Curves of Committee Assignments, 1718–32

Figure 6-2. Lorenz Curves of Committee Assignments, 1733–52

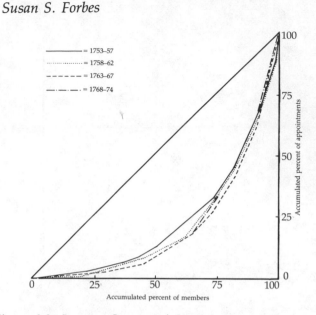

Figure 6-3. Lorenz Curves of Committee Assignments,
1753–74

ing, New Garden was left with only forty-one members. While
these men were only 54 percent of its former membership, the
meeting still assigned 371 jobs, or 80 percent of the past number of
appointments. The distribution of these appointments showed a
substantial movement toward greater equality in participation.
From 1738 to 1743, 27 percent of the population functioned as
elders, while 73 percent were backbenchers. During a period of
internal tension due to loss of members, those who did participate
were more likely to receive their equal share of appointments.

After the meeting adjusted to the loss of Nottingham and Sadsbury, with the addition of London Grove, it returned to its original
pattern of ever-increasing inequities in the distribution of jobs. Until
1753, the underrepresented portion of the backbenchers remained
fairly stable at 55 percent to 57 percent, but the proportion of elders
decreased to about 20 percent of the population. From 1753 to 1757,
the number of elders decreased still further to 15 percent, while the
underrepresented reached a high of 69 percent. At the same time,
the number of appointments was increasing so rapidly that the
officeholder with the greatest number of appointments held at least
sixty-four times as many jobs as did the one with the lowest num-

Table 6-1. Numerical Distribution of Committee Assignments, 1718–74

Years	Number of men	Percentage of men	Number of Appointments	Percentage of Appointments
1718–22	28	68	1–4	33
	5	12	5–6	16
	8	20	7–16	51
1723–27	40	60	0–5	20
	14	20	6–10	29
	13	20	13–22	51
1728–32	48	62	0–5	22
	13	17	1–12	22
	16	21	13–22	56
1733–37	32	55	0–7	14
	13	22	8–16	31
	13	23	18–39	55
1738–42	22	54	1–8	24
	8	19	9–13	24
	13	27	14–22	52
1743–47	27	55	0–5	16
	13	27	6–11	34
	9	18	12–30	50
1748–52	28	57	1–6	20
	11	18	7–12	24
	12	25	13–22	56
1753–57	38	69	0–8	28
	8	15	9–17	20
	9	16	18–42	52
1758–62	40	61	0–10	18
	15	24	11–21	31
	10	15	22–64	51
1763–67	46	68	0–14	22
	12	17	15–33	28
	10	15	24–69	50
1768–74	50	64	1–16	18
	17	22	17–41	32
	11	14	42–103	50

ber. While these sixty-four appointments were not a higher proportion of all appointments than previous elders had achieved, the greater activity of the meeting made the elders do more than they had to do formerly. Therefore, the elders appeared to be more active vis-à-vis the backbenchers.

This analysis of the activities of members of the New Garden monthly meeting from 1718 to 1775 reveals inequities from the beginning in the distribution of appointments. At all times, a minority of the population was able to command a majority of the appointments, while the majority of men could be considered underrepresented. Only in a period of internal change was this pattern alleviated, but even here it was not reversed.

Any discussion of activism in the monthly meeting must consider a second index of individual participation: the total number of appointments accumulated by each member during his entire period of service. The Lorenz curve in Figure 6-4 shows that the distribution of appointments corresponds to the distributions found during the five-year periods studied. Still defining elders as the smallest percentage of the population able to control over 50 percent of the available appointments, we find 12 percent of the members

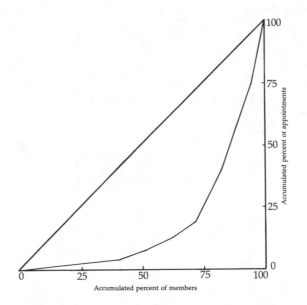

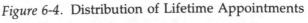

Figure 6-4. Distribution of Lifetime Appointments

were lifetime elders. Eighty-eight percent were backbenchers, with 70 percent underrepresented. While some men received their appointments during only one of the five-year periods studied above, others participated during the course of forty or fifty years. The majority of members, however, could have averaged no more than one appointment per year for a term of ten years. Fifty-seven percent of the members served less than ten years, while about the same proportion held ten appointments or less during their stay in New Garden. Table 6-2 summarizes the information about the number of years each member served on committees. Twenty-seven men had over twenty-five years of service. Of these, only fourteen were elders, and of these fourteen, only five averaged more than the twenty assignments per five-year period characteristic of elders when judged by periods. Ten other elders who did not serve more than twenty-five years also averaged over twenty assignments per period. Hence, fifteen men could be considered elders in both categories of activism, while an equal number accumulated their large numbers of appointments solely through longevity.

While length of service might account for the centrality of a portion of the elders, it does not explain the differences in activism amongst members within particular five-year periods. At any given time all members could theoretically divide the appointments equally amongst themselves. As the Lorenz curve reflects, however, the distribution was far from equal. Were there any characteristics of the highly active that distinguished them from their less active neighbors? Differences in wealth are a possibility calling for study. Because New Garden was in a rural, predominantly farming area, landownership is a useful index of wealth. We can use the tax

Table 6-2. Length of Service of Members of New Garden

Number of men	Number of years of service
90	1– 5
45	6–10
49	11–15
19	16–20
7	21–25
12	26–30
5	31–35
6	36–40
1	41–45
3	46–50
0	51–57

records for New Garden, London Grove, the Marlboroughs, Nottingham, and Sadsbury to determine the variance in wealth. In 1718, thirty-one of the forty-one participating members, or 76 percent, could be found on the local tax sheets. Those not located were adult sons who owned no land of their own, men living in unincorporated areas, and a small number of servants and indentured servants. The distribution of land among Quakers corresponded quite closely to the general distribution of land in the town of New Garden. The Lorenz curve in Figure 6-5 reflects a high degree of equality in landownership, although a large portion of the owners held less than an equal share, while 31 percent owned a majority of the available acreage. This degree of variance in ownership warranted an examination of differences in wealth as a source of division between elders and backbenchers. Applying regression theory to the data on amount of land owned and the number of committee positions assigned, we obtained an r^2 statistic of .19, indicating that wealth (measured in amount of land owned) accounted for 19 percent of the variation in number of assignments. Landownership in the first years of New Garden's meeting thus had some positive effect on the number of assignments an individual obtained, espe-

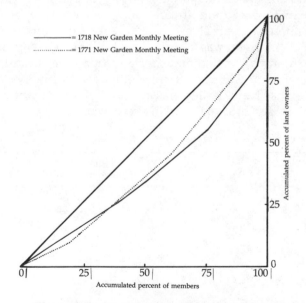

Figure 6-5. Distribution of Land among Monthly Meeting Members

cially considering the broad base of ownership. The correlation is not strong enough, however, to assume that wealth was the primary factor.

In the following years, the tax rates were listed, rather than the acreage under which these rates were assigned. Taxes in the New Garden area in 1727 ranged from two to thirteen shillings, and in 1740 from one shilling three pence to thirteen shillings. Again, the range in taxes was not excessive, but it was sufficient to allow us to examine the rate vis-à-vis the distribution of appointments. In 1727, the r^2 statistic obtained in studying the correlation between taxes and committee assignments was .0049, while in 1740 the r^2 was .0064. Within the nine years from 1718 to 1727, landownership had ceased to be any factor at all in determining the number of committee assignments. By 1771, acreage owned was again recorded in the tax lists. Sixty of the seventy-eight members active at that time, or 77 percent, were located and the amount of land they owned was determined. The Lorenz curve in graph 5 shows the wide distribution, although again it reveals some degree of inequality. The correlation coefficient obtained was no different from that of 1740, when agreement between landownership and committee appointments was random. Hence, disproportionate wealth did not confer higher rank within the meeting, any more than poverty spurred extra devotion resulting in extra duties.

During the last seven years, the tax records list those residents who pursued a trade or profession. Since, in a region in which land is easily obtained, landownership might lose some of its force as a source of stratification, occupation may be a stronger index. It might be reasonable to assume that men who offered their services to the community in their work, might also have offered them to the meeting. They might also have come into contact with the townspeople and, therefore, have had greater opportunity and ability to communicate with them. Dividing the members along the lines of occupation revealed no such alignment, however. The contingency table depicted in Table 6-3 yields a chi-square of .239 with a phi-

Table 6-3. Distribution of Appointments among Farmers and Tradesmen

Representation	Farmers	Tradesmen	Total
Underrepresented	26	11	37
Overrepresented	16	5	21
Total	42	16	58

square of .0041. Since a phi-square of 0 means that there is no relationship between variables, we must reject a null hypothesis that there is a correlation between occupation and activism.

The tax rates and meeting records also furnish information about the townships in which members lived. The town residency of thirty-four members of the 1718–22 meetings were located as shown in Table 6-4. In the meeting as a whole, at that time, 80 percent of the members were backbenchers, while 20 percent were elders. The proportion for the members as divided by residency conforms well enough to these general proportions to conclude that residency within either of the major towns in which a preparatory meeting was held had no effect on activism.

Almost twice as many of the participants from 1718 to 1722 came from Nottingham. After the separation of that preparatory meeting in 1729 and then the departure of Sadsbury Friends, the monthly meeting divided its duties between residents of New Garden and London Grove and the Marlboroughs. The monthly gathering alternated between the two areas. The distribution of assignments as shown in Table 6-5 reflects a proportion between elders and backbenchers that is roughly as would be expected. The years from 1768 to 1774 again show the various towns dividing the assignments of their residents as did the entire meeting, with fourteen percent of the population now serving as elders (see Table 6-6). Specific town affiliation continued to exert no control over the distribution of appointments.

Nor did political expertise affect an individual's share of appointments. Sixteen committee members held political office, yet no

Table 6-4. Town Residency, 1718–22

Town	Elders	Backbenchers	Total
New Garden	3	8	11
Nottingham	3	17	20
Bush River	0	3	3

Table 6-5. Town Residency, 1738–42

Town	Elders	Backbenchers	Total
New Garden	3	10	13
London Grove	4	7	11
Marlborough	4	8	12
Other	2	5	7

Table 6-6. Town Residency, 1768–74

Town	Elders	Backbenchers	Total
New Garden	2	15	17
London Grove	3	16	19
Marlborough	5	15	20
Other	0	22	22

more than 15 percent of them also became elders. The vast majority, even if leaders of the political assembly, remained backbenchers in the meeting. On the other hand, spiritual excellence in ministry was not recognized as a sufficient reason for excessive activism in business matters or vice versa. Of the eight men believed to have a special gift of prophecy and revealing to others the word of God, and therefore appointed to attend the meeting for ministers, seven were backbenchers.

The lack of correlation between any of these factors and committee assignments is striking. In its functions, the meeting acted as a quasi-political unit. Yet the meeting did not draw its leadership from the ranks of those generally associated, by wealth, occupation, neighborhood, or political or ministerial office, with political elites. Indeed, the meeting may well have chosen to ignore these factors exactly as a way of affirming its allegiance to the earliest norms of Quakerism. Perhaps eighteenth-century Friends remembered the advice of a seventeenth-century epistle to a new business meeting, urging that "none . . . exercise lordship or dominion over another, nor the person of any be set apart, but as they continue in the power of truth . . . that truth itself in the body may reign, not persons nor forms."[14] Evidently, neither political expertise nor worldly position was considered absolute evidence that the power of Truth had led an individual to disciplinary acumen.
vidual to disciplinary acumen.

Yet, neither was the meeting completely random in its distribution of assignments. Family membership is a significant predictor of central members. Information about New Garden families came from the meeting, which recorded births and marriages, and genealogies collected by the Historical Society of Pennsylvania.[15] From these sources it was possible to assemble the membership of the men's meeting into nuclear families of three generations, and sometimes into extended families with the addition of uncles and nephews as well. Female members were located in genealogies and then checked in the minutes of the women's meeting. Because the latter did not record all of its activities, information about the committee assignments of the female members was limited to appointments to marriage committees, the only category consistently listed during the fifty-seven years studied.

Sixty men whose fathers also joined committees accumulated a mean score of 37.3 appointments, while the mean score for the meeting as a whole was 26 assignments. As a group, the men with fathers on committees received 2,155 appointments, or 528 more than the 1,527 jobs expected of a group their size. Thirty-two men whose sons also participated registered a mean score of 51 appointments, and a group total of 1,585, as compared with an expected total of 876 appointments. The six men whose fathers and sons held appointments accumulated a mean score of 100 assignments.

The wives of ninety-seven members participated in the women's meetings. Their husbands averaged 42.7 appointments, with a group sum of 4,160 assignments. The expected sum for this group was 2,629. Those who did not have wives who participated held 2,099 appointments, or 1,531 less than would be expected from 48 percent of the population. In addition, men with brothers participating registered a higher mean and group score—43.8 and 2,199 appointments respectively—than would have been anticipated from their proportion of the membership.

In all of these cases in which a member's immediate family participated in meeting affairs, scores of up to four times higher than the norm were recorded. Furthermore, of the thirty-five men who accumulated over fifty-five appointments, thirty, or 86 percent, saw their wives working in the women's meeting. Thirty-four percent of these elders had sons who joined, while 43 percent were themselves the sons of committee members. Forty-five percent of the elders were the brothers of attending members. In the population as a whole, 42 percent had wives, 14 percent sons, 26 percent fathers, and 24 percent had brothers who joined. The participation of members of one's family significantly enhanced one's own chance of accumulating large numbers of appointments.

Most New Gardeners who participated in monthly meeting activities were given their first committee assignment within a few years of their own marriage. An examination of marriage certificate committees may enable us to determine if there were any differences in the early life histories of those who became an integral part of the meeting. Twenty-five elders were married in New Garden. All but three of them were young men, not yet active in the meeting, who were marrying for the first time. The other three were widowers who had been serving on committees for a number of years before their second marriage. In addition, seventy-seven backbenchers contracted a marriage. Table 6-7 indicates whether the member eventually became an elder or a backbencher, and whether the committee investigating him was composed primarily of elders or backbenchers or was equally divided between the two groups. The Goodman-Kruskal test for Tau demonstrated that a knowledge of the type of committee visiting a member reduced the chance of error in predicting his future position by 35 percent. While those who became backbenchers could be investigated by any type of committee, those who became elders were generally visited by the most active in the meeting.

Elders differed from other members in a second way. They entered into the committee life of the meeting at an earlier age. The mean age of members of the monthly meeting at the time of their first committee assignment was 33.9 years of age. The mean age of the backbenchers was 36, while the elders averaged 30 years of age.

It appears that those with the potential to become very active in the meeting were a special substrata of the general population, easily recognizable from family ties. During a newcomer's first major contact with the monthly meeting, in the form of his request for a marriage certificate, he actually went through a rite of passage. The certificate investigation thus enabled the meeting to introduce its young members to the workings of the business meeting, with the potentially active receiving their instructions from those who, from sheer bulk of labor, understood its functionings best.

The meeting could determine an individual's potential for activism from the family that raised him. As we have already seen, family membership was the only important factor that differentiated the activists from the rest of the meeting. Although American Quakers did not formally subscribe to the concept of birthright membership (as did English Friends), during the eighteenth century Friends

Table 6-7. Composition of Committees Visiting Bridegrooms

Type of Committee	Elder Bridegrooms	Backbencher Bridegrooms	Total
Elder committee	18	26	44
Backbencher committee	4	23	27
Mixed committee	3	28	31
Total	25	77	102

increasingly emphasized nurture and education within the Quaker family as the main basis of fellowship. And our examination of activism indicates that family conferred status as well as membership in the meeting. In fact, the family may be seen as the mediator between the individual and the corporate structure of Quakerism—the vehicle through which the spiritual authority of the group was passed on to the individual Friend.

Such mediation was plainly apparent in the process through which marriage certificates were granted. Friends about to marry were assuredly moved by private sentiment, yet they also looked for community approval. As James Moore, a New Garden Quaker, explained to his children in 1761, young people contemplating marriage had to be careful not to let their "affections be drawn away" until they had "the mind of Truth uniting with [them] in their proceedings." They were to "take care" to proceed "orderly in the fear and counsel of God, in the accomplishment of [their] undertaking agreeable to the good rules and order of the Church; that so [their] marriage may not be in or by the will of man only, but of the Lord that hath joined [them] together."[16]

Since the meeting was a gathering of many Inner Lights of God, if the meeting approved a marriage request, an engaged couple could be assured of the rightness and righteousness of their marriage. In addition, they were assured the comfort and aid of their parents and friends if trouble arose out of the marriage, since those who approved the marriage committed themselves to its success. Despite the theological commitment to an individual relationship with God, Quakers nevertheless understood the need for human contact and reassurance, first from their own families and then from the meeting a a whole.

The meeting used the careful investigation of all requesting marriage certificates in order to maintain discipline within the community of believers. While the majority of the applicants were granted their certificates without delay, a sizable number found themselves under scrutiny for un-Quakerlike acts. In addition, not all Friends followed the outlined procedures. Occasionally two Friends were unwilling to wait until the gathering issued the certificate. Others knew that the meeting would raise serious objections about their courtship, a possible pregnancy, or their ability to support themselves. Still others, who did not have their parents' approval, eloped and were married by a magistrate or minister of another denomination. Of course, Friends who married those outside the fellowship were also unable to wed within the meeting. Because of the centrality of the family in Quakerism, the handling of these marital infractions reveals much about the nature of Quaker fellowship.

The proportion of uncertified to all Quaker marriages changed considerably during New Garden's colonial past. Until 1730, only 7 percent of all marriages occurred outside the meeting's auspices, but after 1730 the number rose almost continuously until the end of the period. By 1774, more New Garden marriages were out of than in unity with Friends (see Table 6-8). In addition, the type of marital infraction changed over the same span. During the early period, about one-third of the marriages involved a Quaker/non-Quaker union, while the other two-thirds involved a ceremony performed by a minister or magistrate. After 1755, however, the proportion of exogamous matches increased to 50 percent of all deviant marriages.

The increase in the number of Quakers contracting exogamous unions may be explained by the changes in New Garden itself: the growth of a non-Quaker community within the townships and the growth within the Quaker gathering of a group of physically, economically, and, perhaps, religiously mobile members. When the New Garden area was first settled and the population was almost exclusively Quaker, few Friends purposefully, or even inadvertently, broke the rules of discipline. Few were willing to risk voluntary social ostracism by taking a non-Quaker spouse, even if they were

Table 6-8. New Garden Quaker Marriages in and out of Meeting, 1720–74

Date	Marriages in Meeting	Marriages out of Meeting	Total
1720–1725	15	1	16
1726–1730	26	2	28
1731–1735	44	12	56
1736–1740	26	15	41
1741–1745	29	17	46
1746–1750	46	12	58
1751–1755	44	20	64
1756–1760	42	25	67
1761–1765	45	28	67
1766–1770	29	31	60
1771–1774	25	31	56

able to find one, since in early New Garden loss of religious fellowship would mean loss of community. As the non-Quaker population grew, though, Friends found not only new spouses but new communities that welcomed them into the fold.

In facing the crisis of intermarriage and the potential loss of Quaker families, the meeting had two choices—to allow those who contracted exogamous marriages to remain within the Quaker fellowship and hope that they remained Quaker or to disown them. In some cases, those who married out of unity indicated a desire to retain membership. Then, a committee, usually of elders, would visit the accused until he or she proved properly repentant and presented an acknowledgment of guilt to the meeting as a whole. Before 1755, the acknowledgment was most often a simple expression of sorrow. I.S., after impregnating and then marrying a non-Quaker in 1745, said he was "heartily sorry" for all his "Transgressions against the Truth and real professors thereof" and declared he did "desire forgiveness of God and that his people may so fare pass by mine offenses as to continue their care over me." After 1755, however, the meeting demanded considerably more of an acknowledgment. When P.B. married a non-Quaker, she offered the following statement:

> Whereas I have been educated in the way of Truth and, having also made Profession of it but for want of keeping close to that Principle which would have preserved me from the snare of the enemy; gave way to my own Evil inclinations and suffered my affection to be drawn out by a man not of our Society and was married by a Priest which brought trouble to my friends, therefore having had some sight of the evil of my offenses and is [sic] sorry for it . . . I give this forth for the clearing of Truth and do hereby condemn my misconduct therein.[17]

The meeting that accepted this document as a sincere sign of repentence did not, however, afford the remedy of divorce or even separation to a spouse who had publicly recanted the marriage.

The wording of the acknowledgment was not in itself as indicative of the meeting's response to marital deviance as was the willingness to accept an acknowledgment when offered. Until 1740, the New Garden meeting forgave only 24 percent of all those who married out of unity. Over the next decade and a half, the meeting accepted more and more acknowledgments. During the period 1751–54, it disowned only one of fourteen accused members, accepting 93 percent of the offered acknowledgments. Then the trend reversed. In 1755, four of the five who married out of unity were disowned; during the next twenty-five years, the group disowned 87 percent of marital deviants (see Table 6-9).

When first faced with an increase in exogamous unions, then, the meeting seemed to act as a group whose very survival was problematic. Members seemed to see the surge in deviance, especially in the realm of the family, as symptomatic of a disintegrating community unable to keep its members within the fold. And at first they adapted themselves to the pressures of individuals who wished greater contact with the non-Quaker world by relaxing the discipline. The monthly meeting thus took steps to insure continued membership in the Society of Friends by offering the Quaker participants in exogamous marriages a new type of fellowship—joint membership in two separate and sometimes even conflicting communities, the Society of Friends and the church of the non-Quaker spouse.

Yet, it may be hypothesized, New Garden Friends were uncomfortable with their new Quakerism and, after a while, attempted to cleanse the group from within. During the period of change, New Garden experienced a tightening of leadership as the percentage of those who could be considered elders declined from 25 percent (1748–52) to 16 percent (1753–57). The meeting thus depended even more heavily on a small group of men, presumably those who were distinctively committed to the norms of Quakerism and willing to

Table 6-9. New Garden Quaker Marital Infractions, Disownments, and Acknowledgments, 1720–74

Date	No. of Infractions	No. of Disownments	No. of Acknowledgments	% Acknowledgments
1720–25	1	1	0	0
1726–30	2	1	1	50
1731–35	12	9	3	25
1736–40	15	12	3	20
1741–45	17	9	8	47
1746–50	12	5	7	58
1751–55	20	5	15	75
(1751–54)	(15)	(1)	(14)	(93)
(1755)	(5)	(4)	(1)	(20)
1756–60	25	16	9	36
1761–65	28	23	5	18
1766–70	31	31	0	0
1771–74	31	29	2	6

guide the Society towards internal reform. In 1755, the proportion of those forgiven their deviance decreased dramatically, and thereafter the number accused of deviance rose as radically.

The concern during this period with the state of Quakerism in general may be documented, although no New Gardeners discussed the pattern of disownment itself. John Churchman, Jr., a resident of Nottingham but formerly a member of the New Garden meeting, feared that "a lifeless, Formal spirit has the prevalence of managing the affairs of the church." Churchman was particularly concerned with Quaker youth because he

> thought [he] beheld many of the youth of [the] Society taking their flight as into the air, where the snares of the prince of power thereof are laid to catch them; some of who being already so much ensnared, to their unspeakable hurt, I knew them not, otherwise than by their natural fathers, and a family resemblance, their demeanor and habit being so exceedingly altered.

Reporting on New Garden after the cleansing process began, Churchman expressed much more positive sentiments, believing that "the love of our merciful Father was measurably felt, to the comfort of the humble of heart."[18]

With the disownment of all who married out of the fellowship as a step toward reform of the Quaker community, Quakerism may have found the ultimate expression of its corporate testimony.[19] The Society became not just one among many for its serious members, but the sole group to which the member could give his full allegiance. The members belonged more to a tribe than to a religious congregation. The monthly meeting conformed to the definition of a tribe as a fairly small, simple, independent, self-contained, and homogeneous society in which essential uniformities were shared by all persons despite special modes of behavior associated with age, sex, and occupation.

A contrast of Quaker tribalism with the Puritan tribalism described by Edmund Morgan in *The Puritan Family* is informative. When members of a tribelike group in the midst of a heterogeneous society show stronger loyalty to their particular party than to the society of which it is a part, they reflect a tribalistic attitude. In New England, the group demanding special loyalty was the family. Too fond parents hoped to save their children from what they saw as certain damnation. If the Puritan system failed because, as Morgan believed, "the Puritans relied upon their children to provide the church with Members," their failure came from an all-too-common cause.[20]

In 1755, the Society of Friends entered its own period of tribalism. While Puritans proved overly loyal to their families, the Quakers of New Garden gave their primary allegiance to their religious community. Although they assigned status within the meeting along familial lines, they held the family sacred as an expression of religious fellowship, not in and of itself. For example, if the child of a Quaker married out of meeting, his parents were supposed to sever their ties with him. If the meeting discovered that the child married with his parents' consent or that the parents actually attended the wedding, a committee would visit the parents, and if they continued to support their children, the group disowned them, too. The Quaker owed his allegiance first to his religious group and only after that to his own family.

The tendency towards exclusiveness, which was given full reign in the marital disownments, led the Quaker community into a full-fledged tribalism that was sustained by the theology and sectarianism of the religion itself. In contrast to the all-consuming evangelical Quakerism that had characterized the religion of the seventeenth-century founders, tribal Quakerism lacked an outwardlooking, messianic quality. It looked inward; its corporate discipline created a well-ordered life, even if, sometimes, at the expense of the spiritual experience that had been foremost in the first decades of Quakerism. In his *Sociology of Religion*, Max Weber said of Quakerism that a "congery of ascetics always tends to become an aristocratic, exclusive organization within or definitely outside the world of the average people who surround these ascetics."[21] He was quite correct in his judgment. The Society of Friends indeed became an organization in which a select group of elders commanded the positions of influence while excluding from the ranks of fellowship all those who embraced the outside world.

NOTES

1. Hector St. John Crèvecoeur, *Letters from an American Farmer* (New York, 1912), p. 51.

2. Howard H. Brinton, *Friends for 300 Years* (New York, 1952), p. 14.

3. Quoted in Frederick Tolles, *Quakers and the Atlantic Culture* (New York, 1960), p. 22.

4. Quoted in William C. Braithwaite, *The Beginnings of Quakerism* (London, 1912; 2d ed., Cambridge, 1955), p. 306.

5. See Tolles, *Quakers and the Atlantic Culture*, for a detailed discussion of the relationship between American and English Friends.

6. Tolles, *Quakers and the Atlantic Culture*, p. 29.

7. See Richard Bauman, *For the Reputation of Truth* (Baltimore, 1971), and David Kobrin, *The Saving Remnant: Intellectual Sources of Change and Decline in Colonial Quakerism, 1690–1810* (Ph.D. diss., University of Pennsylvania, 1968), for further exploration of the divisions within Quakerism.

8. The New Garden Monthly Meeting included residents not only of New Garden but also of London Grove, Sadsbury, Nottingham, and the Marlboroughs. By 1732, the residents of Sadsbury and Nottingham were granted the right to establish their own monthly gathering.

9. New Garden figures are based on tax lists, *Pennsylvania Archives*, 3d ser. 11, and Historical Society of Pennsylvania handwritten manuscripts. Information about Chester County may be gained from James T. Lemon, *The Best Poor Man's Country* (Baltimore, 1972).

10. New Garden, in this respect, followed the pattern of other Chester County communities. By 1760, minimum sizes of many farms had been reached, preventing equal division of property among all sons, and therefore requiring sons of the third generation to move away from the family home. Tenant farming also became more frequent, as about 30 percent of Chester's married taxpayers were landless. Movement to new communities was high; between 1774 and 1785 more than 50 percent of the adult males disappeared from Chester County records (Lemon, *Best Poor Man's Country*, pp. 73, 92–95).

11. I have chosen centrality, or the frequency with which each member interacts and the number of other participants with whom he operates, as a measure of status within the meeting because it is easily and objectively measured and because centrality tends to be strongly linked to other properties of status such as conformity to norms and influence upon other members. See Terence Hopkins, *The Exercise of Influence in Small Groups* (Totowa, N.J., 1964).

12. Those whom I have designated as elders were often given formal recognition by the meeting. Ten out of twelve of those who accumulated over 100 assignments were named elders, overseers, or clerks by the meeting.

13. A committee appointment made at one meeting could require labor spread over the course of many months. The initial appointment was the only one counted, however, in determining the number of assignments. If anything, this determination underrepresents the activism of the elders since many of their appointments were to committees, such as arbitrators or discipline visitations, which took a great deal of time and effort. From 1748 to 1762, for example, elders spent 70 percent of their time on committees that settled disputes and investigated infractions of the discipline.

14. Quoted in Braithwaite, *Beginnings of Quakerism*, p. 329.

15. Aside from the genealogical information in the manuscript and published records of the Genealogical Society of Pennsylvania, located in the Historical Society of Pennsylvania, I also consulted copies of the early tax lists and abstracts of wills filed in Chester County. In addition to the information on individual families in the genealogies, I also found pertinent data in Gilbert Cope and J. Smith Futhey, *History of Chester County, Pennsylvania* (Philadelphia, 1881), and Albert Myers, *Immigration of*

the Irish Quakers into Pennsylvania, 1682–1750 (Lancaster, 1901). Also extremely helpful were the many volumes of the *Pennsylvania Archives*.

Full genealogical information is unfortunately not available for each New Garden member. As I could find no evidence of systematic bias to account for the information that I could obtain, I have decided to use the incomplete data in the hope that some imformation is better than none at all.

16. John Andrew Moore Passmore, *Ancestors and Descendants of Andrew Moore, 1612–1897* (Philadelphia, 1897), p. 27.

17. New Garden Monthly Meeting Minutes, 1756.

18. John Churchman, *An Account of the Gospel Labors and Christian Experiences of that Faithful Minister of Christ, John Churchman, late of Nottingham in Pennsylvania* (Philadelphia, 1873), pp. 241, 243, 279.

19. The Society of Friends was seeking other expressions of its corporate testimony during this general period. Perhaps the most famous manifestation of Quaker reform was the withdrawal of many prominent Friends from political life in 1756, when their commitment to pacifism came into conflict with the demands of the French and Indian War. It should be noted that the New Garden reforms that I have documented began prior to the political withdrawal. Although it would be impossible to assign a cause-and-effect relationship, in the absence of data from other meetings, it is very possible that the political leaders were following a trend toward purification that originated in small, rural meetings, such as New Garden. We do know that pressure to vote against war taxes came from rural Quakers, including John Churchman. Further research is certainly needed to pinpoint the exact relationship between these local efforts to disown those guilty of infractions of the discipline and more general attempts to reform Quakerism.

20. Edmund Morgan, *The Puritan Family* (New York, 1944), p. 185.

21. Max Weber, *Sociology of Religion* (Boston, 1963), p. 166.

CHAPTER 7

The Quaker Connection: Visiting Patterns among Women in the Philadelphia Society of Friends, 1750–1800

NANCY TOMES

Sarah Logan Fisher, a Philadelphia merchant's wife, entitled her journal for 1777, a "diary of trifling occurrences." In it she recorded the events that marked the passage of family and community time: the activities of her children, the daily visits with kinfolk and friends, the births, deaths and weddings among her circle of acquaintances. For the most part, historians have shared Sarah Fisher's deprecating attitude toward the everyday matters recorded in women's journals. While genealogists and local historians have ransacked diaries like hers for glimpses of personages and events of the Revolution, they have considered the women's activities themselves unimportant. Even scholars interested in women's status have dismissed these painstaking records of daily life as but one more evidence of female idleness and oppression, and have gone in search of those rare women who ventured beyond the ordinary round of women's concerns.[1]

From the intellectual perspective of the "new social history," however, the "trifling occurrences" recorded in women's journals have become historical events as worthy of note as revolutionary battles or political debates. Over the last decade and a half, historians have increasingly recognized the role of seemingly powerless and inarticulate individuals in shaping society. As a consequence, they have developed a new respect for the "politics" of everyday life, including women's experience. From this perspective, even the most fragmentary records of individual behavior—census records, tax lists, church registers—have become important historical documents. Borrowing extensively from the methods of anthropology and sociology, social historians have used such records to yield significant insights into the past.

The methods of "historical anthropology," as practiced by Alan Macfarlane in *The Family Life of Ralph Josselin*, suggest a particularly promising line of investigation for journals. This imaginative analysis of a seventeenth-century English clergyman's diary demonstrates the wealth of information that can be extracted from even the driest journal entries. Macfarlane used this document to reconstruct every aspect of Josselin's life: his economic activities, relations with wife and children, involvement in the social world of kin and neighbors, even the mental world revealed in his dreams and images. In discussing the relative importance of kin and friends to Josselin, Macfarlane made inventive use of his visiting patterns. Used as an index of intimacy, the clergyman's records of visits revealed that he sustained closer ties with his friends than with his relations.[2]

Macfarlane's analysis of visiting patterns is an especially useful model for interpreting eighteenth-century women's journals, since they so often recorded information on social activities. From women's visiting patterns, as Macfarlane's work demonstrates, the historian can reconstruct the network of family, kin, and friendship ties that shaped the journal writer's life. When examined over time, the brief entries of names and activities form patterns. People seen regularly and informally can be distinguished from those encountered less frequently and in less intimate settings. From genealogical records, kinship relations between the woman and the circle she visited can be established. Further detail comes from her remarks about individuals, including terms of address and endearment. Taken together, this information provides an idea of the journal writer's "emotional universe": the people who mattered most to her, the ways she formed and sustained emotional ties over time, and the relative importance of kin and friends in her life.[3]

This internal view of journal writers' personal relationships takes on even greater significance when compared with knowledge of the larger society in which they lived. Information about visiting patterns, particularly the function of kinship and religious affiliation in determining the range of personal contacts, can profitably be used to speculate about the role of women's personal networks in shaping larger social groupings. The social rituals perpetuated by upper-class women, for example, undoubtedly played an important role in the maintenance of male political and economic elites. Thus the charting of visiting patterns among women of an elite group may provide insight into the specific mechanisms by which its boundaries were formed and defended.[4]

This study will focus on visiting patterns among women of the Philadelphia Society of Friends between 1750 and 1790. The women chosen for this study—Elizabeth Drinker, Sarah Logan Fisher, Anna and Peggy Rawle, Ann Warder, and Sally Wister—were all daughters or wives (sometimes both) of wealthy and influential Quaker merchants.[5] In no sense were they "average" women of the time (if such a type ever really existed); rather, their male relations had accumulated substantial fortunes that enabled these women to be both literate and leisured. All the journal writers had attended private schools; all had sufficient freedom from household chores to keep journals and to make the visits recorded therein. Such advantages in and of themselves set these diarists apart from the great majority of colonial women.

In addition to their high economic status, these Quaker women also shared their families' prominent status within the Society of Friends. The journal writers' male relatives and family friends played important roles in the Friends' affairs during years of crisis and change. The Quakers had long possessed substantial political influence in the colony founded by William Penn, himself a prominent English Friend. In Philadelphia, the Friends held a variety of political posts that enabled them to influence local and provincial government. But they were not without rivals, for by mid-century a wealthy group of non-Quakers had arisen who increasingly contested and circumscribed the Friends' political power over the next thirty years. Belonging to the Quaker elite at a time when its political supremacy was being challenged, the journal writers' sense of group identity must have been particularly intense. Their daily activities can reasonably be expected to reflect the social strategies used by a group striving to sustain its authority and cohesiveness in a time of unprecedented change.[6]

To determine the relevance of women's visiting patterns to the maintenance of an elite group, then, no better set of diarists could be selected. The journals of these Quaker ladies allow us not only to chart the dimensions of their "female world of love and ritual," but also to identify the links between that world and the larger community within which they lived.[7] By examining the forms and functions of visiting performed by elite women, and determining the familial and religious bonds reinforced by their ceremonial acts, we can gain a better understanding of the role women's activities played in sustaining the Quaker polity.

The amount of time spent visiting by these six Quaker women, and the prominent place it occupied in their journals, indicate its importance in their lives. Under ordinary circumstances, it was a daily activity. "No person, our family excepted, has been here this day that I can recollect, which is rather an uncommon circumstance," Elizabeth Drinker noted in her journal.[8] Visiting included a wide range of activities, from "grand visits," when guests were received in the drawing room, to a brief walk in the garden. Ann Warder's observations on Philadelphia society reflect the significance as well as frequency of social calls. A native Englishwoman, she used her journal to record the strange customs of Americans for the benefit of her sister in England. Ann commented frequently on the unusual "sociability" of her new acquaintances: "I have now a great heap of work that decreases very slowly through gossiping about, which is unavoidable without giving my kind friends offense, for the great number before I have got once around renders it necessary to begin again. . . . It is the custom to visit here more than with us, and they destroy the social freedom of it by too much dressing."[9]

The visits recorded by the journal writers varied greatly in both form and function. At the most formal extreme were the ceremonial calls made solely to convey the sense of obligation and respect felt by one family for another. By these honorary calls, a woman signified that she recognized certain social relationships as particularly important. Formal visits were made infrequently but systematically, usually at tea time. Ann Warder, as might be expected, found this practice very tiresome. Her complaints provide good evidence that a woman "in society" could not fail to make formal visits without incurring censure. After tea with one sister-in-law, Ann confided to her journal that "I now feel at liberty to begin afresh with visiting the more distant connections—the idea of being obliged to without giving offense proves to me a burden in such very warm weather." Evidently her grudging efforts did not satisfy her relations, for her mother-in-law told her later that "Sister Morris and Sister Emlen [her sisters-in-law] thought I rather slighted them by my few visits, and conscious that every moment of my time seemed too engaged with such trifles, I could not help weeping, which did me good."[10]

The Philadelphia-born journal writers may have felt similarly burdened but recorded no such complaints about duty calls, probably because they had been raised to expect them. As an outsider, Ann Warder undoubtedly found them more onerous.

Similar to these ceremonial calls, but with a more specific purpose, were visits made to mark some change in an individual's life that warranted community notice. Travelers received special visits on the eve of their departure and the day of their return. Ann Warder, for example, recorded that "many in their own carriages have honored me with their company" after her arrival from England. The community observed special visiting customs for newly married couples. For a week after the wedding, women called to drink tea with the bride and men to have punch with the groom. The couple's young friends and relations played an especially active role in celebrating their new marital status. Elizabeth Drinker wrote on the day after her son's marriage that his sisters "Sally and Nancy spent this afternoon with ye Bride, with many other young persons, who were not invited to ye wedding, her uncle's house being small." Rather than presuming that newlyweds or travelers might enjoy some privacy, their friends seemed to make a concerted effort to keep them company as they readjusted to community life.[11]

A woman's lying-in was an equally public occasion for her women friends and relatives. As soon as her labor began, married and unmarried women alike came to her bedside to comfort and tend her. On rushing to her sister-in-law's home, Sarah Fisher found "Sister Hannah" already attended by several women as well as her doctor. After the baby's birth, more formal calls of congratulation were made. Sarah Fisher noted in her journal a criticism of these lying-in customs that testifies to their prevalence: "At monthly meeting, Susy Lightfoot appeared in testimony, entreating young mothers not to make such great preparations for their lying-in as they generally do, and to avoid those formal visitings upon the occasion which are too much made use of among us, but rather wish'd they might be thankful to their Divine Helper who had brought them through that time of difficulty and danger with safety."[12]

The journal writers recorded many less formal visits made in times of sickness and death. When a member of her family lay ill or dying, a woman called her close female friends and kin to advise and comfort her. Sarah Fisher wrote in a typical entry that she "walk'd up this morning to see cousin Sally Emlen, as she had sent word her child was dying, but found it rather better on my getting there tho' very ill with the hives." She noted that "several good women . . . administering their advice and skill" had preceded her there. Elizabeth Drinker responded quickly to a message from "Neighbor Waln" that the watching women thought her friend Sucky's daughter "near the close." Elizabeth wrote, "I went in the backchamber to Sucky who was in deep distress; she desired me after some time to go into the front chamber and enquire if she was gone." After the death, a group of women and men stayed to watch over the corpse. When her friend Caty Greenleaf died of consumption, Elizabeth Drinker's daughter performed this service. Her mother noted proudly that it was "the first time Sally sat up all night" on such an occasion. For days after the funeral, a family received consolation visits. Sarah Fisher, for example, received a constant stream of visitors who came to condole her on the death of her parents.[13]

Along with these various visiting customs, the Quakers also observed specialized forms of religious visiting. The monthly meeting regularly appointed several members as "family visitors" to visit each family on its rolls for prayer and personal counsel. They also appeared at times of crisis: to mourn the dead, comfort the distraught, and reprimand the wayward. When Elizabeth Drinker's daughter Molly eloped with a young man her parents did not approve of, the meeting appointed two women to visit her. Family visitors were often women; Hannah Catherall and Rebecca Jones formed an established pair who appeared regularly in several of the journal writers' households.[14]

Beyond the purposive calls made to show respect, mark a special community event, or attend a friend during a crisis, the journal writers recorded many visits paid only for pleasure. The women considered these informal social events as uniquely "agreeable" or "pleasant." Often their activities consisted of no more than a walk, a chat, a shopping trip, or an evening spent reading or sewing together. Frequent, spontaneous visits involved a small circle of intimate friends or kin who were entertained in the kitchen or bedchamber rather than in the drawing room. Peggy Rawle wrote of a visit with friends, "We came up here [to her bedroom] to enjoy a little of our own chat, and spent an agreeable evening." Even Ann Warder, who disliked making formal visits, enjoyed those occasions when, after dinner, she took "a general ramble among my friends." On a larger scale, the women organized outings and small parties with friends and relatives. The unmarried women often paid each other overnight visits.[15]

The balance of formal and pleasure visits in a woman's social life changed over the course of her life cycle. Depending on her age and marital status, her visits varied not only in their purpose but also in the social group they encompassed. Visits can be categorized by the social "unit" involved: some visits were paid to individuals ("stepped up to see Sally Emlen") or to groups ("George Emlen, Myers and Sally sup'd with us"), while others were aimed at couples ("called on Francis and Becky Rawle") or at a whole household ("to Aunt Fisher's for awhile"). A comparison of both the purpose and the social unit involved in visits by the young unmarried women—Sally Wister, the Rawle sisters, and Elizabeth Drinker before her marriage—with the young matrons—Sarah Logan Fisher and Ann Warder—and the older married women—Sarah Fisher and Elizabeth Drinker in their later journals—reveals some significant differences in their visiting patterns.

Of the three groups, the young unmarried women did the most pleasure visiting and paid the fewest formal calls. Their social activities centered primarily on a set of unmarried girl friends, with one particular "best friend" usually distinguished from the others. The single girls also had many contacts with older women, both married and unmarried, and enjoyed lengthy stays in the households of friends and kinfolk. In comparison with the married journal writers, they spent more time exclusively in the company of women. This does not mean that the girls were rigidly isolated from men. The circles of unmarried girl friends often had male admirers from the same age group attached to them. Anna Rawle, for example, identified two boys as the "beaux of our circle." But contact with older men outside the family was indeed fairly limited.[16]

Marriage brought a very different pattern of visiting. Once established in her own home, a young matron had to assume responsibility for the formal calls. It was her duty then to show the proper regard for her new in-laws and to participate in important community events by observing established visiting customs. Consequently the married journal writers did less unceremonial socializing among women their own age. Instead they attended more mixed gatherings of men and women. At such events, some informal sex segregation took place. Ann Warder noted of one dinner party, "when we were well satisfied, left the men to their pipes and went upstairs to our chat."[17] On the whole, however, the married women spent less time in all-female groups. The difference between single and married women's visiting patterns indicates that at marriage, a young woman no longer belonged so exclusively to a peer-group, pleasure-oriented social life, but rather had to take up more formal responsibilities for visiting.

The journals kept by Sarah Logan Fisher and Elizabeth Drinker in the later years of their lives suggest another life-cycle change in visiting patterns. While in their forties, both women became increasingly housebound due to ill health. As they could do little visiting, the older women's activities consequently centered more and more on members of their own families, particularly children and grandchildren. Both women expressed feelings of loneliness and isolation brought about by this curtailment of movement. They became all the more dependent on the few intimate friends who could be relied upon to come see them at home. Sarah Fisher wrote on a day when her husband and daughter had gone on a trip, "felt very lonely, poorly in body and heavily oppressed in mind, sent for my dear friend M. Houlton to spend the day with me."[18] The journals of the older women indicate that when sickness and old age made visiting difficult, women felt a sense of loss, again suggesting the centrality of this social activity in their lives.

Changes in visiting customs and patterns over a woman's lifetime suggest the larger purposes that visiting served in community life. Not surprisingly, the journal writers participated in many informal social occasions purely for pleasure; in these instances, visiting involved no more than a natural desire for recreation and companionship. But beyond this pleasurable intent, the extent and complexity of formal visiting indicates that it played a larger role in this society. Visiting served as a ceremonial way of "paying one's respects" to relatives or friends to whom one felt a particular obligation. It also provided a means for involving the wider community in the life of each household. Through observance of the proper visiting customs, neighbors and kin helped a young couple adjust to the first days of married life, surrounded a lying-in woman with sympathetic female friends, shared a parent's grief over a child's death. From the first prompt response to a call for help to the more formal recognition of a birth or death, visiting involved people in the most intimate events of their neighbors' lives. In this fashion, the community built a network of mutual obligation and social knowledge in a society where few institutional forms of assistance existed. Visiting helped to maintain an informal social "insurance"; it represented an investment in rituals which created "a store of good will which may be drawn upon in emergencies."[19] And in observing those rituals, especially those designed to cope with sickness and death, women's activities played a crucial role.

In light of the enormous psychological and practical value of visiting, it becomes all the more important to know with whom women visited. From the universe of individuals around them, they chose only certain ones to participate in these visiting rituals. Their selection thus established the boundaries of mutual obligation recognized by the journal writers. An analysis of their visiting patterns, by revealing the factors which determined these boundaries, can illumine the basic structure of the society in which the journal writers lived.

At the center of each woman's network of mutual obligation stood the nuclear family, both the one into which she was born and the one she formed at marriage. The emotional and practical ties created in these units—those between husband and wife, parent and child, brothers and sisters—strongly affected her social activities yet can only be partially evaluated with information on visiting patterns. As long as family members lived in the same household, the journal entries provide little idea of the frequency and intensity of contact. The closest relationships, especially that between husband and wife, may have received the least attention because they were so all-encompassing. Alan Macfarlane, encountering this phenomenon in Ralph Josselin's diary, referred to it as an "optical illusion," or emotional foreshortening of the diarist's most intimate relationships. Due to this foreshortening, the women's journals provide a more reliable index of ties *between*, rather than *within*, their households.[20]

The journal writers' visiting patterns clearly demonstrate the importance of parent-child relationships in forming links of mutual affection and support between households. When living apart from parents or children, the journal writers maintained frequent and intimate contact with them. Sarah Logan Fisher, for example, visited "Mammy and Daddy" daily after her marriage. Their deaths sent her into a deep depression. "This four weeks," she wrote after her father died, "I must pass over in silence, words being incapable of expressing the grief I have felt in the loss of my dear, my excellent Parent in whom I mourn a Father, Brother, and Friend."[21] Ties between parents and children were not solely emotional, for in a crisis, women often turned to their parents for help. Rebecca Rawle Shoemaker sent her daughters to live with her mother when her husband's Loyalist sympathies forced her to flee Philadelphia with him. Peggy and Anna Rawle kept their journals for "dearest mother" during their separation. Elizabeth Drinker's children drew upon their mother's considerable skills as a healer; Elizabeth nursed her grandchildren through a variety of childhood diseases. Ann Warder's mother-in-law raised the seven orphaned children of her daughter Lydia Warder Parker.[22]

In addition to the parental ties maintained after leaving home, the journal writers continued very close relationships with siblings. A particularly strong intimacy seemed to exist between sisters close in age, such as Anna and Peggy Rawle. Three years apart in age, they attended school together, had the same set of friends, paid calls together and shared a bedroom. Their journals recorded many nights spent together reading and sewing in their room. Peggy went to live with her sister after Anna's marriage to John Clifford in 1784.[23] Elizabeth Drinker and her sister Mary Sandwith sustained a similar closeness throughout their lives. Unmarried herself, Mary Sandwith lived with the Drinkers as almost a second mother. She often accompanied Henry Drinker and the children on trips that Elizabeth could not make because of her health. The Drinkers' eldest daughters, Sally and Nancy, formed another strong attachment. After they married, they contrived to live next door to each other in Downingtown.

Brothers and sisters formed strong but seemingly less intense ties. Sarah Fisher, who had no sisters, expressed fondness for her brothers but appeared to share more experience with their wives. Sally and Nancy Drinker showed a special concern for their brother William, who had tuberculosis. When he became ill on a visit to New York, they took turns traveling there to nurse him. In larger families, bonds between older and younger children seem to have been weaker, regardless of sex. Sally Wister, for example, often mentioned her sister Betsy, three years younger than herself, while rarely referring to her much younger sisters and brother. In the Drinker family, the youngest children, William and Molly, also spent the most time together.

The journal writers' relationships with parents and children, brothers and sisters, obviously formed the most important emotional nexus for their social activities. When viewed against the background of the women's other personal contacts, however, it appears that these bonds were only the core of a much larger set of kinship relations that structured their visiting patterns. When all the individuals a woman mentioned visiting over a period of several months are examined together, the predominance of kin ties is quite striking. With the exception of Elizabeth Drinker, an orphan with few kin even by marriage, the other journal writers were related to between 40 and 90 percent of those visited. These percentages include members of the nuclear family not resident in the journal writer's household; but even when they are removed from the total, the percent of kin-based visiting remains between 40 and 60 percent of the total visits.[24]

The range of kin recognized by the journal writers was not extensive, although it was well within western European tradition. Relatives acknowledged by the women included grandparents, great aunts and uncles, aunts and uncles, first cousins, nieces and nephews. Only Sarah Logan Fisher identified any number of second cousins; these cousins were mostly Pembertons, one of the most prominent Quaker families in Philadelphia, which may explain her recognition of that degree of kinship. But if the journal writers did not recognize a wide range of kin, their kinship relations did become very complicated by marriage. Marriage created a whole new set of connections regarded as binding as a woman's own blood relationships. A wife accepted her husband's relatives as her own, never distinguishing them as "in-laws" in her references to them. This practice led to the acknowledgment of rather remote degrees of kinship, as in the case of Ann Warder's "Uncle Roberts," who was her husband's brother's first wife's father.[25]

The mutual affection and support manifested by visiting among relatives in eighteenth-century Philadelphia illustrates the dangers inherent in using household structure as the sole index of kinship relations. Historians have too often assumed that since western European families lived almost exclusively in nuclear households, they were inherently more isolated from relatives than the extended household groups found in other cultures. It may be, though, that families lived in nuclear households yet provided services and support to an extended family group. If a married woman did not live with her parents or siblings or cousins, yet visited them daily, the fact that they lived in separate households seems less significant than it otherwise might. The visiting patterns revealed in these women's journals suggest that household composition alone cannot be used as a measure of family structure.

184

The journal writers obviously lived within a dense web of kin relations. Relatives formed the staple of both their formal and informal social contacts. Yet family relationships did not constitute the totality of these women's emotional bonds. Their visiting also brought them into contact with individuals, of all ages and positions, to whom they were not related. As a result, each journal writer formed friendships of differing intensities outside her kinship circle. "How greatly is a near, dear and feeling friend to be prized," wrote Elizabeth Drinker, a sentiment echoed in the other journals.[26] Among her varied acquaintances, each woman singled out a few special friends for whom her love rivaled the intensity of family ties.

The journal writers' intense friendships almost all developed from a circle of school friends made before the woman married. Sally Wister kept her journal for her school chum Debby Norris. She wrote in it, "I long to see thee, to embrace thee and to assure thee of my love. . . . If wishes could avail I wou'd be in your garden with Sally Jones, Polly Fishbourne and thyself." Anna and Peggy Rawle cultivated a similar set of friends made at the Benezet school, among them Peggy's favorite, Polly Foulke. She described to her mother the qualities that drew her to Polly. "such a flow of good humor, and so much unaffected cheerfulness, that she is the delight of all her acquaintances; join'd to these she has a heart remarkably affectionate and kind."[27]

These friendships may have started as schoolgirl affections, but they lasted far beyond the women's school days. In Elizabeth Drinker's journal, it is possible to see how these ties matured over time. Elizabeth's best friend, Betsy Moode, moved away after her marriage to Samuel Emlen and died soon after. Thirty years later, Elizabeth marked the anniversary of her death, referring to her still as "my very dear friend." Hannah Moode, Betsy's sister, also had been Elizabeth's particular girlhood friend. After her marriage, she moved to New York; it was with her family that Elizabeth's son William went to stay when he became ill on a trip to the city. Other schoolgirl friends like Sally Wharton, Sucky Hartshorn, and Hannah Hicks remained Elizabeth's friends and neighbors throughout her life.[28]

The journal writers' choice of special female friends from among their schoolmates suggests that peer groups formed in girlhood played a special role in the structuring of their social world. While this influence seems slight in comparison with the centrality of kin in their lives, such relationships are significant nonetheless in what they may indicate about women's changing personalities. The journal writers were among the first generation of women to attend schools outside the home with girls their own age. The self-conscious cultivation of female friends that schooling allowed may have encouraged a shift from a familial orientation—where a girl's friends were either relatives or individuals encountered only in a family setting—to a more individualistic attitude—where her social relationships expressed her personal needs or preferences. Obviously the journal writers still had a predominantly familial outlook, yet the connection between schooling and some individuation on their part is suggestive. Perhaps what can be seen here is the beginning of that sororial frame of mind, that sense of connection with women outside the family, which made possible the reform activities of later generations of Quaker women.[29]

Despite their seemingly individualistic nature, the journal writers' intimate friendships still formed part of the larger pattern of community life. For the women's choice of intimates reflected an obligation no less transcendent than the ties of kinship: the bond of shared religion. In the most individualistic preferences they expressed, the journal writers did not stray beyond the circle of their coreligionists. Even in the less intense encounters of everyday life, the women observed the principle of exclusivity. With the exception of Sally Wister, who rather daringly flirted with the non-Quaker soldiers billeted on her cousin's farm during the British occupation of Philadelphia, the journal writers visited only with other Friends.

The striking religious insularity evidenced in these women's visiting patterns undoubtedly reflected the trend toward "retreatism" in the Quaker community during the last half of the eighteenth century. Finding it difficult to maintain its principles in political and social affairs, the Society chose to withdraw from "the world" rather than compromise its religious identity and beliefs. This withdrawal can be seen in many aspects of Quaker community life. Jack Marietta has shown how increasingly stringent ecclesiastical discipline in the monthly meeting enforced behavioral standards designed to set the Friends apart from their worldly neighbors. Sydney James has indicated the ways in which the Friends' retreat from the larger community led to their increased philanthropic efforts on behalf of the poor, sick, and uneducated among their coreligionists.[30]

But while women's social activities reinforced increasingly rigid boundaries between the Quakers and the outside world, the visiting of the women also played a complex role *within* the Society, establishing social ties among Friends of different backgrounds. In a 1772 census, the Philadelphia monthly meeting numbered over 1,000 members.[31] Obviously, in a community of that size, Quakers could indulge a variety of personal or political preferences in the choice of friends. Even among their coreligionists, the women had to choose which individuals and families they would visit. Without extensive information on each visitor's background, it is difficult to ascertain all the factors that determined the formation of social circles within the Society. From the internal evidence of the journals, however, some speculations can be made about the dynamics of the Quaker community.

Despite the growing emphasis on conformity in the Society, divisions existed among the Quaker community in the decades between 1750 and 1790. Studies by scholars such as Richard Bauman and Frederick Tolles have shown that even among Quakers in good standing there were serious disagreements on religious and political issues. Prosperity had fostered in many Friends a new worldliness, including an increasingly secular outlook on life and open enjoyment of wealth, which provoked criticism from their more austere brethren. The same factions disagreed over the political stance dictated by their religious principles on such issues as military defense and Indian policy in the 1750s and support for the Revolution in the 1770s. Throughout this period, tension between the worldly, secular instincts of many Quakers and the intense quietistic zeal of others created deep cleavages within the Society.[32]

As indicated by their positions on the Revolutionary conflict, the journal writers' male relations clearly belonged to different factions in these disputes. Elizabeth Drinker's husband, Henry, and Sarah Fisher's husband, Thomas, were among the twelve Quaker leaders arrested and exiled to Virginia in 1777 for refusing on religious grounds to support the Revolutionary government. Samuel Shoemaker, the Rawle sisters' stepfather, had to flee the same patriots for different reasons: he broke with the peace testimony upheld by Friends like Drinker and Fisher, and openly expressed his Loyalist sympathies. Daniel Wister maintained a nominal opposition to both sides in the conflict, yet allowed his daughter Sally to fraternize with American soldiers. The political position of the Warder family is not evident.[33]

The journal writers themselves rarely commented directly on political or religious issues, or even remarked on the relative piety of their visitors. Yet fragmentary evidence from their diaries suggests the effect of religious and political controversies on their social behavior. In various ways, they exhibit the same tension between worldliness and piety that shaped their menfolk's political viewpoints. Elizabeth Drinker and Sarah Fisher appear through their journals as conservative, pious women who disapproved of the growing worldliness they observed among the Friends, especially in the younger generation. Drinker, for example, often expressed her dislike of the idle diversions such as ice-cream parties so popular among her children's friends. Both Drinker and Fisher used their journals in part for religious devotions. In contrast, the other journal writers kept entirely secular records of their lives. The Rawle sisters felt uncomfortable around their devout acquaintances. Anna noted that her sister Peggy would not go see a friend since she had taken "a religious turn." Anna claimed to like the woman still, "tho' the length she carries her scruples seem more likely to make people despair (if they imagine all she does is necessary), than to induce them to follow her example." Ann Warder, who had a keen appreciation of feminine dress and charm, expressed similar reservations about a pious friend's appearance. Her dress, Ann wrote, "looked so old and awkward made that if her person was not so agreeable it would be disgusting."[34]

These signs of distance between the more pious and worldly sets of Quaker women indicate that certain divisions in the community extended from the public to the private spheres of life. Yet such differences among Quaker women should not obscure the points of contact between them. Despite their divergent values, the journal writers still belonged to the same community. They shared visitors in common, and while often choosing different intimates from among them, undoubtedly knew many of the same people. While distinct circles existed, they were by no means exclusive. For example, political differences between their menfolk did not prevent Elizabeth Drinker from receiving a call from Rebecca Shoemaker, Anna and Peggy Rawle's mother, on her return from Loyalist exile in 1782.[35]

Nothing better illustrates the underlying continuity of the Quaker community than Ann Warder's first months in Philadelphia. In the course of her introduction to Quaker society, in 1786, she met all the journal writers except Elizabeth Drinker, who was by then an invalid. She did meet Elizabeth's eldest daughter, Sally, and styled her a very pleasant girl. She admired Sarah Fisher's brother-in-law

Miers and his wife as models of the "strictest gentility" among the Friends, while at the same time acknowledging Anna Rawle Clifford and her husband as the social leaders of the younger set. In time, Ann, like other journal writers, settled into her own special circle of friends. Yet her first introduction to the Philidelphia Quaker community reveals that its larger boundaries included Friends of varied persuasions.[36]

Women's visiting patterns suggest that, however serious political and religious disputes became among Friends, the Quaker community did not become completely factionalized in a social sense. Women may have favored like-minded Friends as intimates, but they by no means rigidly excluded those who disagreed with them. The real rigidity in social patterns appears in the women's complete exclusion of non-Friends from their activities. Thus the daily practices of women suggest the existence of more shared experience than one might be led to expect from the heat of political and religious debates within the Society. While it by no means made Friends a homogenous or unified group, shared religion still united Quakers more than it divided them on specific doctrinal or political issues.[37]

Quaker women's visiting patterns suggest the primacy of two social relations in structuring their social world: kinship and religious affiliation. Inevitably we must compare the relative strength of these two allegiances. Scholars have given much attention to the tension between family and religious ties among the Friends, especially in the transition between generations of "believers." In particular, the debate over the religious status of believers' children, which resulted in the Society's adoption of a birthright membership policy in 1737, brought into sharp focus the conflicting claims of family and religion.[38] Yet, in concentrating exclusively on this particular aspect of religious doctrine, historians have overemphasized the anatagonism between those two forces in the Quaker community. The patterns revealed in the women's journals suggests a fundamentally different perspective on the relationship between family and religion among the Friends.

In so frequently choosing kinfolk as their visiting partners, the journal writers clearly acknowledged the centrality of family ties in establishing networks of mutual obligation and support. In limiting all other social relations to coreligionists, the journal writers offered equally eloquent testimony to the solidarity of the Quaker community. The Society of Friends, by confining all the ceremonial, pragmatic, and pleasurable uses of visiting to its members, thereby assured its own insularity and strength. Yet the relative importance of kinship and religious affiliation in creating a sense of community among the Quakers proves almost impossible to assess. While the amount of kin-visiting done by the journal writers is impressive, it is no less dramatic than the religious insularity they exhibited. Trying to unravel the two affiliations soon leads to the recognition that they became all the stronger as they were so effectively intertwined.

From this perspective, the requirement that all Friends marry within the meeting takes on new significance. As Richard Vann pointed out in his study of the social development of English Quakerism, the first Friends placed great emphasis on marriage between believers. Vann attributed this custom to the Friends' concern with the parental role in children's religious upbringing. The "vital task of forming character" dictated that a husband and wife not be "unequally yoked" in the matter of religious belief.[39] While this may have been the original intention of the prohibition against marrying out of meeting, it had far wider consequences. For by enforcing endogamy, the only other affiliation that could possibly have competed with religion, that of kinship, was made to reinforce the Society's boundaries. Rather than being a rival allegiance, kinship became a model for the group solidarity the Quakers wished to foster. For example, family visiting—the practice of sending representatives from the meeting to celebrate family rituals and help in times of crisis—seems a conscious adaptation of older, kin-oriented customs. Underpinning as it did the Society's more formal, institutional modes of organization, such visiting served to create mutual respect and support among the kin group and probably constituted the most effective means for building a strong collective identity.

In this fashion, the Society of Friends adapted the methods once used to foster an older, organic sense of community—that of a collection of individuals unified more by blood and propinquity than by belief—to promote a radically different identity—as a voluntary, self-conscious sodality. Quaker society thus represents a transitional stage in the evolution from traditional to modern attitudes toward kinship and community. All too often this shift has been portrayed as a simple linear development from the individual's immersion in a collective life of relatives and neighbors to the isolation of existence in the nuclear family. While the simplistic categories of "traditional" and "modern" provide a convenient means for identifying long-term changes in family function, they are of little use in comprehending the process of change.[40] The underlying assumption that economic and social change in the eighteenth and nineteenth centuries immediately and irrevocably destroyed traditional attitudes toward kin and community has to be substantially revised; ample evidence has now accumulated from studies of immigrant and slave communities, for example, that suggests that in certain phases of economic and social change, kin-based systems of informal community support intensified rather than deteriorated.[41]

Historians have long recognized that both kinship and religious affiliation played an important role in the formation and maintenance of colonial political and economic elites. Frederick Tolles first noted the propensity of Quaker "grandees" to intermarriage in his classic *Meeting House and Counting House.* Bernard Bailyn, Edmund Morgan, and Peter Dobkin Hall have recognized the function of kinship in creating business and political alliances among other colonial elites. Colonial kinship patterns show no simple evolution from immersion in a wide kinship group to isolation in intense nuclear families. Rather, the importance of kinship has varied significantly in different economic and social situations.[42]

While these and other studies have contributed greatly to our knowledge of the role of kinship in forming colonial elites, they are all incomplete in their focus only on male arenas of activity such as business and politics. While recognizing the function of marriage in cementing kinship ties, they focus primarily on its consequences for male concerns. The importance of women's social activities in maintaining group cohesion has been given much less attention. Yet this analysis of women's visiting patterns strongly suggests that women played a critical role in sustaining a sense of community among the Philadelphia Quakers. Although men participated in some visiting customs, the bulk of this activity fell to their womenfolk. Through visiting, women affirmed significant relationships, celebrated rituals of community life, and provided emotional and practical help in times of crisis. In particular, the assistance women gave one another in coping with disease and death lent special strength to their bonds. In a society where professional medicine had limited scope, such services were indeed important. Thus, while one aim of family and religious cooperation may have been the formation and preservation of business concerns or political power, the value of social networks perpetuated by women in providing essential psychological and practical services in a precarious urban environment must not be overlooked.

In choosing their partners in this system of mutual help, the journal writers exhibited the strong influence of kinship and religious affiliation in setting their social boundaries. The importance of those two relationships in women's daily activities provides a persuasive argument for their primacy in the organization of the larger society. While male-forged links of commerce and politics have long been recognized as influences on social structure, the networks formed by women's social activities have never been given the acknowledgment they deserve. Historians have for so long accorded primacy to male activities that the equivalency of female concerns must be boldly stated. Yet once examined with care, it becomes clear that women's activities shaped the social world inhabited by men and women alike. On a daily basis, women's interactions translated the structure of the community into a process through which a variety of individuals lived together. Without the myriad "trifling occurrences" that made up the fabric of female lives, the community as all knew it would never have existed.

NOTES

1. One local historian described a colonial woman's journal as "mostly personal in character. The parts of general interest are not numerous" (George Vaux, "Extracts from the Diary of Hannah Callender," *Pennsylvania Magazine of History and Biography* 12 [1888]: 432–56). This attitude seems to have been the prevalent one until very recently. Gerda Lerner, "The Lady and the Mill Girl," *Midcontinent American Studies Journal* 10 (1969): 5–15, links the erosion of women's economic productivity with the development of the "cult of the lady." According to prevailing values, "idleness . . . had become a status symbol" for the lady, and her chief role in life consisted of "displaying her husband's wealth" (p. 12). Most historians have dismissed women's social activities in much the same terms. Notable exceptions are Nancy Cott, *The Bonds of Womanhood* (New Haven, 1977), and Carroll Smith-Rosenberg, "The Female World of Love and Ritual," *Signs* 1 (1975): 1–29.

2. Alan Macfarlane, *The Family Life of Ralph Josselin* (Cambridge, England, 1970).

3. The term "emotional universe" is my adaptation of Raymond Firth's concept of the "kinship universe." See Firth's *Two Studies of Kinship in London* (London, 1956).

4. Leonore Davidoff, *The Best Circles: Women and Society in Victorian England* (Totowa, N.J., 1973), has made this point convincingly in her study of women's social activities in early Victorian England.

5. All the journals used in this study are in the manuscript collection of the Historical Society of Pennsylvania, Philadelphia. Three of the journals—the Sarah Logan Fisher diaries, 1776–95, and the diaries of Anna and Peggy Rawle—have not been published. A typescript of the Rawle diaries, entitled "Letters and Diaries of a

Loyalist Family of Philadelphia, written between the years 1780 and 1786," has been prepared and is on deposit at the Historical Society. The page numbers used in these footnotes refer to that typescript. The originals of the other three journals are also in the Historical Society collection, but have been published in part. For easier reference, I have used these published versions for my study: Henry D. Biddle, ed., *Extracts from the Journal of Elizabeth Drinker* (Philadelphia, 1889); Albert Myers, ed., *Sally Wister's Journal* (Philadelphia, 1902); and Ann Warder, "Extracts from the Diary of Mrs. Ann Warder," *Pennsylvania Magazine of History and Biography* 17 (1893): 444–61 (part 1), and 18 (1894): 51–63 (part 2).

6. For general accounts of the Philadelphia Society of Friends in this period, see Frederick Tolles, *Meeting House and Counting House* (Chapel Hill, N.C., 1948); Sydney James, *A People among Peoples* (Cambridge, Mass., 1963); Richard Bauman, *For the Reputation of Truth* (Baltimore, 1971); and Stephen Brobeck, "Changes in the Composition and Structure of Philadelphia Elite Groups, 1756–1790" (Ph.D. diss., University of Pennsylvania, 1972).

7. The phrase "female world of love and ritual" is taken from Carroll Smith-Rosenberg's article (see note 1). My approach in the first half of this essay owes much to her influence, as will be obvious.

8. Biddle, *Journal of Elizabeth Drinker*, p. 257.

9. Warder, "Diary of Mrs. Ann Warder," part 2, pp. 51–52.

10. Ibid., part 1, p. 456.

11. Ibid., p. 446; Biddle, *Journal of Elizabeth Drinker*, p. 139. See also Warder, "Diary of Mrs. Ann Warder," part 2, p. 56; Fisher mss., Jan. 15, 1786.

12. Fisher mss., April 20, 1786, and Dec. 24, 1776.

13. Fisher mss., Jan. 18, 1777; Biddle, *Journal of Elizabeth Drinker*, pp. 270, 147; Fisher mss., Nov. 24, 1776, and Feb. 6, 7, 1777.

14. Biddle, *Journal of Elizabeth Drinker*, p. 31. For mentions of Catherall and Jones, see Fisher mss., Jan. 28, 1777; Biddle, *Journal of Elizabeth Drinker*, p. 7; A. Rawle mss., p. 400.

15. A. Rawle mss., p. 404; Warder, "Diary of Mrs. Ann Warder," part 2, p. 51.

16. A. Rawle mss., p. 417. Sally Wister's socializing with American soldiers presents one exception to this generalization.

17. Warder, "Diary of Mrs. Ann Warder," part 2, p. 55.

18. Fisher mss., April 17, 1794.

19. Macfarlane, *Family Life of Ralph Josselin*, pp. 153–54. Macfarlane described this motivation only as it applied to visiting with kin, but I think it extends to friends as well.

20. Ibid., p. 106. Although, for example, the married women presumably saw their husbands daily, spouses played only a minor role in the journals. Macfarlane's explanation of this phenomenon may be too charitable, for no "foreshortening" affected the journal writers' children, who figured prominently in the narrative even when under their mother's roof. This might mean merely that a woman's offspring took up more of her time than her husband or that she felt more comfortable expressing her emotions about them. It might, on the other hand, indicate that women had a stronger attachment to their children than to their spouses.

21. Fisher mss., Nov. 23, 1776.

22. A. Rawle mss., p. 401; Biddle, *Journal of Elizabeth Drinker*, p. 408; reference to the Parker orphans appears in the handwritten notes affixed to the original mss. of Ann Warder's diary, Historical Society of Pennsylvania.

23. Warder, "Diary of Mrs. Ann Warder," part 1, p. 460. In 1787, Ann Warder noted a visit paid to Peggy Rawle at Anna Rawle Clifford's home.

24. I calculated these percentages simply by making a list of all the people mentioned in the journals (for the longer ones, I took several months as a sample) and using the Historical Society of Pennsylvania's vast collection of genealogies to determine their relationship (if any) to the journal writer.

25. Warder, "Diary of Mrs. Ann Warder," part 1, p. 448.

26. Biddle, *Journal of Elizabeth Drinker*, p. 325.

27. Myers, *Sally Wister's Journal*, p. 194, 180; P. Rawle mss., p. 408.

28. Biddle, *Journal of Elizabeth Drinker*, p. 355; see also pp. 248, 349. These relationships are remarkably similar to those Carroll Smith-Rosenberg describes among nineteenth-century women in "The Female World of Love and Ritual."

29. This argument is certainly consistent with Nancy Cott's thesis in *The Bonds of Womanhood*.

30. Jack D. Marietta, "Ecclesiastical Discipline among the Society of Friends" (Ph.D. diss., Stanford University, 1968); James, *People among Peoples*.

31. Figure cited in Jack D. Marietta, "A Note on Quaker Membership," *Quaker History* 59 (1970): 40–43.

32. Bauman, *Reputation of Truth*, pp. 37–46; Tolles, *Meeting House*, pp. 316–34.

33. For information on the political stances of the journal writers' menfolk, see Bauman, *Reputation of Truth*, pp. 61, 164; introduction to "Letters and Diaries of a Loyalist Family . . . ," Historical Society of Pennsylvania; and Myers, *Sally Wister's Journal*, pp. 33–34.

34. Cecil K. Drinker, *Not So Long Ago* (New York, 1937), p. 17; A. Rawle mss., p. 403; Warder, "Diary of Mrs. Ann Warder," part 1, p. 447.

35. Biddle, *Journal of Elizabeth Drinker*, p. 138.

36. Warder, "Diary of Mrs. Ann Warder," part 1, pp. 451, 459–60, and part 2, p. 59.

37. Of course political and religious differences in the Quaker community were not the only factors that structured the journal writers' choice of friends from among their coreligionists. Personal affinities and dislikes, long-standing family alliances and feuds, propinquity of households in a neighborhood—all must have shaped women's social circles. Unfortunately these types of influence cannot be reconstructed from their journals.

Although extensive information on the financial relationships between the women's families and their visitors could not be obtained, in at least two cases visiting patterns and business ties among the Quakers ran parallel. Henry Drinker's business partnership with Abel James had its counterpart in the social activities recorded in Elizabeth Drinker's journal. The whole Drinker family frequently stayed weeks at a time at James's home in Frankford, a small town outside Philadelphia. The Drinker and James children played together and shared the same tutor. Elizabeth acted as an overseer (along with Sarah Fisher) at the wedding of the James's daughter, Becky. See Biddle, *Journal of Elizabeth Drinker*, pp. 141, 144. Sarah Logan Fisher's numerous visits to "Sisters" Gilpin and Fisher paralleled the kin-based business founded by her husband's father. Joshua Fisher's shipping firm included Sarah's husband Thomas, his brothers Samuel and Miers, and their sister's husband Thomas Gilpin. See John Jordan, *Colonial Families of Philadelphia* (New York: Lewis Publishing Co., 1911), p. 664. While these examples are hardly overwhelming, to the extent that visiting patterns strengthened both religious and kinship ties the remarkable social insularity of the Quakers may also have reinforced the economic cooperation for which they were noted.

38. See, for example, Bauman, *Reputation of Truth*, pp. 37–38.

39. Richard Vann, *The Social Development of English Quakerism, 1655–1755* (Cambridge, Mass., 1969), pp. 181, 187–88.

40. Edward Shorter, *The Making of the Modern Family* (New York, 1975), demonstrates the strengths and weaknesses of the traditional-modern categories in analyzing the evolution of kinship and community ties.

41. See, for example, Michael Anderson, "Family, Household and the Industrial Revolution," in Peter Laslett, ed., *Household and Family in Past Time* (Cambridge, England, 1972), and Herbert Gutman, *The Black Family in Slavery and Freedom* (New York, 1976).

42. Tolles, *Meeting House*, pp. 119–20; Bernard Bailyn, *The New England Merchants in the Seventeenth Century* (Cambridge, Mass., 1955); Edmund Morgan, *The Puritan Family*, rev. ed. (New York, 1966,); and Peter Dobkin Hall, "Marital Selection and Business in Massachusetts Merchant Families, 1700–1900," in Michael Gordon, ed., *The American Family in Social-Historical Perspective*, 2d ed. (New York, 1978), pp. 101–14.

CHAPTER 8

Diversity and Its Significance in an Eighteenth-Century Pennsylvania Town

Laura L. Becker

Physical proximity does not guarantee meaningful interaction between individuals. This obvious yet often ignored principle underlies our increasingly sophisticated understanding of community in early America.[1] At the same time, it impels us to probe more deeply into the ways in which people who lived in a given place related to one another: how they were similar or different, what brought them together or kept them apart. This essay will pursue these questions through an investigation of Reading, Pennsylvania, on the eve of the American Revolution.

Reading was a heterogeneous town in a remarkably heterogeneous region. Differentiation exists in all societies, but during the eighteenth century the middle colonies were markedly more diversified than other parts of English America. Historians such as Patricia Bonomi and Milton Klein have suggested that New York, with its wide range of ethnic, religious, and economic groups, prefigured much of later American life, while Peter Wacker has argued much the same for New Jersey. Other scholars, including James Lemon and Alan Tully, have suggested that Pennsylvania was even more prototypical of our subsequent pluralism. Under the tolerant policies of the Penn family, it was perhaps the most heterogeneous colony in the British empire, with several large minorities and dozens of smaller ones.[2]

While the political implications of Pennsylvania's diversity have been recently explored,[3] few attempts have been made to examine the ways in which members of different groups related at the more elemental social, civic, and economic levels within communities. This question is particularly pressing with respect to places such as Philadelphia, where all kinds of people jostled one another in an urban setting. But it is scarcely less intriguing, and perhaps ultimately more important, to apply it to the smaller, more typical colonial settlements in which people lived mainly among their own kind. Many towns and areas within Pennsylvania were dominated by one particular group or another: English or Welsh Quakers, pietist Germans or "church Dutch," transplanted New England Congregationalists or Scotch-Irish Presbyterians.[4] Yet even in these places, minority elements were often sizable enough to give the local population a diverse flavor, and to impose the challenge of intergroup interaction.

A case in point is Reading, Pennsylvania, a secondary urban center and carefully planned county seat in the heart of the colony's heavily German backcountry. Founded in 1751, the town lay fifty-six miles northwest of Philadelphia and had approximately 250 taxpayers by the mid-1770s. Like the Berks County farmers who lived around them, Reading residents were predominantly "church Dutch." Yet this group recognized its minority status in the province at large, and Reading still contained a wide variety of other peoples. It is an interesting place to examine social interactions in colonial Pennsylvania.

In the decade before the Revolution, Reading's taxpayers included men from at least six different national backgrounds.[5] Five-sixths of them were Germans, another eighth were English, and a baker's dozen were French, Dutch, Scottish, or Irish, though these were probably too few to have maintained a strong sense of ethnic identity.[6] The French (Huguenots) and Dutch attended the German Reformed Church in Reading and chose German spouses, while the Scottish and Irish generally associated with the English, for reasons of language if nothing else. Thus the ethnic division in Reading was clearly between the Germans and the English, even though not every resident fit precisely into those categories.

The religious picture is less clear. Prior to the Revolution, the town's taxpayers included men of at least nine different faiths, and though the Lutherans and Reformed were by far the largest groups, neither could claim so much as half the whole. Anglicans, Quakers, and Catholics also had local congregations to support their denominational identities, and Mennonites, Presbyterians, Baptists, and

Jews were present as individuals. While only the four largest groups were sufficiently numerous to permit statistical analysis, Reading was clearly characterized by religious diversity.[7]

The economic situation was still more complex. The townsfolk provided goods and services to the surrounding countryside and to people passing through, as well as to their neighbors. As a result, Reading's occupational structure was remarkably diversified for a community of its size, with at least fifty-nine distinct occupations pursued by fewer than 250 taxpayers in 1773. A majority were artisans, but they themselves were a highly varied group, with specialists in thirty-five different crafts. Another fifth of the citizens were businessmen, including a brewer, a tobacconist, nine shopkeepers, and twenty-eight taverners. There was also a circle of professional men: three doctors, two lawyers, two surveyors, a clerk, two teachers, several ministers, and eight political officials. Sixteen others were laborers, and two more were farmers.[8]

Amid such occupational diversity, it is not surprising that Reading men varied extensively in wealth as well. Historians cannot state with confidence where earlier societies drew their class lines, but they have often found relative wealth a useful indicator of economic differentiation, and Reading's taxpayers can readily be divided into a bottom 30 percent, a middle 30 percent, an upper 30 percent, and a top 10 percent. Such a division reveals that the bottom 30 percent controlled barely an eighth of the town's wealth in 1773, the middle 30 percent less than a fifth of that wealth, and the top 10 percent almost one-third.[9]

Yet such a division also raises a crucial question: Just how meaningful were the wealth differences these categories reveal? Was someone in the middle 30 percent really distinguishable from someone in the upper 30 percent? And though the question is perhaps most relevant to such a statistical matter as wealth distribution, it can also be raised more broadly. Prerevolutionary Reading appears to have been a complex community with a variety of identifiable ethnic, religious, occupational, and wealth groups. But were these divisions significant? Historians have ordinarily simply *assumed* the importance of group labels such as "German," "Anglican," "shopkeeper," or "top 10 percent," without troubling to explore the meaning of those labels. In order to thoroughly understand social relationships, however, it is imperative to get behind such labels and ask whether they represented meaningful differences among people.

The answer, with respect to Reading, is yes.

Wealth differences in Reading may have been less pronounced than they were in larger colonial cities, but they were nonetheless noticeable, and since a man's tax was based on his property, they represented real differences in life-style. There was a broad base of prosperity in Reading—two-thirds of all residents in 1773 owned a house, a lot, and a cow—but the location, size and furnishings of the home varied considerably with wealth. Men in the upper 30 percent and top 10 percent tended to have a lot on or near the town square, and their personal possessions, as revealed in inventories, were markedly more extensive and fine than those of men in the lower wealth groups. Such items as delft or china dishes, wine decanters, tea sets, silver spoons, pictures, curtains, and leather chairs were found only in the homes of the "better sort."[10] Similarly, servants and slaves were exclusively in the hands of Reading men ranking in the top 20 percent. So were most of the important political offices and much of the local legal activity. Nine out of ten elected county officials and all appointed ones living in prerevolutionary Reading came from one of the top two wealth groups.[11] The rich also appeared most often in lawsuits, as auditors of estates, and as guardians to orphaned children in the community.[12]

Men of differing wealth tended to differ in occupation as well. The numerically dominant artisans were spread over all four wealth brackets, but men pursuing certain crafts were richer than others. For example, in 1773, clockmakers in Reading paid an average tax of £7-0-0, bakers paid £6-0-0, and gunsmiths paid £5-10-0, while tailors, weavers, and coopers all averaged under £3-0-0. Moreover, most occupational groups were more consistent with respect to wealth than craftsmen. As might be expected, professionals and businessmen were almost all in the upper brackets, while laborers were almost all at the bottom.[13]

Thus the economic divisions clearly represented significant differences among men. The same was true of religious divisions. A very large proportion of the townspeople seem to have been associated with one of the local churches. Despite incomplete records for all denominations except the Quakers and the Lutherans, almost nine-tenths of the 1773 taxpayers left evidence of an association with a particular congregation. (In Germantown, the figure was closer to one-half.)[14] In some cases, of course, our only evidence of affiliation is that the individual was baptized or buried in a certain church— hardly proof of active involvement. But among the Lutherans, the only denomination that left extensive records, an average of 40 percent of the known Reading members took communion on the occasions it was recorded, while over three-fourths signed the Revised Ordinance of 1772, affirming the goals and the governing structure of their church.[15] Moreover, in the three congregations for which we have lists of officers, thirty-two men, or one out of every eight married male taxpayers in town in 1773, held a church office in the decade before the Revolution.

Ironically, the recurrent internal squabbles that plagued the Lutheran and Reformed congregations in Reading are also proof that people took their religion seriously. Although the quarrels were rarely over strictly theological matters, struggle for control of church affairs do indicate that members were "involved."[16] In fact, among all the major denominations in Reading, only some Quakers gave overt indications that they were not firmly tied to their sect. During the period 1767–91, fourteen of the fifty-one Reading men of Quaker background were disciplined by the monthly meeting for violation of Quaker principles, and nine of them were disowned for failing to show proper remorse. Others appeared in the county courts, contrary to Quaker codes calling for private settlement of disputes. Nevertheless, even the Quakers maintained a definite religious community in Reading. As with other local denominations, services were held regularly, and there was even sufficient demand to warrant the founding of a school in which Quaker principles were taught.[17] Clearly, religion and religious affiliation were important in this town.

In addition to attending different churches and adhering to different creeds, members of the major denominations in prerevolutionary Reading varied with respect to a whole set of secular traits. Most of the Lutherans and Reformed were German, while local Quakers and Anglicans were almost exclusively English in background. The Anglicans as a group were highly distinctive within Reading society: on the average they were younger and settled in town for a significantly shorter time than their Lutheran, Reformed or Quaker neighbors; they were substantially wealthier than any other group; and they dominated the ranks of the professionals and county officeholders living in Reading. The Quakers were also above average in wealth, and there were proportionately more Reformed than Lutheran men in business and fewer in general labor.[18]

Indeed, Reformed men outshone their Lutheran brethren in a variety of ways. On the average they were slightly wealthier, they were more economically mobile, and they held a disproportionate number of political posts. Although almost all Reading men of either denomination were literate, the wives of Reformed men were considerably more likely to be literate; and both Reformed men and women were more likely to have learned English than their Lutheran counterparts, despite the fact that they all emigrated to America at approximately the same time.[19] In general, one might say that the Reformed citizens of Reading showed a Calvinist drive and activism that distinguished them from the Lutherans.

Despite these differences, however, the Germans as a group differed markedly from men and women of English background. Indeed, the ethnic division was the most pronounced division within the community. At the root of this pattern is the fact that most of the Germans were not simply "ethnics" who had inherited a culture from parents or grandparents; rather, most were actually born in Germany. Moreover, they arrived in America only a couple of decades before the Revolution, so their German heritage had hardly faded by the 1770s.[20] That heritage included a lower middle-class economic status, familiarity with (though not necessarily approval of) a rigid class system, limited experience with British style law, government, and language, and, apparently, a distinctive social style.[21] All of those elements were manifested in the New World, differentiating the Germans from their neighbors.

Thus the Germans in Reading were less elevated in their economic profile than the English. They were underrepresented in the upper wealth brackets, in business, and in professions, and their average tax was noticeably lower.[22] This is not to say that the ethnic division in Reading was one between rich and poor. On the contrary, some of the wealthiest men in town were German, and even those in the bottom 30 percent seem to have been reasonably comfortable.[23] However, on the whole the Germans did tilt toward the lower end of the scale, the English toward the upper.

Furthermore, the English were predominant in the town's civic life. They were more likely to participate in legal activities of one kind or another, and although they comprised only 12 percent of the men in Reading on the eve of the Revolution, they held 82 percent of the appointed offices and 26 percent of the elected ones. Their domination of appointed offices may have reflected the importance of "connection" in colonial Pennsylvania politics, but their overrepresentation in elected offices must have been something more. Perhaps the German majority, coming from such a highly structured society, deferred to the wealthier English minority. More likely, the Germans failed to exercise their potential political strength because they were relatively unfamiliar with the political system and, above all, the language of their adopted country.[24]

There is no way to determine precisely how many Germans in Reading were comfortable with English during this period, but we do know that they continued to use their native language extensively. Most Reading advertisements were printed in German rather than English newspapers, tacit proof that the former were more widely read by the local population. In fact, the first newspaper published in Reading itself, which did not appear until 1789, was in German. Even in the 1790s an observer reported that court proceedings were greatly complicated by the fact that many inhabitants did not understand English. And German continued to be used in both Lutheran and Reformed church services in Reading well into the nineteenth century.[25]

Germans could undoubtedly be differentiated from Reading citizens of English background in other ways as well. Regarding those elements of behavior and temperament that fall under the heading "national character," the descriptions left by such astute observers as Dr. Benjamin Rush suggested that the Germans in Pennsylvania were distinctive in many aspects of culture, ranging from diet to diligence.[26] Reading's German citizens were particularly likely to have maintained traditional customs and modes of behavior because they were such a large majority in town and so recently arrived in America. It is interesting, for example, that when the Reverend Henry Melchior Muhlenberg came to preach in Reading in June of 1775, he found himself "escorted . . . to the church after the old German manner . . . practiced in the ancient and distinguished Hansa towns and imperial cities.[27]

To summarize briefly, the different customs, language, and socioeconomic traits which characterized Reading's German and English citizens made the ethnic division within the town highly significant. Similarly, the high rate of religious participation, frequent church controversies, and socioeconomic differences among members of Reading's various denominations strongly suggest that religious affiliation was an important element in the community's social stratification. Wealth and occupation likewise were more than empty labels, since taxpayers differing in those areas also varied in a whole series of other traits.

And yet, all these people were neighbors; they shared a common space. Technically, the town of Reading covered 950 acres, but the section in which everyone lived and worked covered only 235 acres, less than half a square mile. With approximately 1,350 people there in 1773, the population density was nearly 3,700 per square mile. There was even a town square—a central gathering place. Clearly, Reading residents would have been hard pressed to avoid contact with each other. They almost *had* to interact.

The question is, just *how* did they interact? How frequent and how intimate were their dealings with each other? These are indeed difficult questions to answer, especially for a town whose inhabitants left few personal records to provide clues.[28] And yet, from impersonal documents such as court and church records, wills, deeds, and mortgages, a surprising amount of evidence concerning intergroup interactions can be uncovered.

This evidence suggests that the ethnic barrier in Reading was very strong in private, personal relationships. On the most intimate level, English-German intermarriage was extremely rare: only 0.6 percent of the taxpayers there during the prerevolutionary decade had this kind of "mixed" marriage. The figure was also low for friendships, as indicated by men's choices of nonrelatives as executors and witnesses to their wills or sponsors to their children's baptisms.[29] Of the 148 local men for whom this kind of data is available, only seven (4.7 percent) selected men outside their own ethnic group to serve in any of those capacities.

The few organized social institutions in town were as segregated as the informal social groups seem to have been. The Reading Library Company, which met as early as 1764, was comprised almost entirely of Englishmen, while the Rainbow Fire Company, founded in 1773, seems to have been almost entirely German in membership.[30] And the largest and most important organizations in Reading, the churches, were also unmixed. Of the 305 men in prerevolutionary Reading whose religion is known, only four (1.3 percent) belonged to a church dominated by a different ethnic group (for example, an English Lutheran, a Dutch Quaker). Only the local Catholic church had a congregation that cut across ethnic lines: 25 percent of its parishioners were English or Irish, 75 percent were German. But that was the smallest organized church in town, with most of its members living outside of Reading.

The lack of close social contacts among Reading's German and English citizens undoubtedly stemmed from the fact that the ethnic division had so many highly visible facets. The language difference obviously presented a major barrier to interaction, but the immigrants' "foreign" customs, lower economic status, and separate denominations must have hindered it as well. Taken as a whole, however, that last was a less significant factor than one might have expected, because religious lines seem to have been crossed rather frequently—a striking pattern, given that religious affiliation was so high, that some interdenominational mixing would have required interethnic mixing, and that certain groups (Quakers and Catholics in particular) had religious scruples against marriage outside the fold.

Of the forty-five prerevolutionary cases where we know the religion in which both spouses were raised, no fewer than nineteen (43.2 percent) involved spouses from different religious backgrounds. Obviously, members of small denominations had few of their own kind to choose from locally, and therefore some could be expected to find mates outside their group. However, the majority of intermarriages were between members of the larger churches, suggesting that the citizens of Reading were quite broad minded in their attitudes toward other faiths.

This tolerance is confirmed by the number of friendships that crossed denominational lines. Of the 148 men who named a nonrelative as executor, witness, or sponsor, sixty-five (44.6 percent) chose one or more men of another religion. On a less intimate but still voluntary social level, different Reading congregations cooperated with each other in significant ways. For example, members of one denomination gave freely to others for such projects as a new church building. When the local Lutherans undertook a fund-raising drive for this purpose, 37.8 percent of the contributors from Reading were non-Lutherans, including one-third of the men who gave £5-0-0 or more. Quakers did refrain from this and most other forms of interdenominational cooperation, but Catholic, Reformed, and Episcopalian as well as Lutheran citizens gave generously.[31]

Moreover, facilities were shared, and ministers frequently performed services for members of other denominations. The Reverend Alexander Murray preached to, baptized, and married a number of non-Anglicans, while some members of his own flock attended local worship led by visiting Methodist preacher Joseph Pilmoor. Henry Melchoir Muhlenberg recorded that he "preached an English sermon in the courthouse because the English people [Anglicans] have no church there as yet," while a Presbyterian minister from Philadelphia named James Sproat conducted services in the German schoolhouse when he came to Reading. Reverend William Boos of the local Reformed Church married couples of English background, and the lengthier records kept by Lutheran ministers reveal that they baptized, married, and buried some Anglican and many Reformed individuals.[32]

Relationships between the Lutheran and Reformed churches seem to have been particularly cordial in Reading, and elsewhere. Both contemporary observers and historians have asserted that those two denominations "always lived in harmony in America," drawn together by the many similarities in their creeds and practices.[33] Calvinism in Germany apparently followed the founder's ideals in doctrine only, "and even this in modified version," according to scholars. The Heidelberg Catechism of 1563, which set forth the basic tenets of German Calvinism, downplayed predestination, and the church itself was always organized by territory under state control, just like the Lutherans.[34] In this regard, the Lutherans and Reformed together fell into the category "church Dutch," as distinguishable from the numerous independent German sects that made their way to America, such as the Mennonites, Dunkards, and Brethren. Furthermore, neither the Lutherans nor the Reformed were pacifist, and both believed in an educated ministry—two more traits which set them apart from the sects.[35]

In fact, Lutheran and Reformed immigrants were so compatible that they often worshiped jointly, or at least shared a joint church until their congregations grew large enough to support separate ones. In Berks County alone, during one decade late in the eighteenth century, four of the eleven German churches established were "mixed." Such mixing many not have occurred in Reading, yet in a will written in 1753, one man left half his estate to the "United Church" in Reading, while in 1788 another specified that money from the sale of his property was to go to his daughter, "with reversion to the Lutheran and Reformed congregations of Reading."[36] And although the two denominations maintained separate schools, they may very well have used the same religious primer. Local blacksmith Henry Hahn, who sold publications of a Philadelphia printer on the side, offered the town's citizens the *Hochdeutsch Evangelish-Lutherishe und Reformerte ABC und Namen Buchlein.*[37]

Not all interdenominational relationships were harmonious. This was, after all, an eighteenth-century community, and certain prejudices were clearly present. However, the evidence suggests that prejudice in Reading was isolated rather than systematic. Mathias Bush, who lived or at least owned property in Reading from 1784 to 1790, was pointedly labeled "the Jew" on several tax lists, while no other person's religion was given. More open hostility was directed at Catholics, probably because they were much more numerous than Jews in the town and the county. During the French and Indian War, local justices wrote to the governor that "the people of the Roman Catholic Church are bound by their principles to be the worst subjects and the worst of neighbors," and suggested they be disarmed. Furthermore, at least two citizens of Reading disinherited daughters who married Catholics.[38]

Taken as a whole, this evidence of prejudice is very limited indeed, especially since Jews and Catholics comprise a mere 3 percent of Reading's population prior to the Revolution. It is highly significant that apart from some snide remarks by the local Anglican missionary concerning the Lutherans' frequent quarrels with their ministers, there is no indication of prejudice or discrimination towards any member of a Protestant denomination.[39] Indeed, despite the importance of religion in this town, and historians' assertions that the Great Awakening brought about "a new denominational consciousness" set in a framework of "competitive coexistence,"[40] there is little evidence of interchurch tension among Protestants. Within denominations, however, the situation was anything but peaceful: there were troubles with ministers, squabbles among congregants, and a near-schism. Those problems reflected the generally weak organization of Reading's congregations: the lack of a formal church among the Anglicans, the Quakers' small numbers, the difficulties in obtaining and keeping satisfactory ministers experienced by the Lutherans and Reformed. But in Reading, as elsewhere, those tensions did not spill over into interdenominational problems.[41] Reading's Anglican minister was frustrated that the Lutherans did not see their way clear to joining his denomination,[42] but otherwise the general attitude in town seems to have been "live and let live," if not outright friendliness.

Experience and practicality as well as ideals contributed to this peaceful pattern. Most members of the major denominations represented in Reading were probably raised with people of different faiths. The German immigrants came mainly from Baden, Wurtemburg, the Palatinate, and other principalities of the southwest, all of which contained quite a mixture of religious groups. The Anglicans and Quakers living in Reading came mainly from Pennsylvania and

New Jersey (the Quakers largely from predominantly German Berks County), so they, too, grew up as members of one denomination among many.[43]

In Reading itself, of course, there were some strong practical reasons for tolerating people of other faiths. No single group dominated the community, and the largest—the immigrant churches—were preoccupied with internal problems and were, after all, a minority in the colony as a whole. As for members of the smaller denominations in Reading, it was obviously in their interest to maintain good relations with their numerous Lutheran and Reformed neighbors, and common ethnicity probably bound the small number of Anglicans and Quakers closer together in this town than in communities where men of English background predominated.

Ideological considerations came into play, too. As a rule, sects such as the Quakers, Dunkards, Schwenkfelders, Moravians, and early Baptists were more exclusive than the Lutheran, Reformed, Presbyterian, Anglican, and Catholic churches.[44] Reading contained mostly "church" groups, and the Quakers, the only significant exception, were clearly committed to tolerance. Indeed, one must not underestimate the importance of the broad-minded atmosphere they created in Pennsylvania. At no time was one specific denomination granted privileges denied to others, and all groups settling in the colony appreciated or at least accepted that policy.[45] Thus experience, practicality, and ideology combined in Reading to produce a community in which members of different churches lived together in peace without a strong sense of exclusiveness.

Members of different wealth groups in town also showed little sense of exclusiveness. In fact, wealth lines were crossed regularly in marriage and friendship. Of sixty-six Reading men who married local women (enabling us to determine the relative wealth of both families), twenty-four (36.4 percent) chose a bride whose father was in a higher wealth bracket than his own, twenty (30.3 percent) chose a bride from a lower wealth bracket, and twenty-two (33.3 percent) chose one from the same bracket.[46] The distribution of friendships was almost as even. Of the 148 men in prerevolutionary Reading who selected nonrelatives as executors, witnesses, or sponsors, 45.9 percent had at least one friend from a higher bracket, 59.5 percent had a friend in a lower bracket, and 43.2 percent had a friend from the same bracket.[47]

Some of this apparent lack of snobbishness may be accounted for by the fact that the distance between wealth groups in Reading was not extreme. Indeed, given our reliance on a relative measurement, men at the top of one bracket and the bottom of the next could have been very similar in wealth. However, in nearly one out of every six marriages cited above, the father and father-in-law were more than one bracket apart, while over half of the 148 men with friends had at least one who was two or more brackets away. Moreover, it should be noted that there was substantial range *within* brackets (especially within the upper two). Thus it is clear that close personal relationships in this town often cut across wealth lines.

Perhaps the major factor behind this pattern was the great extent to which people of varying wealth had casual contact in Reading. While churches obviously segregated people by religion (and as we have seen, ethnicity), each denomination had only one church in town, and there is no evidence that seats were assigned by wealth, as sometimes occurred elsewhere.[48] Therefore, families of differing wealth must have mingled in this sphere. Neighborhoods were also mixed. There was some tendency for residents on individual streets to be concentrated in certain wealth brackets, but even the owners of Reading lots 1 through 32, which surrounded Penn Square and were the most valuable in town, included one man in the bottom 30 percent and four men in the middle 30 percent, along with seven in the upper 30 percent and eleven in the top 10 percent. The most common occupations among these men were shopkeeper and taverner—a predictable pattern, given that this was the town center—but there were also a variety of craftsmen and several professionals. Other blocks likewise showed central tendencies in the wealth and occupational characteristics of residents, but they, too, were economically mixed.[49]

Significantly, they were ethnically and religiously mixed as well. The blocks on either side of Penn Square held six German Lutherans, seven German Reformed, four English Anglicans, four English Quakers, one German Catholic, and one German Mennonite. Another block, farther from the town center, had six German Lutherans, four German Reformed, one English Anglican, and one English Quaker. These men, their wives, and their children undoubtedly mingled frequently, at least on an informal basis, since they lived in such close proximity. (Blocks were less than 500 feet long.)

Casual mixing also took place in the town's taverns. Indeed, judging from book debts owed to Reading's innkeepers, patrons varied widely in ethnicity, religion, wealth, and occupation. When

German Lutheran taverner Frederick Gosler died, the Reading men who owed him money (and therefore presumably had patronized his establishment) included twenty Germans and seven Englishmen representing all four of the major local denominations, all four wealth brackets, and occupations ranging from carter to carpenter to clerk.[50] Since there were local taverns run by men of other ethnicities and religions (so people could have stayed with their own kind had they so desired), this data underscores the general lack of barriers between Reading citizens in their informal relationships.

Even those who were exclusive in their choice of companions intermingled freely with all kinds of people in the economic sphere. The semiweekly markets and semiannual fairs held in Reading were important community events, probably attended by a majority of the local population. Moreover, the debts listed in certain inventories indicate that Reading citizens had extensive dealings with members of different groups through their need to draw on each other's goods and services. Table 1 summarizes the characteristics of townsmen owing money to the recorder of deeds, a brickmaker, and a tinner living in Reading.[51]

This evidence that economic relationships consistently cut across ethnic, religious, occupational and wealth lines is strongly supported by the economic patterns revealed in lawsuits. Suits were very common in the colonial period, and since they were usually initiated over an unpaid debt, they, too, provide clues about economic interaction.[52] Of the 237 suits between Reading men in the decade before the Revolution, 79 (33.3 percent) involved men of different ethnicities, 168 (70.9 percent) involved men of different religions, 128 (54.0 percent) involved men from different wealth brackets, and 207 (87.3 percent) involved men with different occupations.

Those lawsuits also indicate that considerable intergroup interaction took place in the courthouse. But while suits involved antagonistic contact, other legal proceedings had men working together as teams—for example, to evaluate a dead man's estate or to form a jury—and many of those teams were very definitely "mixed." Table 8-2 lists attributes of the men who served as a jury in the Court of Quarter Sessions in May of 1775.[53] Legal activities clearly provided an important point of contact, and often cooperation, for Reading's heterogeneous citizenry.[54]

Despite fragmentation along ethnic, religious, wealth, and occupational lines, then, there was widespread and significant interac-

Table 8-1. Debt Patterns in Reading

Characteristics of Debtors	Creditors		
	Henry Christ, Jr., Recorder	Jacob Rabbold, Brickmaker	Henry Degenhart, Tinner
German	25	28	41
English	7	7	8
Lutheran	18	14	21
Reformed	7	13	18
Anglican	2	4	3
Quaker	5	2	5
Catholic	0	0	1
Jewish	0	0	1
Laborer	2	2	2
Farmer	0	1	1
Craftsman	17	19	26
Businessman	8	4	10
Professional	1	1	2
Officer/Gent.	3	2	2
Bottom 30%	4	8	15
Middle 30%	13	9	14
Upper 30%	10	12	13
Top 10%	5	4	7
Total	32	35	49

NOTE: This data is drawn from the inventories of these three men (BCCH). These particular inventories were used because they represent citizens in different occupations and wealth brackets, and because they were among the very few from this period to provide the names of individual debtors, rather than simply a grand total for "book debts." Christ died in 1789, Rabbold in 1783, Degenhart in 1786; the wealth and occupation of the debtors is taken from the last sample tax list on which they appeared prior to the death of the creditor. Complete information was not available on all creditors; hence, totals are not always consistent.

tion among the various groups in prerevolutionary Reading. It is true that the ethnic barrier was a formidable one, rarely surmounted in intimate relationships, and that the few formal institutions in town were also segregated by ethnicity or religion. However, these institutions did include members of varying economic characteristics, and it is noteworthy that religious as well as wealth lines were frequently crossed in marriage and friendship.

Furthermore, people in Reading seem to have mingled freely on the streets where they lived, in the taverns, in the marketplace and in the courts. Thus, local Anglican lawyer John Price received a complimentary obituary in *Der Wochentliche Staatsbote*, the newspaper favored by Reading's German residents. And while leading

Table 8-2. Characteristics of a Reading Jury, May, 1775

Name	Ethnicity	Religion	Occupation	Wealth
John Fulweiler	German	Reformed	Turner	Middle 30%
Peter Rapp	German	Lutheran	Butcher	Upper 30%
Thomas Youngman	German	Reformed	Tanner	Bottom 30%
John Collier	English	Quaker	Tailor	Middle 30%
Nicholas Lutz	German	Reformed	Gentleman	Upper 30%
George Schultz	German	Lutheran	Hatter	Top 10%
John Goodheart	German	Reformed	Skinner	Middle 30%
Daniel Hiester	German	Reformed	Gentleman	Top 10%
Christopher Merkle	German	Lutheran	Blacksmith	Upper 30%
Thomas Warren	English	Anglican	Weaver	Middle 30%
Durst Phister	German	Reformed	Butcher	Upper 30%

citizen James Read invited only men of his own kind (wealthy English professionals) to share "the pleasure of dusting a bottle of excellent madeira," he still referred to middle-class Lutheran blue-dyer Ludwig Imler as "my good neighbor."[55]

This general lack of antagonism in the face of diversity is significant, and at the most fundamental level, it stems from the basic structure of the community. In essence, this town was built around the common pursuit of nonagricultrual occupations in a definable physical space small enough to permit people to get to know each other, at least casually. There was none of the New England Christian Utopian Closed Corporate Community in Reading. Although it was almost as carefully planned as Massachusetts towns such as Dedham, the planning was the work of a handful of officials, not of the settlers themselves, who came as individuals and earned the right of residency simply by purchasing a lot.[56] "Community" in the New England sense was also lacking in that Reading never had only one church, or even one ethnic group. Diversity was present from the start, and while people developed formal institutions and informal ways to meet their spiritual and social needs, none of these linked all or even most of the citizens. There wasn't even a town meeting.

The very fact that Reading was open and individualistic and profit-oriented rather than closed and corporate and utopian meant that its people probably left each other alone to a much greater degree than in New England towns. Within the boundaries of Pennsylvania's overarching civic institutions, the government and the courts, Reading's citizens were largely autonomous.

Equally significant in explaining the general harmony in the town is the fact that no group was truly dominant over the others. The English held a disproportionate number of political offices and were overrepresented in the top wealth brackets, but the Germans still filled a majority of places in both cases. While power and wealth might not have been so well shared had the Germans been less overwhelming in numbers, the fact remains that both groups were well represented in the local elite. Furthermore, most people participated in the town's civic affairs, and even those at the bottom of the wealth scale seem to have shared in the town's economic prosperity.[57] Thus, despite its diversity, Reading lacked significant sources of strife such as an attitude of exclusiveness or the presence of an underprivileged minority.

The town's revolutionary experience at once reflected and tested its legacy of peaceful coexistence. In the early 1770s, Pennsylvanians engaged in a heated debate over the future of their government and society—a debate that provided a perfect opportunity for latent local antagonisms to surface.[58] Even after independence was declared, struggles for political power and military privilege could have revealed or created fissures in Reading's seemingly harmonious atmosphere. But the Revolution did not upset the town's social equilibrium. On the contrary, in the long run it seems to have knit the community even closer together by providing a common cause, a shared experience, and new areas of intergroup contact and cooperation.

Reading residents responded to the Revolution with remarkable unity, as staunch and consistent Whigs.[59] In other places, socioeconomic differences fed the formation of opposing camps on the issues raised by the crisis with England.[60] But in Reading, such differences had never led to conflict, and none appeared at this juncture. In fact, there were only two cases of overt loyalism in the town, aside from the Anglican minister who returned to England.[61] Reading did have some self-acknowledged pacifists. On September 1, 1775, a group of citizens "conscientiously scrupulous of bearing arms" passed a number of resolutions pledging support to the Revolutionary cause and offering contributions to further it.[62] Significantly, these patriotic pacifists were accepted and their position respected. County officials did not discipline conscientious objectors as they did others who refused to join the military "associations" (militia companies), and the spokesman for the pacifists, William Reeser of Reading, served on both the Committee of

Observation and the Committee of Correspondence, was appointed by the Assembly to take subscriptions for the Continental Loan in 1777, and continued to hold a judgeship throught this period.[63]

The accommodation of such views is clear evidence of the extent of tolerance in eighteenth-century Reading. And the prosecution of the Revolution by a wide spectrum of town residents reinforced the tradition of intergroup cooperation. Wealthy English professionals predominated among Reading representatives on the earliest county committees (perhaps in part because they were more closely connected to leaders in Philadelphia and knew what was going on before others did). But all committees contained a mixture of peoples, and later committees included a significant number of Reading's "average" citizens: Germans, craftsmen, and men in the middle wealth brackets. Reading citizens elected or appointed to regular county offices during the Revolution likewise were drawn from a variety of groups.[64]

Thus the political side of the revolutionary movement in Reading was clearly a cooperative effort involving different types of people. The same was true of the military aspect of the conflict. Military service was widespread among Reading men and well distributed across ethnic, religious, and economic lines. With the exception of the largely pacifist Quakers, between two-thirds and three-quarters of each group served.[65] Military officers were also drawn from a broad spectrum of citizens, and while those holding the higher ranks tended to be wealthy, a surprisingly even proportion of the overall number came from each of the four wealth levels.[66]

Moreover, militia units were not segregated in any way. That is not something to be taken for granted; there was, after all, a special German Regiment within the Pennsylvania Continental Lines. But virtually all Reading militiamen served under, alongside, or at the head of men of other backgrounds. For example, Captain Daniel DeTurck of neighboring Alsace Township commanded a company including Reading men with a wide assortment of traits; there were Germans, Englishmen, Lutherans, Reformed, Anglicans, craftsmen, businessmen, and laborers from three of the four wealth brackets.[67]

Through such groups the Revolution undoubtedly furthered the intermixing of different peoples in the town. But it is clear that even before the war, Reading partook of the "social flexibility" that was one of the major "underpinnings of stability" in eighteenth-century Pennsylvania.[68] Indeed, with its heterogeneity, individualism, un-

Laura L. Becker

equal distribution of wealth, market economy, and dense settlement pattern, colonial Reading was already a "modern" community relative to the more traditional settlements elsewhere in the colonies. Moreover, the townspeople had been forced to contend with these patterns right from the start. In a sense, Reading was "born modern," and thus never faced the adjustment problems inherent in the social transformations other communities experienced.[69] Instead, Reading passed through the eighteenth century in peace and harmony amidst diversity.

NOTES

1. Two useful articles on approaches to the study of community in colonial America are Darrett Rutman, "The Social Web: A Prospectus for the Study of Early American Community," in William O'Neill, ed., *Insights and Parallels* (Minneapolis, 1973), pp. 57–89; and Richard R. Beeman, "The New Social History and the Search for 'Community' in Colonial America," *American Quarterly* 29 (1977): 422–43.

2. Patricia Bonomi, *A Factious People: Politics and Society in Colonial New York* (New York, 1971); Milton Klein, "New York in the American Colonies: A New Look," in Jacob Judd and Irwin Polishook, eds., *Aspects of Early New York Society and Politics* (New York, 1974), pp. 8–28; Peter Wacker, *Land and People: A Cultural Geography of Preindustrial New Jersey* (New Brunswick, 1975); James Lemon, *The Best Poor Man's Country: A Geographical Study of Early Southeastern Pennsylvania* (Baltimore, 1972); Alan Tully, *William Penn's Legacy: Politics and Social Structure in Provincial Pennsylvania, 1726–1755* (Baltimore, 1977).

3. See James Hutson, *Pennsylvania Politics, 1746–1770* (Princeton, 1972); Tully, *William Penn's Legacy*; Wayne Bockelman and Owen Ireland, "The Internal Revolution in Pennsylvania: An Ethnic-Religious Interpretation," *Pennsylvania History* 41 (1974): 125–59; Richard Ryerson, *The Revolution Is Now Begun: The Radical Committees of Philadelphia, 1765–1776* (Philadelphia, 1978); Gary Nash, *The Urban Crucible: Social Change, Political Consciousness and the Origins of the American Revolution* (Cambridge, Mass., 1979).

4. See Lemon, *Best Poor Man's Country*, ch. 2, on the settlement of groups within eastern Pennsylvania. Recent studies of German and Scotch-Irish backcountry communities include Laura Becker, "The American Revolution as a Community Experience: A Case Study of Reading, Pennsylvania" (Ph.D. diss., University of Pennsylvania, 1978); George Franz, "Paxton: A Study of Community Structure and Mobility" (Ph.D. diss., Rutgers University, 1974.)

5. When phrases such as "the decade before the Revolution" and "prerevolutionary Reading" are used, the data refers to married male taxpayers in Reading in either 1767 or 1773 (the two selected sample years from that era). In certain specified cases where it was necessary (as in discussions of economic structure), the data will refer to married male taxpayers in Reading in 1773. In other specified cases, where larger numbers were required for meaningful statistical analysis, the data will refer to married male taxpayers in town during any of the five sample years analyzed in the author's more comprehensive study of Reading between 1767 and 1791, cited in note 4 (a detailed discussion of the methodology and sources used in this essay is provided

214

in that manuscript). Tax lists, as well as deed books, wills, etc., can be found in the Genealogical Society Collections, Historical Society of Pennsylvania, Philadelphia (hereafter cited as GSC); The Historical Society of Berks County, Reading (hereafter cited as HSBC); and the Berks County Courthouse, Reading (hereafter cited as BCCH).

6. The precise breakdown of ethnic groups in prerevolutionary Reading was:

	Number	Percent		Number	Percent
German	289	83.3	Irish	3	0.9
English	43	12.3	Scottish	1	0.3
French	6	1.7			
Dutch	3	0.9	Unknown	2	0.6

Ethnicity was determined by one or more of the following: birthplace or ethnicity of parents (for all groups), name (for German, Dutch, Irish), and signature or active membership in a German-speaking church if there were no evidence to indicate other ethnicity (for Germans).

7. The precise breakdown of known religious groups in prerevolutionary Reading was:

	Number	Percent		Number	Percent
Lutheran	170	49.0	Catholic	9	2.6
Reformed	85	24.5	Mennonite	2	0.6
Anglican	19	5.5	Jewish	1	0.3
Quaker	19	5.5	Unknown	42	12.1

The presence of Presbyterian and Baptist individuals is noted by the Reverend Alexander Murray in a letter to the Secretary of the Society for the Propagation of the Gospel [SPG] in Foreign Parts, Jan. 25, 1764. For a reference to other "sectaries," see Murray to SPG, June 25, 1765. Both documents are in SPG Letters, ser. B, vol. 21 (microfilm, University of Pennsylvania). Although the Catholics had a chapel in Reading, most of the parishioners lived outside the town. Hence, statistics on religious groups will cover only the Lutherans, Reformed, Anglicans, and Quakers.

8. The precise breakdown of occupational groups in 1773 was:

	Number	Percent		Number	Percent
Craftsmen	150	61.7	Laborers	16	6.6
Businessmen	44	18.1	Farmers	2	0.8
Professionals–			Miscellaneous	8	3.3
Officers	21	8.6	Unknown	2	0.8

There was an average of 4.1 men per occupation in Reading, a smaller number than that found in either Germantown or Lancaster, Pennsylvania, during this period. See Stephanie Wolf, *Urban Village: Population, Community and Family Structure in German-town, Pennsylvania, 1683–1800* (Princeton, 1976), pp. 106–7; Lemon, *Best Poor Man's Country*, p. 141.

9. The precise breakdown of tax paid in 1773 was:

Wealth Bracket	Tax Paid	Percentage of Total Tax
Bottom 30%	£154	12.8
Middle 30%	£225	18.9
Upper 30%	£427	35.6
Top 10%	£391	32.6

Laura L. Becker

These divisions have become standard among students of early American social structure. See, for example, James Lemon and Gary Nash, "The Distribution of Wealth in Eighteenth Century America," *Journal of Social History* 2 (1968): 1–24; Allan Kulikoff, "The Progress of Inequality in Revolutionary Boston," *William and Mary Quarterly* 28 (1971): 375–412.

10. For a more extensive discussion of the range of pesonal property in the hands of different wealth groups, see Becker, "The American Revolution as a Community Experience," pp. 166–174. Reading inventories, which list personal property, can be found in the Register of Wills (BCCH). Tax lists list real property: houses, lots, livestock, servants, slaves, and luxuries.

11. The precise breakdown of prerevolutionary county officeholding was:

Wealth Bracket	Appointed Officers	Elected Officers
Bottom 30%	0 (0.0%)	0 (0.0%)
Middle 30%	0 (0.0%)	2 (10.5%)
Upper 30%	3 (17.6%)	10 (52.6%)
Top 10%	14 (82.4%)	7 (36.9%)

Reading men holding office in the colonial government were all from the top two wealth brackets. For more details, see Becker, "The American Revolution as a Community Experience," pp. 268–75.

12. The following table shows involvement in court activities by wealth for 1773 married male taxpayers:

Wealth Bracket	Percentage with at Least One Court Appearance During the Decade Before the Revolution	Mean Number of Appearances
Bottom 30%	30.1	1.0
Middle 30%	68.5	2.7
Upper 30%	81.8	4.8
Top 10%	91.7	9.1

For further details on this subject, see Laura Becker, "The People and the System: Legal Activities in a Colonial Pennsylvania Town," *Pennsylvania Magazine of History and Biography* 105 (1981): 141.

13. More extensive analysis can be found in Becker, "The American Revolution as a Community Experience," pp. 121–24.

14. Wolf, *Urban Village*, p. 216.

15. Communicants are listed in Trinity Evangelical Lutheran Church, Reading—Baptisms, Marriages, Burials (GSC, HSBC). The 102 Reading Lutherans who signed the Ordinance of 1772 are listed in Jacob Fry, *History of the Trinity Lutheran Church* (Reading, 1894), pp. 71–73.

16. These quarrels are described in Becker, "The American Revolution as a Community Experience," pp. 228–33.

17. See Exeter Monthly Meeting Minutes, 1765–1808, Friends Historical Society, Swarthmore, Pa.

18. The following table highlights some group differences (excluding unknowns):

1773	Lutheran	Reformed	Anglican	Quaker
Average Age	42.8	40.0	36.3	38.6
Average No. of Years in Reading after 1773	11.6	14.3	8.4	13.5
Average Tax Paid	£4.1	£4.8	£10.9	£5.7
% Laborers	8.0	4.1	0.0	0.0
% Businessmen	10.9	21.9	18.2	23.1
% Professionals	3.6	6.8	54.5	7.7
% Holding County Office	5.0	16.7	61.5	21.4
Number	137	73	11	13

19. See the statistics in note 18 for wealth and officeholding patterns. In terms of economic mobility, 27.5 percent of the Reformed men moved up a wealth bracket between 1767 and 1773, as compared to 17.6 percent of the Lutherans, despite the fact that the Reformed started off higher as a group. The statistics on literacy, based on available signatures, are as follows:

1773	Literate	Percentage Signing in English Script
Reformed Men	100.0	22.2
Lutheran Men	95.2	15.2
Reformed Women	44.4	11.1
Lutheran Women	26.6	3.3

20. At least 190 of the 289 Germans in prerevolutionary Reading (65.7 percent) were born in Germany. Excluding those whose place of birth is unknown, the proportion rises to 90.0 percent. Of the 135 German immigrants whose date of arrival in America can be determined, 88.9 percent came after 1745.

21. These traits are mentioned because they clearly affected intergroup relationships. For a more general study of eighteenth-century German life, see W. H. Bruford, *Germany in the Eighteenth Century* (Cambridge, England, 1965).

22. The following table summarizes these differences (excluding unknowns):

1773	Percentage of Germans	Percentage of English
Bottom 30%	31.7	17.2
Middle 30%	30.8	24.1
Upper 30%	30.3	34.5
Top 10%	7.2	24.1
Average Tax	£4.3	£7.1
Number	221	29
% Businessmen	17.4	22.2
% Professionals	3.8	18.5
Number	213	27

23. Among Reading taxpayers in the bottom 30 percent in 1773, 64.8 percent owned a house and at least half a lot, while 52.1 percent owned a cow. Moreover, inventories indicate that their furnishings were simple but adequate. For a sample inventory, see Becker, "The American Revolution as a Community Experience," pp. 165–66.

24. For a broader discussion of the Germans' political and legal activities, see ibid., ch. 6, and Alan Tully, "Englishmen and Germans: National-Group Contact in Colonial Pennsylvania, 1700–1755," *Pennsylvania History* 45 (1978): 237–56.

25. See Becker, "The American Revolution as a Community Experience," pp. 211–15, for details and an explanation of this pattern of language retention. Comments on the use of German in the courts and churches appear in François, duc de la Rochefoucault, *Travels through the United States of North America* (London, 1800), p. 46; Daniel Wetzel, *History of the First Reformed Church* (Reading, 1953), p. 50; Fry, *History of the Trinity Lutheran Church*, p. 102.

26. Benjamin Rush, *An Account of the Manners of the German Inhabitants of Pennsylvania* (Philadelphia, 1875; ms. written 1789).

27. Theodore Tappert and John Doberstein, trans., *Journals of Henry Melchior Muhlenberg*, 3 vols. (Philadelphia, 1942–48), 2:698.

28. Only a few residents—all of English heritage—left any letters, and no diaries from this period could be located.

29. It is possible that witnesses to wills were simply pulled in off the street. However, the pattern for this group of "friends" was very similar to that of baptismal sponsors, who were obviously chosen with care. Thus it is highly likely witnesses were chosen with care as well.

30. A list of the Library Company members is in the Louis Richards Collection, Documents, HSBC. The Rainbow Fire Company is discussed in Morton Montgomery, *History of Berks County in Pennsylvania* (Philadelphia, 1886), p. 814.

31. The building subcription, undertaken in 1790, is described along with its contributors in Fry, *History of Trinity Lutheran Church*, pp. 111, 113, 286, 287.

32. Alexander Murray to the SPG, Jan. 25, 1764, April 9, 1763, Sept. 25, 1768; SPG Letters, ser. B, vol. 21; Frederick Maser and Howard Maag, eds., *The Journal of Joseph Pilmoor* (Philadelphia, 1969), entry for May 27, 1772, p. 135; *Journals of Henry Melchior Muhlenberg*, entry for May 28, 1767, 2:337; James Sproat Journal, entry for April 15, 1778, pp. 30–31, General Manuscript Collection, Historical Society of Pennsylvania (hereafter cited as HSP); Marriages by the Reverend William Boos (GSC); Trinity Evangelical Lutheran Church, Reading—Baptisms, Marriages, Burials (GSC).

33. Rush, *An Account of the Manners of the German Inhabitants of Pennsylvania*, p. 45; James Knauss, *Social Conditions among the Pennsylvania Germans in the Eighteenth Century* (Philadelphia, 1922), p. 41; Abdel Wentz, "Relations between the Lutheran and Reformed Churches in the Eighteenth and Nineteenth Centuries," *Lutheran Church Quarterly* 6 (1933): 300–327.

34. Hajo Holborn, *A History of Modern Germany*, 3 vols. (New York, 1959–69), 1:260.

35. Knauss, *Social Conditions*, p. 41. On general differences between sects and churches, see Richard Niebuhr, *The Social Sources of Denominationalism* (New York, 1929), pp. 17–22.

36. See the wills of Philip Jacob Majer (Meyer), d. 1765, and Christopher Krauss, d. 1788, Berks County Wills (GSC). On mixed churches in Berks County, see Knauss, *Social Conditions*, p. 47. Church records are somewhat vague on Reading's earliest years. The Lutheran congregation was organized in 1752 (one year after the town was settled), and the Reformed Congregation followed a year later. Both had church buildings by 1755, but the situation between 1753 and 1755 is unclear.

37. Heinrich Miller, ed., *Der Wochentliche Staatsbote* (Philadelphia, 1762–79), Feb. 17, 1779.

38. Montgomery, *History of Berks County*, p. 367; wills of Conrad Weiser, d. 1760, and Conrad Bobb, d. 1790, Berks County Wills (GSC).

39. Alexander Murray to the SPG, Jan. 25, 1764, March 26, 1772, in William Perry,

ed., *Historical Collections Relating to the American Colonial Church*, 5 vols. (Hartford, 1870–88), 2:357–58, 458–59.

40. Dietmar Rothermund, *The Layman's Progress: Religious and Political Experience in Colonial Pennsylvania, 1740–1770* (Philadelphia, 1961), chs. 2 and 3.

41. See note 16. Stephanie Wolf found the same pattern in Germantown; see her *Urban Village*, p. 222.

42. *Journals of Henry Melchior Muhlenberg*, 1:665.

43. A map locating religious groups in early modern Germany can be found in Holborn, *A History of Modern Germany*, 1:286–87. For a discussion of the origins of Reading's citizens, see Becker, "The American Revolution as a Community Experience," pp. 34–35, 48.

44. Tully, *William Penn's Legacy*, p. 59.

45. On Quaker attitudes, see ibid., ch. 8, and Sydney James, *A People among Peoples: Quaker Benevolence in Eighteenth-Century America* (Cambridge, Mass., 1963), ch. 6.

46. The following table gives precise figures on the economic background of spouses chosen by Reading men from the various wealth brackets. In order to get an adequate statistical base, the data was drawn from the author's broader study of all men living in the town in 1767, 1773, 1779, 1785, and 1791.

| | Bride's Father | | | | |
Groom's Father	Bottom 30%	Middle 30%	Upper 30%	Top 10%	Number
Bottom 30%	3 (21.4%)	5 (35.7%)	5 (35.7%)	1 (7.1%)	14
Middle 30%	4 (28.6%)	3 (21.4%)	7 (50.0%)	0 (0.0%)	14
Upper 30%	2 (8.0%)	6 (24.0%)	11 (44.0%)	6 (24.0%)	25
Top 10%	0 (0.0%)	2 (15.4%)	6 (46.2%)	5 (38.5%)	13
Number	9	16	29	12	66

47. The total exceeds 100 percent because a substantial number of men had friends in more than one wealth bracket. The following table gives the precise breakdown of friendships by wealth in prerevolutionary Reading:

| | Percentage with at Least One Friend in Bracket | | | | |
Wealth of Individual	Bottom 30%	Middle 30%	Upper 30%	Top 10%	Number
Bottom 30%	22.2	55.5	77.8	0.0	36
Middle 30%	50.0	66.6	41.7	25.0	48
Upper 30%	63.6	81.8	54.5	18.2	44
Top 10%	20.0	40.0	60.0	0.0	20

48. On this tradition in New England, see Ola Winslow, *Meetinghouse Hill* (New York, 1952), ch. 9.

49. For a more detailed discussion of residential patterns, see Becker, "The American Revolution as a Community Experience," pp. 183–89.

50. A complete breakdown of patrons' characteristics is given in ibid., p. 245. The inventory itself, dated 1789, is in the Register of Wills (BCCH).

51. This data is drawn from the inventories of these three men, all of whom died in the 1780s (BCCH). Complete information was not available on all debtors; hence, totals are not always consistent.

52. Some records of the Courts of Common Pleas (BCCH, HSBC) actually specify the amount being contested. For more detail on lawsuits in Reading, see Becker, "The People and the System," pp. 138–39.

53. This and other jury lists are in the records of the Court of Quarter Sessions (BCCH, HSBC). Most juries also included men from other towns in the county. For teams evaluating estates, see Orphans Court Records (GSC, HSBC).

54. It is a commonly accepted notion that contact between people who are working together as equals promotes positive attitudes and mutual respect. See the classic study by Gordon Allport, *The Nature of Prejudice* (New York, 1954), ch. 16.

55. *Der Wochentliche Staatsbote*, March 23, 1773; James Read to Edward Shippen, Oct. 6, 1772, Nov. 16, 1774, Shippen Collection, vol. 7 (HSP).

56. For the contrasting ways in which Dedham and Reading were founded and settled, see Kenneth Lockridge, *A New England Town: The First Hundred Years* (New York, 1970), part 1, and Becker, "The American Revolution as a Community Experience," pp. 17–22.

57. See Becker, "The People and the System," pp. 138–40, for details on the high proportion of prerevolutionary Reading men involved in legal actions. Political participation is harder to gauge, but 35 to 40 percent of Reading citizens seem to have voted in county elections—a respectable number given the cultural and linguistic barriers the Germans faced. Reading men dominated among officeholders within the county (see Becker, "The American Revolution as a Community Experience," pp. 265–269). Alan Tully has argued that the Germans were able to get along with the English in Pennsylvania in part because they accepted domination by the latter as a workable arrangement during the mid-eighteenth century (see Tully's "Englishmen and Germans," pp. 237–56).

58. On the coming of the Revolution in Pennsylvania, see Charles Lincoln, *The Revolutionary Movement in Pennsylvania* (Philadelphia, 1901); Theodore Thayer, *Pennsylvania Politics and the Growth of Democracy, 1740–1776* (Harrisburg, 1952); David Hawke, *In the Midst of a Revolution* (Philadelphia, 1961); Charles Olton, *Artisans for Independence: Philadelphia Mechanics and the American Revolution* (Syracuse, 1975); Ryerson, *The Revolution Is Now Begun*; Nash, *The Urban Crucible*, chs. 11 and 13.

59. For more detailed coverage of the town's response to the Revolution, see Becker, "The American Revolution as a Community Experience," pp. 296–320.

60. William Nelson, *The American Tory* (Boston, 1961); Bruce Merritt, "Loyalism and Social Conflict in Revolutionary Deerfield, Massachusetts," *Journal of American History* 57 (1970): 227–89; Jessica Kross Ehrlich, "A Town Study in Colonial New York: Newtown, Queens County, 1642–1790" (Ph.D. diss., University of Michigan, 1974); Gregory Nobles, "Politics and Society in Hampshire County, Massachusetts, 1740–1775" (Ph.D. diss., University of Michigan, 1979); Ryerson, *The Revolution Is Now Begun*.

61. These two were Reynold Keen and John Biddle. See "Forfeited Estates," *Pennsylvania Archives*, ser. 6:12 (Harrisburg, 1907) 20–67; *State of the Accounts of the Collectors of Excise for Berks County* (Philadelphia, 1783), HSP. On the experience of the Anglican minister, see Mary Dives, "Alexander Murray, D.D.," *Historical Review of Berks County* 4 (1939) 38–39.

62. "Minutes of the Committee of Berks County, 1775," *Pennsylvania Archives*, ser. 1:4 (Philadelphia, 1851) 649; William Reeser to the Committee of Safety, Sept. 11, 1775, *Pennsylvania Archives*, ser. 1:4 653.

63. Morton Montgomery, *Berks County, Pennsylvania in the Revolution* (Reading, 1894), pp. 28, 29, 297; *Pennsylvania Archives*, ser. 2:3 (Harrisburg, 1896) 701.

64. The following table shows the range in committee members' characteristics. Economic data is drawn from the 1773 tax list.

Date of Committee

Socio-Economic Characteristic	July '74	Dec. '74	Jan. '75	Pre-1776 (cum)	Jan. '76	July '76	Dec. '76	Dec. '76	1776 (cum)
German	1	5	2	42.1%	2	3	4	9	64.3%
English	4	4	3	57.9%	4	2	2	2	35.7%
Lutheran	1	2	1	21.1%	0	1	2	6	32.1%
Reformed	0	3	1	21.1%	2	2	2	3	32.1%
Anglican	3	3	2	42.0%	3	2	1	2	28.6%
Quaker	1	1	1	15.8%	1	0	1	0	7.2%
Craftsman	0	0	0	0.0%	0	2	1	6	32.1%
Businessman	1	3	1	26.3%	1	0	2	3	23.4%
Professional	3	2	2	36.8%	3	2	3	1	32.1%
Officer/Gent	1	4	2	36.8%	2	1	0	1	14.3%
Bottom 30%	0	0	0	0.0%	0	2	2	0	14.3%
Middle 30%	0	0	0	0.0%	0	2	0	3	17.9%
Upper 30%	1	2	0	15.8%	2	1	1	6	35.7%
Top 10%	4	7	5	84.2%	4	0	3	2	32.1%
Number	5	9	5	19	6	5	6	11	28

For a more detailed discussion of these committees, and county officers, see Becker, "The American Revolution as a Community Experience," pp. 412–15.

65. The following table gives the proportion of men in Reading in 1779 who served in the military:

Percentage of Group Serving

German	69.5%	Lutheran	71.3%	Bottom 30%	70.6%
English	66.0%	Reformed	72.9%	Middle 30%	65.4%
		Anglican	73.3%	Upper 30%	70.1%
		Quaker	39.1%	Top 10%	62.9%

A more extensive analysis of military service can be found in Becker, "The American Revolution as a Community Experience," ch. 8.

66. The following table describes the relative wealth of military officers in Reading in 1779:

	Wealth Groups			
	Bottom 30%	Middle 30%	Upper 30%	Top 10%
Percentage of Officers in Group	30.3	28.8	30.3	12.1

67. A roster of this company is provided in Montgomery, *Berks County, Pennsylvania, in the Revolution*, pp. 94–95.

68. Tully, *William Penn's Legacy*, ch. 4.

69. A classic study of this kind of transformation is Lockridge, *A New England Town*.

CHAPTER 9

This Tory Labyrinth: Community, Conflict, and Military Strategy during the Valley Forge Winter

WAYNE BODLE

Relatively little scholarly attention has been paid to the communal context in which the military events of the American Revolution occurred. This is as surprising as it is unfortunate, considering the salience of the issue in the popular historical imagination. Americans have long imagined the Revolution in scenes of ragged farmers and backwoodsmen, hiding behind trees and fences to pick off clusters of uncomprehending redcoats. These scenes suggest that the Revolution was somehow comparable to a modern guerilla war, and individuals as ideologically diverse as Mao Tse-tung and Walt Disney have availed themselves of this imagery. Recent generations, sensitized by the experience of colonial "wars of national liberation," have readily accepted the analogy.[1]

Historians have been slower to address the war in these terms. Despite dutiful acknowledgements that the Continental army was itself an aggregation of "citizen-soldiers," they have only begun to explore systematically the complex relationships between that army and the civilian populations among which it operated. John Shy has made some provocative observations on the subject.[2] The accumulating literature of loyalism has shown, in a general way, the underlying civil implications of martial events.[3] Social historians, by demonstrating the relevance of a communal framework to a wide variety of subjects, have pointed toward new ways of conceptualizing the Revolution. The work that we have in this area, however, has been much more suggestive than definitive.[4]

222

Shy finds the "structural similarities" between the Revolution and modern revolutionary wars "far more important than the differences."[5] A recent study of Concord in 1775 sustains the classic image of an embattled countryside, inhabited by an alert and united population ready to swarm out to chasten a powerful professional army by ignoring the rules of stand-up warfare.[6] An account of the pivotal American victory at Saratoga attributes it, at least in part, to the ability of an armed and mobilizable population to overwhelm a technically superior regular force.[7] And current research suggests the viability of an explanation taking account of unconventional tactics and the effective exploitation of popular support for understanding the ebb and flow of military fortunes in the southern campaigns after 1778.[8] Except for Saratoga, however, these studies are confined to the geographic and chronological extremities of the Revolution. There is a need for a wider range of cases to be explored. If conclusions suggested by rural Massachusetts in 1775 remain even remotely recognizable in the Carolina backcountry in the early 1780s, they may well merit closer attention. It would first be prudent, however, to examine the situation in the middle states between 1776 and 1778.

One way of viewing that period would indeed emphasize continuities bridging the war's early weeks in New England and the later southern campaigns. The interval between the battles at Long Island in August 1776 and at Monmouth nearly two years later, saw more American reversals than successes, retarding George Washington's efforts to build a conventional army on the European model and forcing at least occasional resort to improbable combat ventures. The Trenton-Princeton campaign at the end of 1776, for example, holds a place in Revolutionary mythology almost as cherished as that of Lexington and Concord, as an illustration of the crucial differences between "professional" European and "popular" American modes of armed conflict. The 1777 Pennsylvania campaign also suggests an American disposition to stretch the canons of eighteenth-century warfare. After relatively inconclusive conventional engagements at Brandywine and Germantown early in the fall, the campaign slipped almost inexorably into a dispersed conflict based in the Philadelphia hinterland. Unable to defeat a cautiously deployed opponent by direct assault, the rebels prepared for a winter combining elements of the 1775–76 siege of Boston with the detached patrolling and skirmishing activities used to contest British control of the New Jersey countryside during the previous winter.[9]

Continental authorities, spurred by Pennsylvania's embattled state government, never abandoned hope for more offensive measures. In December, Congress sent a committee to camp to press for a concerted "winter's campaign."[10] At Christmas, Washington himself entertained plans for a Trenton-style surprise attack on Philadelphia.[11] He understood, however, that such an enterprise was beyond the capacity of the army acting alone. Having warned Congress that the army was on the verge of starvation or dispersal, he was reduced to hoping that it might at least spearhead a patriot uprising in the middle states. A successful assault, he observed, would require the "force of Pensa., Maryland, [Delaware] and Jerseys . . . to be pourd In to Crush Howe before he could recovr. from the Surprise or regain his Ships."[12]

There is little evidence, however, that consideration of the scheme advanced beyond the paper stage, and some doubt whether it constituted anything more than a dutiful exercise floated to placate proponents of aggressive resistance to the British invasion of Pennsylvania. By the end of 1777, Washington could hardly have envisioned a southern Saratoga. The regional "force" that he colorfully depicted as being "pourd In" to complete the imaginary rout of the enemy was, in fact, anxiously watching to discover what his regulars might do on its behalf.

Even William Howe, who had chosen to campaign in Pennsylvania partly in hope of reaping the active support of its supposedly loyal population, had been disappointed by the tepid local response to his initiatives. He had no sooner disembarked his troops at the head of the Chesapeake Bay than he had discovered the indifference—or, as it seemed to him, the antipathy—of the area's population. Far from flocking to redcoat protection, he complained, the people had "by far the greater number deserted their dwellings, driving off . . . their stock of cattle and horses." His hope of subduing Pennsylvania would be, he lamented, "greatly impeded by the prevailing disposition of the inhabitants, who I am sorry to observe, seem to be . . . strongly in Enmity against us, many having taken up arms."[13]

Howe was being as unduly pessimistic on the brink of the campaign as he had before been blithely hopeful in planning for it. His observation of the inhabitants' inclination to avoid the conflict was accurate, but his estimate of their active resistance was not. Nevertheless, he found in Pennsylvania something less than the open-armed welcome he had anticipated. While the people readily tendered supplies to purse-heavy British commissaries early in the campaign, they appeared disposed to await events before making decisive political commitments.[14] Indeed, safely quartered in Philadelphia in November, one British general judged the area's people to be "as unanimous against us as in ye Jerseys, or any part where I have been," and called the campaign "as hard an exertion as ever was made by any army, through the strangest country in the world."[15]

The Pennsylvania countryside and its inhabitants seemed little stranger to Englishmen, however, than they did to many members of the Continental army. Armchair strategists in Congress, who hoped that a "native" army might furnish a rallying point around which an embattled citizenry could unite to resist the incursions of a foreign force, must have cringed to discern the nonorganic relationship that seemed to be evolving between the state's inhabitants and the American soldiery. Throughout the winter, Continental troops complained bitterly of being adrift on an unsupportive communal sea.

Connecticut brigadier Jedediah Huntington observed that "any army, even a friendly one, if any can be called so, are a dreadful scourge to any people—you cannot conceive what devastation and distress mark their steps."[16] And American troops were often far from friendly toward the belabored civilians among whom they found themselves restlessly encamped. Five months of enforced intimacy with those civilians, which coincided with a steady decline in their material well-being, had inclined many soldiers to perceive a causal relationship between the two phenomena. A New England officer, considering the "unequal distribution and scanty allowance of provisions" confronting his men, blamed the former problem on the army's own commissaries but railed that "the cursed Quakers and other inhabitants are the cause of the latter." Observing that local residents did not "seem to have any more idea of Liberty than a savage does of Civilization," he shuddered to imagine New England's fate had its citizens "shown the same disposition towards Gen¹ Burgoyne, which the cringing, nonresisting asslike fools of this state have done towards How[e]."[17]

If the equivocal response of many Pennsylvanians to the invasion of their state earned them the contempt of army members, their undisguised preference for British currency if not politics inspired in some of their protectors a spiteful ambivalence about the war's

225

impact on the locality. One officer attributed raging local inflation to the "banditti inhabiting Penn[a] . . . who openly refuse [Continental money] as a tender. . . . 'Tis beautiful," he gloated, "to see the said vestiges of war thro' their plantations." Having unsheathed the sword of resentment, he buried it deeply in the vulnerable underbelly of the community:

> What the English began the Americans have finished—the dutch, the Welsh and the scots & the quaking gentry hailed brother Howe a welcome guest but ruin and devastation indiscriminately befel the friend and foe. Military power that so long deprecated evil must soon take place in the vicinity of our army to curb that spirit of dissention now prevailing throughout the state. The sufferings of the inhabitants are intolerable, but they may thank their own perversity.[18]

Such observations largely reflected the regional biases of men drawn from parochial cultures in a still, at best, imperfectly confederated polity. Rhode Island brigadier James Varnum spoke for many New Englanders when he opined that the salvation of an apparently ungrateful state "ought to cause repentance in us for all our sins," and contemptuously dismissed Pennsylvania as "this Tory Labyrinth." Varnum depicted the state in almost purgatorial terms, noting that he expected "by this Pennance to emerge into the World, after leaving this place, with all accounts fully ballanced. I shall then take care how I sin again, ever having a retrospect to its consequences."[19] Resentment of the locality, however, was also prevalent among middle states natives, and even among some Pennsylvanians.

Predictably, the state's large and diverse community of religious dissenters from war became particular targets for the invective of army members. The Society of Friends stood proxy for much of the offhand bigotry aimed at those presumed to be "disaffected" from the patriot cause. Such phrases as Quaker or "quaking" served as easily available epithets for men who would happily have found others had these not been readily at hand.[20] The cohesive and articulate Friends, however, were also peculiarly equipped to retaliate. The members of one monthly meeting extracted a measure of passive literary revenge for the depredations that they suffered by recording their losses under the mocking rubric "taken . . . by the Army under George Washington, Commonly Called the American Army."[21]

This evidence is both colorful and useful in characterizing civil-military relationships, but it is not in itself definitive. Army members often vilified each other, and their letters are as full of derogatory allusions to the civilians of their home states as to those of their host. Such rhetorical interplay needs to be weighed against measures of behavioral cause and effect. In eastern Pennsylvania during 1777–78, overt group attitudes were firmly grounded in a tangle of dilemmas based on clashes of almost irreconcilable interests. Every contact between soldiers and civilians impinged on issues that recalled what the war was about, such as the right to withhold or dispose of property, to move freely from place to place, or to associate without reference to presumed loyalty to either side. For both armies, however, the critical issue concerned control of the area's resources. Washington and Howe displayed varying degrees of sensitivity to the broader implications of civilian goodwill for their military situations. For both, however, the hearts and minds of the people took a distinctly secondary place to the backs and bellies of the troops under their command.

In this contest, the Continental army found that harsh repression and permissive tolerance were equally unavailable—and unavailing—as consistent methods of dealing with the local community. The establishment of the camp at Valley Forge in late December of 1777 briefly unleashed the army on the community. A temporary collapse of its supply systems caused Washington tacitly to suspend his long-standing policy of avoiding massive seizures from civilians.[22] It was later acknowledged that "plunder" and "abuses" occurred for "three miles in every direction" around the new camp between December 26 and January 6.[23] Unattached soldiers and army attendants roamed the countryside, exercising military authority officially and privately over friend and foe alike. Major General Anthony Wayne, a local resident, was besieged by erstwhile neighbors complaining of abuse at the hands of soldiers. Even the families of militia members, he claimed, were being stripped and insulted, and he recommended "garrison orders" to prevent intramural violence within the Continental establishment itself.[24] This disordered situation also created something of a brigand's paradise for self-appointed guerillas. Private parties, calling themselves "Volunteers," patrolled local roads, stopping and looting both civilians and soldiers.[25]

Some order was restored in January with the stabilization of the supply systems, and Washington took strong steps to limit the movement of personnel to and from the camp.[26] The army had to provide for its own security, however, and held at least formal responsibility for keeping order and protecting patriot citizens in a broad crescent of neighborhoods between Philadelphia and the state's interior counties. These tasks guaranteed that some of its members would remain exposed to the citizenry throughout the winter. Washington sought to delineate this role as narrowly as possible by giving the Pennsylvania militia responsibility for the area east of the Schuylkill River. The militia would thus provide a buffer between the army and as much of the populace as possible, diffusing political responsibility for civil-military relations.[27]

It was this reluctant deployment of the army as a regional police force that defined its relationship with the populace. Its missions of segregating rural inhabitants from British influence, curtailing their trade with the city, and augmenting the work of its own supply departments, developed into an often ugly game of hide-and-seek. The officers responsible for detachments discovered the impossibility of performing their duties effectively. One reported that the "market people" had easily adapted to the presence of his patrols by going on foot, hiding in each others' houses, inquiring of neighbors for the whereabouts of Continental dragoons, and slipping off "through the Plantations" as soon as the patrols had passed.[28]

For the country people, the lure was the British practice of paying for goods in specie, set against the American reliance on rapidly depreciating paper money. By skillfully exploiting a combination of coercion and enticement, William Howe was able to transform the Philadelphia markets into a powerful magnet for local produce.[29] This helped to create a vicious circle of communal disadvantage for the Continental side. Attempts by inhabitants to trade with the city provoked coercive efforts to prevent the practice. These further alienated the inhabitants from the American army and reinforced their inclination to deal with the British. Secure in this initial advantage, Howe adhered through the early winter to a policy of allowing the country people to assume the risks of the road with their goods. This lessened the exposure of his own troops to rebel attack and reduced the likelihood that predictable incidents of soldierly excess would offset the advantages of a reliable treasury.

The consequences of that policy were soon apparent. The commander of a Continental foraging party in Bucks County found the area being literally drained of provisions, and he warned Washington that "not less flour than is sufficient to maintain eight to ten thousand men goes daily to Phila., carried in by single persons, wagons and horses." What could not be accomplished by stealth was sometimes being achieved by force, as recalcitrant farmers turned to paramilitary methods to thwart the restraints of martial law. A drove of cattle had reached the city the week before escorted by "a small party of armed countrymen."[30]

There was evidence of serious American complicity in this process, for which army and militia officers blamed each other. The latter charged that, by giving passes to individuals to trade with the city, their Continental comrades were indulging in open favoritism among civilians.[31] An investigating officer confirmed the charge and attributed the dereliction to the length of detached patrols, which made their members "too well acquainted with the girls and people from town who I fear seduce them and make them commit many things highly improper such as seizing flour . . . from one person and delivering it to their favorites."[32] One officer conceded the presence of outright highwaymen in his patrols, claiming that he had "not confined them as there are not three of the men that I could with any degree of safety trust my life with."[33] These circumstances reinforced Washington's inclination to minimize the involvement of regular troops in this duty, even at the risk of undermining the effort to prevent trade with the city. Throughout the winter he pressed Pennsylvania authorities to furnish more militia to police the countryside. At the same time he sought vainly for ways of supplying the army without earning the enmity of the inhabitants.

In late January of 1778 Washington attempted to capitalize on the entrepreneurial spirit that the British markets had aroused in the populace by establishing emporiums of his own near the Valley Forge camp. His proclamation informing the "good people" of the region of the measure, however, merely demonstrated how far the alienation between the army and its neighbors had proceeded. Washington found it necessary to assure prospective suppliers

> that the Clerks of the market are Inhabitants of this state, will attend on the respective days . . . Whose duty it will be to protect the Inhabitants from any kind of abuse or violence that may be offered to their persons or effects—and to see that they receive pay for their Articles according to the prices hereafter mentioned.[34]

Unfortunately, the good will that the measure was intended to reap was aborted even before the message appeared in local newspapers. February produced a second general collapse of the army's support departments. The result was the worst material deprivation of the winter and the most stringent resort to seizures from the locality. Washington sent Nathanael Greene with several thousand troops to strip the countryside between the Schuylkill River and the Brandywine Creek for fifteen to twenty miles inland from the Delaware River.[35]

Greene's reports provide the sharpest picture of the winter of the war's impact on the locality, and the most haunting indication of the implications of the situation for military events. The "face of the Country," he observed, was "strongly markt with poverty and distress," and his collection of supplies was "inconsiderable."[36] Whigs comprised but a small minority of the population, and they lived in such fear of their Tory neighbors that they refused to cooperate with Greene or even to provide intelligence. One hundred citizens had enlisted in a "Provincial" corps to suppress Whigs and protect marketeers. The latter, Greene observed, had already taken into the city "all the Cattle and most of the best Horses."[37]

Greene had neither the time for drawing fine distinctions among local attitudes nor the occasion for winning friends for the army among the inhabitants. A careful reading of his reports, however, reveals a more complex picture of the political and social fabric of the area than they initially seem to convey. In fact, the district was neither so absolutely drained of resources, nor so sharply divided into dominant Tory and submissive Whig camps, as it initially appeared to him. Rather, there was a large, apolitical, and essentially self-interested middle group, whose guiding principle lay in the protection of their own lives and property.[38] Their continuing experience with the conflict, moreover, was making them increasingly sophisticated at the business of doing just that, especially by hiding their goods from the intrusive attention of army foragers.

In less desperate circumstances the latter group might have presented Greene with a valuable opportunity for winning at least some of its members to the rebel side by a discriminating application of force. Impelled by the gravity of the crisis, however, he found that by cracking down on the inhabitants collectively, he could squeeze significant amounts of supplies from what initially seemed to be a barren terrain. "The Inhabitants cry out and beset me from all quarters," he reported, "but like Pharoh I harden my heart." Finding two civilians on their way to the city with provisions, he "gave them one hundred [lashes] each by way of example. . . . I determine to forage the Country very bare," he promised, "nothing shall be left unattempted."[39] Greene was obstructed at every step, however, by the seemingly ingenious ability of the people to conceal their property. He reported almost daily that the area had been gleaned, only to find more goods in practically every defile and copse of trees that he came to. "Our poor fellows are obliged to search all the woods and swamps after them," he complained, "and often without success."[40] In an effort to forestall this frustrating game of hide-and-seek, he began to withhold receipts for concealed goods and to order the arrest of resisting civilians.[41]

Greene's reports offer an exceptionally revealing portrait of the civil context of the encampment at a time when the very survival of the army stood in grave doubt. Despite the concentration of Continental efforts and resources west of the Schuylkill, the area remained unsubdued and unpropitiously disposed toward the army's welfare. An increasingly militant Tory minority was arming to suppress an already cowed and even smaller Whig minority, and, in the process, was enabling a self-interested middle group to act on its own behalf. Because of the imbalance between the currencies of the contending armies, the behavior of the middle group inherently tended to favor the British side.

East of the Schuylkill, meanwhile, an even graver situation prevailed. Responding to the containment of the regular army west of the river because of the supply crisis, and to a relative tightening of his own provisions reserves, William Howe adopted a more aggressive stance toward the Philadelphia hinterland.[42] Where earlier he had relied on the attraction of British money to bring the country people to the city, leaving it to the Americans to cope with the consequences of restraining these movements, in February he launched a series of assaults on the already weak militia structure east of the Schuylkill. A Provincial corps raised among Pennsylvania Loyalists, supported by regular British army detachments, probed the countryside in a widening arc north and northwest of the city. The raids initially focused on the local militia organization and on the structure of revolutionary civil authority in the area. With the help of sympathetic local residents, the corps seized prominent Whigs, lawyers, "committeemen," and militia recruiting officers, bringing them to Philadelphia for internment.[43]

This outburst of armed loyalism threatened to involve the area in open civil warfare, and brought pressure on Washington to expand

231

the operations of the regular army to both sides of the Schuylkill. He continued to resist that pressure, both because of a lack of troops and from a reluctance to expose the army to the hazards of attempting to contain a burgeoning civil conflict. Instead, he sought more militia, and looked for ways to use the small Continental detachments in the area more effectively. Their officers were ordered to arrest market people for exemplary punishments and to assist the militia in disabling mills on the creeks leading to the city to reduce the availability of flour in the area.[44]

During February, however, the militia ceased to be even a minimally effective force. Its strength hovered between sixty and one hundred men, rather than the one thousand that the state had agreed to maintain.[45] John Lacey, its commander, depicted himself as something between a policeman guarding his own men and a virtual prisoner of that group. "I do by no means approve of the conduct of the militia," he complained, adding,

> They ought to be men who govern their conduct by principle but unhappily for America they fall far short of that character, they are constantly stealing from the inhabitants and from one another, we dare not leave the least thing in their sight nor even in the care of the guards or we are sure to have it stolen our discipline is very bad and impossible to enforce it with the present officers, unless you form in them new ideas and new souls as their whole study is to be popular themselves and to keep in favor with the men, by joining with and taking their part.[46]

So precarious had the situation become that Washington was willing to avail himself of this spirit of brigandage by allowing the militia to keep any goods they could seize from the market people. He insisted, however, that they should "ramble through the woods and byways as well as the great roads," and "fire upon . . . those gangs of mercenary wretches" who traded with the enemy.[47] Increasingly, he looked to deadly force to accomplish what insufficient numbers could not.

Although Washington sought to keep the army disentangled from this ugly conflict, he was forced by events to modify his approach. By late February the Provincial raiders, emboldened by the collapse of militia resistance, began to attack Continental targets in lower Bucks County. Supported by British regulars, they preyed openly on the army's supply line to the northern states by intercept-

232

ing droves of cattle coming from New England.[48] This caused a bowing of the line in a northwesterly direction and threatened the army at its most vulnerable point. Washington reacted by sending strong detachments of regular troops across the Schuylkill on brief missions to protect the line.[49] He continued to insist, however, that the civil consequences of enemy activity in the area would remain the responsibility of the state.[50]

Lacey's difficulties with the militia, however, increased rather than diminished. A native of Bucks County, he seemed strangely ignorant of much of the territory near the British lines and found himself dependent on a populace so hostile that its members refused even to tell him "the direction of the roads."[51] He met bitter accusations that he was using his position to favor friends and relatives and received threats that he would be caught by the British or by the Provincial units within a week.[52] He countered with a remarkable proposal to depopulate the area between his lines and those of the British by requiring its residents to "move back into the country" for fifteen miles.[53] Besides reflecting his personal difficulties, the idea testified eloquently to the futility that Lacey and others felt toward their mission of enforcing revolutionary order over a fractious population in the Philadelphia hinterland. Lacey floated the proposal informally and received a delegation of angry Quakers demanding to know his "reasons for ordering them to quit their habitations." Caught in a storm of complaint, Lacey belatedly sought approval of the plan from headquarters.[54]

Washington rejected the proposal, but not before deeming it "rather [more] desirable than practicable" and reflecting on how "little consideration the Majority of the parties concerned may deserve from us." Ultimately, his unwillingness to countenance the "horror of depopulating a whole district" prevailed over his belief that the plan would "undoubtedly put an end to the pernicious illicit Commerce which at present subsists." Instead, the officers patrolling the area were directed to continue their selective intimidation of suspected wrongdoers. While he retained the authority to do so, Washington would support the military trial and punishment of notorious offenders captured by the militia.[55] When that authority expired in April, he ordered miscreants sent to the state for detention. Those of good character, or with reputable friends in the area, would be released and warned that they would be hanged for a second offense.[56] Deprived of the legal power to punish formally recalcitrant civilians, Washington advised a militia officer to "begin shooting some of the most notorious offenders wherever they can be found *in flagrante delicto.*"[57]

Well into the spring the countryside remained unsecured by American forces. While Lacey struggled to impose order on its inhabitants, he found it difficult even to control his own men.[58] The militia continued to tread warily, if at all, in the vicinity of the city. Instead of serving as a visible symbol and enforcer of revolutionary authority, its members learned to act covertly.[59] While they sought personal security in anonymity, "strolling parties" of furloughed soldiers and would-be brigand civilians readily embraced the identity of state forces as a disguise with which to commit "villainous roberys" on unwary travelers.[60] In this unsettled environment, Lacey soon concluded that he had "not the least hope, or encouragement to believe [that the market people] will refrain from their evil ways."[61]

British pressure on the militia continued during the spring. After a brief respite in March, new raids occurred in April northwest of Philadelphia. These fell particularly heavily on the militia, culminating on May 1 with a devastating predawn attack, spearheaded by Robert Simcoe's corps of Queen's Rangers, on Lacey's camp near the Crooked Billet. The attack broke the back of the militia for the season. Most of the ambushed party were newly mustered troops, who received their first taste of combat that morning. Even for a partisan conflict, the episode constituted an unusually brutal initiation. Accounts from both sides agreed that some victims were burned to death, while American witnesses insisted that wounded men were bayoneted and thrown into heaps of burning straw.[62] The survivors were reduced to an even more timid and ineffective force than the state had fielded earlier in the winter. Simcoe acknowledged that the affair "had its full effect, of intimidating the militia, as they never afterwards appeared, but in small parties, and like robbers."[63]

This circumstance threw Washington back on the regular army as the only force capable of securing the countryside. After May 1, the division of the area into districts defined by the Schuylkill became an increasingly hollow fiction. Washington recognized the essentially rhetorical import of his continued efforts to extract militia reinforcements from the state and began to maintain large detachments of regular troops east of the Schuylkill. The significance of that development was underlined by the fact that these parties were commanded by general officers with broad responsibilities for providing security and collecting intelligence.[64]

In one sense, this expansion of Continental responsibility betrayed the ultimate failure of Washington's persistent effort to use the militia as a buffer to minimize the army's contact with the populace. To call it such, however, may be to overlook its partial, or at least its relative, success. By resisting pressure to supplement or replace the militia east of the Schuylkill during the early months of 1778, Washington purchased time for the army to recuperate from the ravages of the 1777 campaign and for its support departments to be revitalized. By May, the army had been reinforced, and its health and field-readiness had improved as a result of smallpox vaccinations and the distribution of new clothing. It had also received six weeks of training under "Baron" Friedrich Steuben. While this training did not have the immediate and almost miraculous transforming effect with which Revolutionary folklore has sometimes credited it, it did improve the discipline and confidence of the troops. After March, the emphasis at Valley Forge moved from survival to the implementation of reforms and to preparations for the summer campaign. The improving climate, the new efficiency of the support departments, and the closer attention to discipline all raised morale and blunted internal dissention. They also softened the expression of external resentment. During the spring, disparagement of the local community virtually disappeared from the army's discourse.

Thus the army that Washington had to expose to the countryside in May was a somewhat more tempered instrument than the one that he shielded from such exposure earlier in the winter. Its mission had also changed. More reliably supplied, it no longer occupied itself so urgently with seizures from prostrate neighborhoods. Instead, security and intelligence were the main objects of its detachments. The secondary objective of restraining civil traffic with Philadelphia also seemed to ease in response to changes in the military climate. As the prospect loomed that the British might leave the area, political currency—based on pragmatic calculations of future events—began to outweigh the monetary kind in shaping patterns of local commerce. One American officer even noted a "great change in this state since the news [of a treaty of alliance] from France—the Tories all turned Whigs. . . . They begin, mercenary wretches," he disdainfully reported, "to be as eager for Continental Money now as they were a few weeks ago for gold."[65]

If this observation of a political shift is conjectural for the country-side, it is established for Philadelphia, where rumors of a British retreat proliferated after Sir Henry Clinton arrived on May 8th to take command of the army from William Howe. The rumors were based on a firm strategic decision made in London and outlined in orders that Clinton received, and they threw the town's Loyalist community into consternation. Howe's advice to his collaborators to seek private terms with the rebels destroyed the communal advantage that he had nurtured throughout the winter.[66] Despite Clinton's refusal to permit negotiations for civil rapprochement, the mystique of Royal invincibility had been broken forever in Pennsylvania.[67]

During the Continental army's last week at Valley Forge, the neighborhood of the camp came to resemble, if only in symbolic microcosm, the diverse and heterogeneous Pennsylvania community that the movement of the war into the state had disrupted and dispersed ten months before. State and Continental officials alike descended on the camp in anticipation of an early opportunity to reenter the city.[68] They found themselves in the company of large numbers of displaced Philadelphia Whigs, who had begun "hovering around the camp" with similar expectations. The latter, in turn, mingled uneasily with swarms of "country refugees," who had fled into the city during the winter. These individuals, whose actions had marked them as politically suspect in revolutionary eyes, had come out, notwithstanding Clinton's prohibition, to sue privately for terms of peace.[69]

It remains to assess the broader significance of the Valley Forge winter, with reference to the questions about the character of the American Revolution raised at the beginning of this essay. Did the winter involve "revolutionary" conflict in anything more than the rhetorical sense of that word? Does the episode support or modify the popular image of the Revolution as a contest between a powerful regular army and a tattered but resourceful band of men who prevailed mainly by stubborn resort to unconventional combat methods and the effective mobilization of civilian support? What does the event signify about patterns of American loyalty, group conflict and cohesion, and the impact of organized force on communal life?

If by unconventional warfare is meant a tactical reliance on small, mobile fighting units, "hit-and-run" combat, at least an occasional resort to brutal force, and a kind of interpenetrability between civil and military enterprises, then the term may be at least partially applicable to this period. Between October of 1777 and May of 1778, few large-scale offensive movements were essayed by either side, and little serious consideration was given to general engagements. Instead, the two armies cautiously probed the area between and around their respective strongholds and opportunistically attacked each other's patrols and detachments when chance or brief imbalances of strength made it safe to do so, but otherwise failed to contest seriously the right of the other side to remain in the area.

In response to the failure of either side, or of both, to control the countryside, patterns of civilian behavior consistent in some ways with what we know about modern guerilla warfare evolved. The evidence is fragmentary, but some Pennsylvania countrymen seem to have banded together to protect their right to exploit what few opportunities attended the burden of hosting the "seat of war." They provided intelligence to apprise each other of the occasional presence of military forces. They sheltered purveyors of illicit commerce. A few even took to the roads in small armed convoys.[70] These activities created a degree of local disorder that fostered a kind of marauding "third force" in the area. Bands of outlaws, reportedly including American and British deserters as well as opportunistic civilians, preyed indiscriminately on luckless wayfarers.[71]

Plainly, to the degree that these phenomena were general, the Pennsylvania countryside was a dangerous place for everyone, and its dangerousness lay precisely in the ambiguities it presented. In James Varnum's phrase, its perils were inherent in its apparently labyrinthine character. Soldiers passed as civilians, while gangs of local outlaws masqueraded as official detachments. Both Whigs and Tories of an occupied interior town united in outrage at the perceived abuse of authority by state-appointed officials, and their aggrieved petition was endorsed by Continental medical officers![72] Army and militia officers alike struggled to execute their duties while wondering about their own safety at the hands of their possibly criminally inclined troops.[73]

Significantly, these phenomena impinged more on Continental than on British forces. It was the rebels who struggled with the constant—if never happily or conscientiously embraced—responsibility for maintaining local order, and the British who enjoyed the occasional luxury of disrupting that order. Ironics abounded in this situation. At Valley Forge, the same popular fear of the excesses of culturally alien soldiers that helped to assure security near the camp undermined Washington's efforts to entice local inhabitants to enter into commercial relations with his army. On the fringes of Continental power in lower Bucks County, John Lacey's attempts to exercise penumbral revolutionary authority were rebuffed with sneering impudence by residents with whom he shared a tangled history of attachments and antagonisms.[74] And though the British theoretically shared the liability of alienness, if not of familiarity, they were largely able to skirt its consequences by permitting their opponents to run afoul of them first.

In such circumstances, it is not surprising that both sides, but particularly the Americans, saw more pitfalls than possibilities in the local communal environment and went to considerable lengths to avoid involving themselves deeply in it. Washington was especially concerned about minimizing these risks. He arranged to use the Pennsylvania militia to absorb much of the brunt of policing the region and, when confronted with the breakdown of that arrangement, willingly blinked at the business of blockading the city to avoid embroiling the army in partisan conflict. Indeed, such conflict would have flown directly in the face of Washington's plan for the use of the winter, which envisioned the reorganization and training of the army on the contemporary European model for use in essentially conventional combat situations.[75] That we should find this surprising speaks eloquently of our habit of forgetting that history is largely a one-way street. Washington was, after all, operating without a received body of theory or doctrine for the use of guerilla warfare, one that would have permitted the careful calculation of risks versus benefits. This is too little appreciated in the rush to discover through analogy the relevance of the past to the present. In 1944 Mao could hunker in his cave in Yenan and picture Washington at Valley Forge, defeating a mechanized British opponent through the skillful manipulation of popular loyalties. In 1778, however, Washington could not reach for Mao's little red book.[78]

The convergence of the actual proliferation of irregular conflict with the lack of an articulated doctrine for its use—indeed, with American resistance to it and British reservations about its implications—provides a point of departure for an interpretation of the "revolutionary" character of the Valley Forge winter. Attempts to measure the concept have been weakened by anachronistic and sentimentally clichéd usage, and especially by a failure to make clear whether the term implies mostly methods and tactics, underlying conditions of communal structure, or some combination of both.

John Shy has provided a suggestive alternative approach to this problem with the concept of "triangularity." In a revolutionary conflict, he argues, "two armed forces contend less with each other than for the support and control of the civilian population." The "government" is reluctant to perceive the situation in these terms, while the "rebels" use every means to "break the links between the governor and the governed." These links are attacked by

> going beneath the normal level of governmental operations, reaching the smallest social groups and even individuals, indoctrinating every-one so recruited, and of course using those forms of violence, particu-larly threats, terrorism, and irregular or guerilla warfare, that are at once most difficult to stop and most likely to change docile, obedient subjects into unhappy, suggestible people.

Violence is "less an instrument of destruction than one kind of persuasion; the aim is to destroy popular responsiveness to the state."[77]

There is a measure of congruence between this model and the events sketched above, but to be useful it must be carefully qual-ified. In particular, the applicability of the terms *government* and *rebels* is problematic. In the American Revolution, the government most immediately in question and the rebel army were presumably on the same side, notwithstanding prevalent friction and discord within the Continental establishment. We will have to look more closely at the situation, measuring the revolutionary nature of the conflict by the relationship—both intended and actual—between the contending forces and the populace, to clarify its ironies and isolate its contradictions.

These began with the ambiguity over who governed and who rebelled. The contradiction between incumbency and insurgency was the one around which all others arranged themselves. In effect, the incumbent-insurgent configuration was an unstable one, con-stantly subject to circumstantial definition. There was no question of transforming docile subjects into unhappy, suggestible people. The descent of the war on the locality had already done that. Rather, the question of "persuasion" was the central one. In this case, persuasion meant convincing the people that the other side was responsible for their unhappy circumstances or, failing that, that the other side was not likely to prevail.

It was the signal accomplishment of the king's "invading" army that it was at least initially able to do a better job of persuasion in this matter than its presumably "native" Continental counterpart. Until giving indications of being ready to abandon Pennsylvania, the British were able to exploit their monetary advantage to cast their opponents into the role of an apparent oppressor, an enforcer of unfair and unpopular restrictions on personal liberty, and a discounting consumer of local resources. In so doing, the British forced the American army to assume many of the burdens, but few of the advantages, of incumbency. In fact, the government to which most members of the community were accustomed to responding, however, reluctantly—that of the state—was placed in the position of authorizing, or even exhorting, the army to take measures that contradicted its own radical constitutional ideals.[78]

By encouraging the inhabitants to defy restrictions against withholding supplies from the rebels or trading with the city, and by resorting at least occasionally to force to protect them in their defiance, the British directly attacked the umbilical link of popular responsiveness to the government of record in the area. Thus, at least by the criteria of triangularity, it is William Howe rather than Washington who appears to emerge as the wily guerilla tactician. Indeed, in attempting to ignore this dimension of the conflict—or, more precisely, to shield his army from its implications—Washington seems almost willingly to have accepted the role that that formulation assigns to the incumbent.

However discordant this reversal may be with traditional images of the Revolution, it poses no insurmountable obstacles to applying the triangularity model to Valley Forge. Two "important points of dissimilarity" that Shy discerns between the Revolution and modern guerilla wars are the "relative ease with which local instruments of government fell into the hands of the American rebels" and the "relative dependence of the rebels on conventional forms of military action."[79] The Valley Forge winter suggests a relationship between these qualifications that may have significant implications for understanding the military dynamics of the Revolution. Simply put, having to deal with actual, relatively autonomous "local instruments of government" (as opposed to the portable "provisional" governing entities that are the political artifacts of modern revolutionary movements) may have importantly affected the army's ability to prosecute the war. The "forms of military action" realistically available to it at any point partly depended on the nature of its relationships with whatever governments existed in the area where it happened to be operating.

For Pennsylvania during 1777–78, the tension between the state's executive body and senior army officers is evident in the documents of the period, as is the strong preference of many of those officers that the army retire to some secure, interior place to recover from the previous campaign. In choosing Valley Forge, Washington effected a compromise generously slanted toward the expressed concerns of state officials, which largely related to the security of the state's "well-disposed" citizens and to those officials' own political responsibilities as the implicit guarantors of that security. His intermittent indulgence in a rhetoric of barely contained exasperation with those leaders during the subsequent winter, however, suggests that Washington held many of the same reservations about the situation that his general officers did.[80]

It was as much an understanding (rather grudgingly arrived at in army circles) of the need to give at least the appearance of protection to the political turf and legitimacy of one of the Continental establishment's most precariously situated constituent parts, as it was adherence to any presently recognized strategic imperative, that kept the army dutifully engaged in its often thankless mission on Philadelphia's frozen doorstep. Thus engaged, it embraced that mission cautiously, in a spirit as tactically conventional as possible, always mindful that the potential risks of any act of enterprise or intervention probably outweighed the benefits. Even with this conservative approach, the army endured all of the difficulties and liabilities that fall to any military force required to act as a partial surrogate for a functioning government in a convoluted cultural and political environment. Because of that approach, however, those difficulties proved to be more disconcerting than harmful to the army's long-term well-being, and the British were unable to capitalize substantially on the situation.[81]

Indeed, if the most interesting point here is the apparent estrangement of an American army from the nurturance of a native community, the most important point may ultimately be the degree to which *both* sides floundered for want of that nurturance. Throughout the winter, neither side displayed a sustained willingness to rely on the local community for anything more than material support. Neither perceived itself as having an assured organic relationship with the community, and neither, in fact, had any reason for perceiving one. Such communal leverage as the British were able to muster depended mainly on their ability to harness the engines of avarice in a fractured polity, and then to exploit the powers inherent in this initial advantage.

Even over the brief span of the winter, however, this advantage proved extremely difficult to sustain. If a fragmented, calculating, politically circumspect population was relatively easy to galvanize with a combination of hard cash and apparent ascendancy, it was also difficult to keep in any given configuration of loyalty. In essence, money and momentum proved to be weak pillars on which to erect a reliable or stable order of occupation. Perhaps more than anything else, the winter demonstrated the relatively narrow boundaries within which armed force could impose political order under such circumstances.

The caution with which both sides came to approach this situation was only occasionally articulated. In discussing his reluctance to send regular army troops to New Jersey to help local Whigs cope with an eruption of civil conflict ignited there by a Continental foraging expedition, Washington poked glumly at the point. "A few hundred Continental Troops," he conceded, "quiet the minds and give satisfaction to the people of the Country,"

> but considered in the true light, they rather do more harm than good. They draw over the attention of the Enemy, and not being able to resist them, are obliged to fly and leave the Country at the Mercy of the foe. But, as I said before, the people do not view things in the same light, and therefore they must be indulged, tho' to their detriment.[82]

The point went to the heart of a difficult, almost intractable problem that both American and British commanders faced throughout the winter. In a communal environment of fragmented, doubtful, or mercurially shifting loyalties, neither side could lay unequivocal claim to being the protector of the populace, nor could either be irrevocably painted as the invader or oppressor of that populace. Such claims could, of course, be implicitly entered, as the initial and partial success of British efforts showed. They could also, however, be challenged. If the situation was subject to circumstantial definition, it was also constantly subject to counter-definition.

As Washington recognized, it was almost impossible to insure consistency. In a contest predicated mainly on the creation of political trust, however, nothing was surer to be abhorred or rejected than inconsistency. Both sides could and did recognize their responsibility toward civilians who claimed their protection, or on whose behalf they purported to act, in any given situation. In the case cited above, Washington overcame his reservations and sent a few troops to New Jersey. In other circumstances, however, both sides ignored or evaded that responsibility, responding to the imperative that their own narrow interests came first. When those interests seemed vital, moreover, both were prepared to behave in ways that abused or distressed their own adherents. Nathanael Greene's indiscriminate foraging through Chester County, and Henry Clinton's pragmatic deafness to the appeals of the Philadelphia constabulary, dramatically illustrate this point.

For the apolitical middle group, the mobilization of whose attachments, however temporarily, provided whatever communal advantage was available to either side, this ambiguity was all the greater. That group, itself internally diverse, was absolutely subject to the perverse vicissitudes of the daily situation. Would-be neutrals with neither the acumen nor the mobility to calculate and instantly act on the relative advantages of trading with one side or the other often found themselves compelled to contribute in rapid succession to both. Nor would the material nexus itself offer reliable insurance of ongoing security. British patrols attempted to keep area highways open on market days, but they did not offer to escort the country people back to their homes, much less remain around to ward off retribution. Indeed, to heed the blandishments of either side in particular situations might well be to have the worst of both worlds, by identifying oneself politically in the area of one's residence without becoming more than an abstract consideration at the headquarters of either army.

Such circumstances placed an absolute premium on prudence. As Shy has observed, however, the "sheer busyness" of the conflict—its rapid movement in space and its dizzying fluctuations of fortune—"made it difficult to know how to be prudent."[83] The observation pertained to the civilian populations that struggled to accommodate their lives to those movements and fluctuations, but the events sketched above suggest that it applies as well to the military managers of the war. Both Washington and Howe made rhetorical and practical use of such concepts as "well-affected" and "disaffected" citizens whenever it suited their interests to do so. When they warily paused to survey the actual environment in which they were operating, however, both recognized the perilous consequences of relying too literally on such concepts. If it was difficult to know exactly how to be prudent, it was easier to know how not to be. In a military situation relying on small detached parties dispersed over wide, imperfectly charted areas, to stake too much on glib assurances of the exploitability of civil attachments or divisions was easily recognizable as the essence of imprudence.[84]

Ultimately, neither side succeeded in policing the population, much less in forging it into an effective auxiliary weapon in what was still essentially a conventional military contest. Such use as either side made of the community followed the existing contours of the war. The British maintained the initiative, and the Americans remained basically reactive. William Howe fished somewhat more aggressively in troubled communal waters than Washington was willing to do. His meddling there, however, was circumspect, halting, and experimental in a manner that suggests the absence of a calculated policy. British strategic planners had still not formulated the communally oriented policy that would result in the civil conflagrations of the southern campaigns of 1779–81.[85]

Washington, meanwhile, made only tentative attempts to counter these British thrusts. When immediate military needs or political pressures required it, he was capable of turning on wayward civilians in a manner that recalls twentieth-century efforts at counterinsurgency. His injunctions to seize provisions for the army yielded gradually to requests to detain willful market people; to orders to shoot repeat offenders and even suspected wrongdoers; and, finally, to threats to hang even reputable citizens who succumbed to temptations to evade the demands of martial law. For the most part, however, Washington endeavored to keep the army isolated from the consequences of this ugly and unwinnable contest.

In the end, James Varnum's perception of the local social and political landscape as a murky labyrinth informed the responses of both sides to the opportunities of the winter. Both reaped whatever advantage they could from specific situations but shrank from the hazards of any wider application of the possibilities of irregular warfare. Washington resisted being drawn into a civil conflict, and Howe and Clinton—one retiring and the other under orders to extract the British army from Pennsylvania—did not unduly press the point.

244

This Tory Labyrinth

NOTES

1. See Theodore H. White, *In Search of History: A Personal Adventure* (New York, 1978), pp. 196–97; Leonard Maltin, *The Disney Films* (New York, 1973), pp. 140–42.

2. John Shy, *A People Numerous and Armed: Reflections on the Military Struggle for American Independence* (London, 1976), especially pp. 195–224.

3. See especially Paul H. Smith, *Loyalists and Redcoats: A Study in British Military Policy* (Williamsburg, Va., 1964); Robert M. Calhoon, "Civil, Revolutionary or Partisan: The Loyalists and the Nature of the War for Independence," in Stanley J. Underdal, ed., *Military History of the American Revolution: Proceedings of the Sixth Military History Symposium* (Washington, D.C., 1976), pp. 93–109; Shy, *People Numerous*, pp. 183–92.

4. Charles Royster, *A Revolutionary People at War: The Continental Army and American Character, 1775–1783* (Chapel Hill, N.C., 1979), offers an especially perceptive treatment of this general subject. While Royster does not touch directly upon many points raised herein, his characterization of the role of military crises in sharpening the "differing assumptions" between soldiers and civilians that increasingly made the army a unique institution in revolutionary society (pp. 192–93), and of the army itself as "one of America's great spectacles," the popular reaction to which demonstrated "both the army's popularity and the distinctiveness that set it apart from the public" (p. 242), are particularly relevant to the context of this essay.

5. Shy, *People Numerous*, p. 201.

6. Robert A. Gross, *The Minutemen and Their World* (New York, 1976), especially pp. 109–32. It should be noted that, while the rest of Gross's study is based on recent original research, his treatment of the critical events of April 19, 1775, is reconstructed largely from a somewhat older secondary literature.

7. John S. Pancake, *1777: Year of the Hangman* (University, Ala., 1977), pp. 179–91. While the battles that resulted in Burgoyne's surrender were basically conventional in execution, the mobilization of the northeastern states was an essential precondition to them. Shy's conclusion that Burgoyne "simply drowned in a hostile sea which [he] . . . had not foreseen and done little to calm" seems a fair one (Shy, *People Numerous*, p. 207).

8. Clyde R. Ferguson, "Carolina and Georgia Patriot and Loyalist Militia in Action, 1778–1783," in Jeffrey J. Crow and Larry E. Tise, eds., *The Southern Experience in the American Revolution* (Chapel Hill, N.C., 1978), pp. 174–99; Ferguson, "Functions of the Partisan Militia in the South during the Revolution: An Interpretation," in W. Robert Higgins, ed., *The Revolutionary War in the South: Power, Conflict, and Leadership* (Durham, N.C., 1979), pp. 239–58; Patrick J. Furlong, "Civilian-Military Conflict and the Restoration of the Royal Province of Georgia, 1778–1782," *Journal of Southern History* 38 (1972): 415–22; Ronald Hoffman, "The 'Disaffected' in the Revolutionary South," in Alfred F. Young, ed., *The American Revolution: Explorations in the History of American Radicalism* (De Kalb, Ill., 1976), pp. 275–313; John Shy, "British Strategy for Pacifying the Southern Colonies, 1778–1781," in Crow and Tise, *Southern Experience*, pp. 155–73; Shy, *People Numerous*, pp. 209–13; and Russell F. Weigley, *The Partisan War: The South Carolina Campaign of 1780–1782* (Columbia, S.C., 1970), address an at best loosely jointed constellation of issues, and are by no means in complete agreement on the points they consider in common. Nevertheless, they all share an

appreciation for the complex social context of the fighting in the South, and of the importance of the combatants' ability to exploit that context.

9. John F. Reed, *Campaign to Valley Forge, July 1, 1777 to December 19, 1777* (Philadelphia, 1963), provides a generally reliable narrative account of the Pennsylvania campaign. For the winter of 1776–77 in New Jersey, see Leonard Lundin, *Cockpit of the Revolution: The War for Independence in New Jersey* (Princeton, N.J., 1940), pp. 221–26.

10. Worthington C. Ford, ed., *Journals of the Continental Congress* (Washington, D.C., 1904–14), 9:972 (hereafter cited as JCC); Elbridge Gerry to John Adams, Dec. 3, 1777, Elbridge Gerry Papers, Library of Congress (hereafter cited as LC).

11. George Washington, "Orders for a Move That Was Intended against Philadelphia by Way of Surprise," Dec. 25, 1777, in John C. Fitzpatrick, ed., *The Writings of George Washington* (Washington, D.C., 1931–44), 10:202–5.

12. Ibid., p. 205.

13. William Howe to Lord George Germain, Aug. 30, 1777, Sackville-Germain Papers, William L. Clements Library (hereafter cited as WLC).

14. For the British collection of supplies from Pennsylvania civilians, see Daniel Wier to John Robinson, Esq., Oct. 25, 1777, Daniel Wier Letterbook, Historical Society of Pennsylvania (hereafter cited as HSP).

15. Major General Charles Gray to ? , Nov. 28, 1777, Andre de Coppet Collection, Princeton University Library.

16. Jedediah Huntington to Jabez Huntington, Jan. 7, 1778, Private Collection of John F. Reed, King of Prussia, Pa.

17. John Brooks to ? , Jan. 5, 1778, Miscellaneous Collection, Massachusetts Historical Society.

18. Anonymous, Jan. 7, 1778, Joseph Reed Papers, New York Historical Society (hereafter cited as NYHS).

19. James Varnum to (Mrs?) William Greene, March 7, 1778, Private Collection of John F. Reed; James Varnum to Col. Nathan Miller, March 7, 1778, Houghton Library, Harvard University.

20. For evidence of army members struggling to comprehend Pennsylvania's pluralistic religious culture, see A. Chapman to Theodore Woodbridge, Feb. 1, 1778, Woodbridge Papers, Connecticut Historical Society (hereafter cited as CHS); George Gibson to Washington, Feb. 17, 1778, George Washington Papers, LC; Isaac Gibbs to his brother, March 5, 1778, photostat copy on file at Valley Forge National Historical Park, Valley Forge, Pa. (original archive unknown).

21. "Sufferings of Friends: Minutes of the Radnor Monthly Meeting," various dates, 1777–78, microfilm, Friends Historical Library, Swarthmore, Pa.

22. For the several emergency powers that Congress granted to Washington to sustain the army from the local community, and for that body's occasional impatience with Washington's reluctance to exercise them, see JCC 8:752; 9:784, 905, 1014–15, 1068.

23. Memorandum specifying criteria for honoring civilian claims for payment for goods seized by the Continental army, Jan. 1778, Washington Papers, LC.

24. Anthony Wayne to Washington, Dec. 26, 1777, ibid.

25. John Clark to Washington, Dec. 30, 1777, ibid.

26. Washington, "General Orders," Dec. 26, 27, 1777, Fitzpatrick, *Washington*, 10:206–7, 214–15.

27. John Armstrong to Washington, Dec. 30, 1777, GWP, LC; Washington to

Thomas Wharton, Jan. 1, 1778, Fitzpatrick, *Washington*, 10:246–47; Thomas Wharton to Washington, Jan. 3, 1778, Washington Papers, LC.

28. John Jameson to Washington, Dec. 31, 1777, Washington Papers, LC; see also Benjamin Talmadge to Jeremiah Wadsworth, Dec. 30, 1777, Jeremiah Wadsworth Papers, Correspondence, CHS.

29. See John Clark to Washington, Dec. 26, 1777, Washington Papers, LC. Bernhard A. Uhlendorf, ed. and trans., *Revolution in America: Confidential Letters and Journals, 1776–1784, of Adjutant General Major Baurmeister of the Hessian Forces* (New Brunswick, N.J., 1957), p. 150, gives an account of the ease with which country people were able to reach the city at this time, and of the resulting glut of rural produce at declining prices in the city markets. Joseph P. Tustin, ed. and trans., *Diary of the American War: A Hessian Journal* (New Haven, Conn., 1979), p. 117 (the journal of Captain Johann Ewald), provides a diametrically opposite view of the same phenomena, but, on balance, Baurmeister's account seems to accord better with the available evidence.

30. Walter Stewart to Washington, Jan. 18, 1778, Washington Papers, LC.

31. James Potter to Washington, Jan. 11, 1778, and Charles Craig to Washington, Jan. 15, 1778, ibid.

32. Walter Stewart to Washington, Jan. 29, 1778, ibid.

33. John Jameson to Washington, Feb. 2, 1778, ibid.

34. Washington, "Proclamation to the Inhabitants of the States of Pennsylvania, New Jersey and Maryland" (copy), Jan. 30, 1778, Theodore Woodbridge Papers, CHS.

35. Washington to Nathanael Greene, Feb. 12, 1778, Fitzpatrick, *Washington*, 10:454–55.

36. Nathanael Greene to Washington, Feb. 15, 16, 1778, in Richard K. Showman, ed., *The Papers of Nathanael Greene* (Chapel Hill, N.C., 1980), 2:285, 287.

37. Nathanael Greene to Washington, Feb. 16, 17, and 18, 1778, Showman, *Greene*, 2:287, 288, 289.

38. For a discussion of this point and its significance, see Shy, *People Numerous*, pp. 215–16.

39. Nathanael Greene to Washington, Feb. 15, 1778, Showman, *Greene*, 2:285.

40. Nathanael Greene to Washington, Feb. 17, 1778, ibid., p. 288.

41. Nathanael Greene to Washington, Feb. 16, 17, 1778, ibid., pp. 286–90.

42. It is impossible to draw a direct causal relationship between British supply fluctuations and Howe's strategy, but there are some suggestive indications. An apparently steady decline in the British magazines at Philadelphia, evident since October of 1777, stabilized abruptly coincident with the adoption of the more aggressive policy toward the hinterland. See R. Arthur Bowler, *Logistics and the Failure of the British Army in America, 1775–1783* (Princeton, N.J., 1975), pp. 265–66.

43. Ernst Kipping and Samuel Stelle Smith, trans. and ed., *At General Howe's Side, 1776–1778: The Diary of Captain Friedrich von Muenchhausen* (Monmouth, N.J., 1974), pp. 47–48, traces these activities.

44. Washington to Israel Angell, Feb. 1, 1778, and Washington to John Lacey, Feb. 1, 1778, Fitzpatrick, *Washington*, 10:412–13.

45. John Lacey to Thomas Wharton, Feb. 2, 1778, Gratz Collection, HSP; John Lacey to Washington, Feb. 11, 1778, Washington Papers, LC.

46. John Lacey to Col. Joseph Hart, Esq., Feb. 11, 1778, John Lacey Papers, NYHS.

47. Washington to John Lacey, Feb. 18, 1778, Fitzpatrick, *Washington*, 10:478–79.

48. Kipping and Smith, *At General Howe's Side*, pp. 47–48.

49. Washington to Lachlan McIntosh, March 21, 24, 1778, Fitzpatrick, *Washington*, 10:120–21, 135–36.

50. John Laurens to Henry Laurens, Feb. 17, 1778 (typescript), Laurens Papers, Long Island Historical Society.

51. John Lacey to Washington, March 9, 1778, Lacey Papers, NYHS.

52. John Lacey to Joseph Kirkbride, March 10, 1778, Lacey Papers, NYHS; Joseph Kirkbride to John Lacey, March 14, 1778, Lacey Papers, NYHS.

53. John Lacey to Washington, March 29, 1778, Washington Papers, LC; see also John Lacey to Washington, March 9, 1778, Lacey Papers, NYHS.

54. John Lacey to Washington, March 29, 1778, Washington Papers, LC.

55. Washington to John Lacey, March 31, 1778, Fitzpatrick, *Washington*, 11:179.

56. Washington to John Lacey, April 11, 1778, ibid., pp. 243–44. Washington's emergency powers within a radius of seventy miles of his headquarters, established in September of 1777 and extended in December of that year until April 10, 1778 (see JCC 10:1068), were not renewed after the latter date.

57. Washington to Joseph Kirkbride, April 20, 1778, Fitzpatrick, *Washington*, 11:284.

58. See, for example, John Lacey, "General Orders," March 19, 1778, Lacey Papers, NYHS; John Lacey, "Proceedings of Courts Martial," April 6, 1778, Washington Papers, LC.

59. Uhlendorf, *Revolution in America*, p. 166; George Emlen to John Lacey, April 3, 1778, Lacey Papers, NYHS.

60. John Lacey to Nathanael Greene, April 27, 1778, Lacey Papers, NYHS.

61. John Lacey to Washington, April 12, 1778, Washington Papers, LC.

62. For American accounts, see John Lacey to Washington, May 2, 1778, Lacey Papers, NYHS; John Lacey to Thomas Wharton, May 4, 1778, Lacey Papers, NYHS; William Stayner, F. Watts, Samuel Henry, Thomas Craven, Samuel Irvin, "Depositions," May 14–15, 1778, Lacey Papers, NYHS. For British accounts, see Uhlendorf, *Revolution in America*, pp. 168–69; Kipping and Smith, *At General Howe's Side*, p. 51; and especially Robert Simcoe, *A Journal of the Operations of the Queen's Rangers, from the End of the Year 1777, to the Conclusion of the Late American War* (Exeter, n.d.), pp. 56–60.

63. Simcoe, *A Journal of the . . . Queen's Rangers*, p. 60.

64. Washington to William Maxwell, May 7, 1778, Fitzpatrick, *Washington*, 11:357–58; Washington to the Marquis de Lafayette, May 18, 1778, ibid., pp. 418–20.

65. George Fleming to Sebastian Bauman, May 14, 1778, Sebastian Bauman Papers, NYHS. For another account of the rising value and negotiability of Continental currency in the late spring, see George Thomas to Richard Thomas, June 14, 1778, ms. 1487, Chester County (Pa.) Historical Society. At about the same time, a British officer noticed that the Philadelphia markets had "fallen off very much"; see "Journals of Capt. John Montressor," *Collections of the New York Historical Society*, 14 (1881): 494.

66. John W. Jackson, *With the British Army in Philadelphia, 1777–1778* (San Rafael, Ca., 1979), pp. 231–32, 251–54.

67. Sir Henry Clinton, "Minutes of a Conversation with Lord Howe and Joseph Galloway," May, 1778, Henry Clinton Papers, WLC.

68. John Bayard to George Bryan, June 5, 1778, Reed Papers, NYHS; Joseph Reed to his wife, June 9, 1778, ibid.

69. Joseph Reed to his wife, June 9, 1778, ibid.

70. This activity is traced in the reports and correspondence of the officers

assigned to prevent it, especially in the Washington Papers. See, for example, John Clark to Washington, Dec. 19, 1777; John Jameson to Washington, Dec. 31, 1777; Richard K. Meade to John Jameson, Jan. 1, 1778; James Potter to Washington, Jan. 11, 1778; Charles Craig to Washington, Jan. 15, 1778; Walter Stewart to Washington, Jan. 18 and Jan. 29, 1778; and John Jameson to Washington, Feb. 2, 1778, all in Washington Papers, LC. See also Lt. Col. Richard Fitzpatrick to his brother, Jan. 31, 1778, Richard Fitzpatrick Papers, LC; and Joseph Reed to ? , Feb. 1, 1778, Reed Papers, NYHS.

71. See, for example, John Clark to Washington, Dec. 30, 1777, Washington Papers, LC; John Lacey to Nathanael Greene, April 24, 1778, Lacey Papers, NYHS.

72. "From Dr. W. Brown, Physician General of the Hospital at Ephrata," May 12, 1778, *Pennsylvania Archives*, 2d ser. 3:190–91.

73. John Jameson to Washington, Feb. 2, 1778, Washington Papers, LC; Nathanael Greene to Washington, Feb. 17, 1778, Showman, *Greene*, 2:289.

74. See Lacey's evocation of the character of the community in lower and central Bucks County during the Revolution, and of the deterioration of political cohesion there during the year between the Battle of Trenton and Valley Forge, in "Memoirs of Brigadier General John Lacey of Pennsylvania," *Pennsylvania Magazine of History and Biography* 25 (1901): 1–13, 191–207, 341–54, 498–515; and especially 26 (1902): 101–11, 265–70.

75. See Shy, *People Numerous*, pp. 135–62 and especially pp. 154–55.

76. White, *In Search of History*, p. 196.

77. Shy, *People Numerous*, p. 199.

78. This was a special, and in many ways an extreme, example of a broader predicament in which Pennsylvania's civil authorities found themselves throughout the war. Even in circumstances less precarious than those of an armed occupation, the adaptation of a frame of government explicitly based on a libertarian ideology, as was the 1776 Pennsylvania constitution, to the exigencies of a prolonged military crisis, was no easy business. See Douglas McNeil Arnold, "Political Ideology and the Internal Revolution in Pennsylvania, 1776–1790" (Ph.D. dissertation, Princeton University, 1976), pp. 100–147.

79. Shy, *People Numerous*, p. 109.

80. For the choices of the Continental general officers on the site of the army's winter encampment, see Fitzpatrick, *Washington*, 10:133. Of eighteen generals offering opinions, only one expressed support for the Valley Forge area, and one suggested a winter campaign. The rest divided fairly evenly between a cantonment at Wilmington and a line of camps between Bethlehem and Lancaster. The response of Pennsylvania political authorities to a report that Wilmington had been selected is in "Remonstrance of Council and Assembly to Congress, 1777," *Pennsylvania Archives*, 1st ser. 6:104–5. Washington's criticisms of the state leaders, implicit and otherwise, are found throughout his correspondence during the winter; see especially his letters to the President of Congress, Dec. 22 and 23, 1777, Fitzpatrick, *Washington*, 10:186–88, 195–96. See also Washington to Thomas Wharton, March 7, 1778, Fitzpatrick, *Washington*, 11:45–48; Washington to General John Armstrong, March 27, 1778, ibid., pp. 157–59; Washington to William Livingston, April 15, 1778, ibid., pp. 262–63.

81. The issues raised in the three preceeding paragraphs can only be sketched at this point, but they suggest some possibly fruitful avenues for comparative analysis. Our understanding of the evolving character of the war might be enhanced by considering the implications of an increasingly "national," increasingly institutional-

ized, increasingly self-aware Continental army, moving from one relatively provincial political context to another, as strategic needs dictated. Its ability to deploy elements from its bag of military tricks would be shaped not only by a new set of British purposes, and resources for carrying them out, and by a previously unencountered local population, but by a different state government. The latter would at once reflect the population that it purported to govern and be an entity unto itself, with its own needs and interests, its own sources of strength and weakness, and its own relation to Continental political authority. It is not necessary to expand the "triangularity" formulation to one of "quadrangularity," but these differences in the "local instruments of government" might well be a good place to begin in explaining broad military developments during the course of the Revolution.

82. Washington to Governor William Livingston, April 14, 1778, Fitzpatrick, *Washington*, 11:256.

83. Shy, *People Numerous*, p. 217.

84. For one Continental officer's acute perception of the ramifications of this point, see Stephen Moylan to Washington, Feb. 24, 1778, Washington Papers, LC.

85. Shy, *People Numerous*, pp. 209–10; Shy, "British Strategy for Pacifying the Southern Colonies, 1778–1781," in Crow and Tise, *Southern Experience*, pp. 155–73.

Contributors

LAURA BECKER is an assistant professor of history at Clemson University. She has published articles on legal activities in colonial Reading and on the singing controversy in eighteenth-century New England, and she is presently preparing a book on Revolutionary Reading. Her larger interest is in the immigrant ethnic experience.

WAYNE BODLE recently completed a three-year research and planning project at Valley Forge National Historical Park. He is currently engaged in a study of settlement and community development in the Upper Delaware Valley during the eighteenth century.

SUSAN FORBES is a research consultant specializing in immigrant and refugee policy. She was Research Director of the Select Commission on Immigration and Refugee Policy and co-author of *United States Immigration Policy and the National Interest: The Staff Report of the Select Commission*. She has taught American studies at Brandeis University and is the author of *The Jewish Woman in America*.

VALERIE GLADFELTER is Director of Marriage and Family Therapy Associates, Marlton, New Jersey. She has taught at the School of Social Work at the University of Pennsylvania and the Graduate School of Social Work at Rutgers University, and she has written on family therapy and other clinical topics. She is a member of the faculty at the New Jersey Center for Family Studies.

DEBORAH GOUGH has taught history at the University of Arizona and now teaches history and works in the Office of

Contributors

Academic and Career Advising at the University of Wisconsin at Eau Claire. She has also written on widows in early America.

NED LANDSMAN is an assistant professor of history at the State University of New York at Stony Brook. He has published several articles on the middle colonies and is currently completing a book on the Scottish migration into the middle colonies.

BARRY LEVY is preparing a book on the Quakers and the rise of the modern family and has already published articles on the subject. He is an assistant professor in the Department of History and Director of the Charles Rieley Armington Research Program on Children at Case Western Reserve University.

NANCY TOMES has written on asylum-keeping in mid-nineteenth-century America, on the history of nursing, and on wife abuse, and is now finishing a book on the nineteenth-century mental hospital, which will be published by Cambridge University Press. She is an assistant professor of history at SUNY–Stony Brook.

MICHAEL ZUCKERMAN teaches history at the University of Pennsylvania. He is the author of *Peaceable Kingdoms: New England Towns in the Eighteenth Century* and of articles on such subjects as modernization, early American identity, the American Revolution, Horatio Alger, and Doctor Spock. He is writing a book on the colonial southern family.

Index

253

Index